Financial Crises

and

Periods of Industrial

and Commercial Depression

Theodore E. Burton

First Published 1902
by D. Appleton & Co.
New York

Fraser Publishing Company Edition
© Fraser Publishing Company 1966
Wells, Vermont

Library of Congress Catalog Card Number: 66-23328

Printed in the U.S.A.

CONTENTS

v

APPENDIX A

APPENDIX B

DIAGRAMS

PREFACE

This penetrating book, first published in 1902, brings out numerous thought-provoking and contrary thoughts on the nature and causes of crises and depressions. These practical suggestions, based on thorough inquiry and not biased with preconceived notions, are still useful today. Fascinating facts and authoritative arguments enhance your reading.

Strangely enough, America's past growth in riches may be due to the violence of her disturbances. In our own era of affluence for most, we still have intervals of time where the demand for certain things exceeds the supply, leading to periods of unequal economic activity. The beginning of trouble may be found in this abundance rather than in scarcity.

Accordingly, it is not so silly as it may seem to go back and read a standard work on the subject of business cycles, one that is as interesting now as it was popular then. Fresh insights, though written over six decades ago, give us a better perspective of what events were like and how people reacted to these events. Limitations in human judgment and misdirected energy are currently the chief hindrances to perpetual prosperity. Progressive government and rapid growth are not the ultimate guarantees. They never are.

James L. Fraser
Wells Vermont

FINANCIAL CRISES
AND
PERIODS OF INDUSTRIAL
AND COMMERCIAL DEPRESSION

INTRODUCTION

No subject of economic discussion has provoked a greater variety of conflicting opinions than that of financial crises and periods of depression. Numerous explanations of their causes have been advanced. Some of them will be found in Appendix A of this book. It will be seen that they display irreconcilable differences. Nor is it in explaining their causes alone that differences appear. Those who review the history of business in past years do not agree upon the seasons which can be considered as prosperous or the contrary; some maintaining that certain years were years of crises or depression, while others deny that such was the fact.

Notwithstanding the general dread of these periodical visitations, the question has recently been much discussed whether they are, after all, calamities. It has been strenuously asserted that crises are a necessary and beneficial check to increasing expansion and extravagance; also, that periods of depression, while bringing misfortune to some, afford

1

an equivalent advantage to others. In support of
this latter assertion, attention has been called to the
advantageous position which, during a period of
stringency, is held by the large number who have
fixed incomes from investments or salaries. It has
also been maintained that, while the lower prices
prevailing during and after a crisis seriously injure the producer and, to a large extent, the wholesale dealer, they benefit the retail dealer and
wage-earner, because the selling prices, charged
by the retailer, and wages respond to the changing movement of affairs much more slowly than
the prices obtained by the producer or wholesale
dealer.

A more important problem is the explanation
of the conceded fact that during crises and periods
of depression, the aggregate wealth of the communities affected does not give indication of such decrease as would be expected, and that those countries which seem to suffer most from these disturbances show, from decade to decade, the greatest
increase in wealth and material prosperity.   M.
Clément Juglar, the veteran French financial writer,
says:

"Paradoxical as it may seem, the riches of
nations can be measured by the violence of the crises
which they experience." *

It is not probable that such vital differences of
opinion can exist unless the question presented is
an intricate one. Its intricacy is due to the multi-

---

* Des Crises Commerciales, 1889, pp. 44–45.

tude of influences at work, many of which operate concurrently, and to the exceptional play of various human motives and caprices, the effects of which, though largely responsible for the conditions which exist, are extremely difficult to trace. There is great danger of confusing *effect* with *cause*, and of mistaking that which is subordinate or incidental for the principal fact of the situation.

In speaking of certain English writers, M. Charles Coquelin says:

" I will venture to say that their authors have almost always gone astray, not from want of knowledge, but rather from refining too much. Their chief mistake has been to dwell upon the particular circumstances of commercial crises, without stating sufficiently their general and dominating character, to consider their variations instead of their resemblances, and consequently stopping almost always at the immediate or secondary causes by which they are determined, instead of going up to the primordial cause which engenders them." *

In this country most of the few brief books upon the subject show a bias derived from preconceived notions about banking, currency, tariff, or other disputed questions of economic policy. The views of their authors regarding the sources of industrial prosperity or adversity vary according to their opinions on these questions. The periodical literature pertaining to the subject, while much

---

* Bankers' Magazine, London, vol. x, p. 309; a summary of an article in the Revue des Deux Mondes, vol. xxiv (1848), p. 464.

more abundant and valuable, is largely tainted with the same defect.

The purpose of this book is to discuss the nature and causes of these recurring disturbances, and to offer some practical suggestions concerning indications of their approach and the possible means for their prevention or mitigation.

With the conviction that much of the uncertainty which belongs to the discussion is the result of confusion in the use of terms, especial attention is given to definitions and classification. The task is not an easy one. As is pointed out by Professor Cairnes and others, the terms employed in treating economic subjects must be obtained from popular language, and that precision which is obtained in the physical sciences by the use of terms employed for those sciences alone is unattainable.*

Much of this confusion is clearly traceable to the indiscriminate use of the words *panic, crisis,* and *depression* for the description of phenomena, which, although usually intimately associated, are nevertheless distinct in their essential nature. An effort is made to describe the distinguishing features of events properly designated by each of these terms.

The unparalleled development of the past thirty-five years has, moreover, furnished the basis for an inquiry whether seasons of business depression are not unavoidable features of a *transition period*, during which a change occurs in methods

---

* The Character and Logical Method of Political Economy, pp. 145–146.

and instruments of production and exchange, resulting in a great increase of useful articles and facilities, but, in the adjustment to new conditions, attended also by serious derangement and loss.

It will also be profitable to investigate the so-called *periodicity* of crises and depressions, and to inquire whether in fact there is a regular recurrence of these disturbances, and if so, whether it is the result of fundamental causes or due to chance.

In the successive chapters, attention is separately given to the different phases of the subject. Under this plan it is difficult to avoid repetition. But the method chosen has seemed essential to the clearest presentation of the facts and arguments pertaining to the various questions arising.

The portions of Chapter VIII, entitled, The Present Outlook, and Increase in the Supply of Gold, were written in May, 1901, and revised in the following August.

A bibliography is appended which is thought to contain a more complete list of books and periodicals specifically relating to this subject than any yet prepared.

CHAPTER I

AT the very outset, the consideration of this subject is embarrassed by the confusion and lack of precision which common usage has sanctioned in the use of terms.

The substantives most frequently employed to designate financial, industrial, or commercial disturbances are: *panic, crisis,* and *depression.* Each of these words, in numerous cases, has been used to describe events more properly characterized by one of the others. With each of these substantives are used the qualifying adjectives above mentioned—*financial, industrial,* and *commercial.*

SUBSTANTIVES

Panic.—The word *panic* is defined as—

" A sudden fright, especially a sudden fright without real cause." *

Also as—

" A sudden, unreasonable, overpowering fear, especially when affecting a large number simultaneously."†

---

* Webster.   † Standard Dictionary.

When relating to trade or finance, it is defined as—

"An exaggerated alarm which takes possession of a trading community on the occurrence of a financial crisis, such as may be caused by the failure of an important bank, or the exposure of a great commercial swindle, inducing a general feeling of distrust, and impelling to hasty and violent measures to secure from possible loss, thus often precipitating a general financial disaster which was at first only feared." *

The term *punic* correctly describes the prevalent disposition during a *brief period*, in which the real situation, serious perhaps, is made much worse by the general excitement and alarm. We cannot say that under the more modern and improved facilities for information and organization, business communities are for a *considerable period* overcome by "sudden fright" or "exaggerated alarm."

Crisis.—The word *crisis* is defined as—

"A decisive point or moment, a turning-point, a critical time, a decisive turn." †

"The high-wrought state of any affair which immediately precedes a change." ‡

"A state of affairs in which a decisive change for better or worse is imminent; now applied especially to times of difficulty, insecurity, and suspense in politics or commerce." #

---

* Century Dictionary.   † Worcester.
‡ Crabb's English Synonyms.
# Murray's New English Dictionary.

John Stuart Mill gives this definition of a *commercial crisis:*

" There is said to be a *commercial crisis* when a great number of merchants and traders at once either have, or apprehend that they shall have, a difficulty in meeting their engagements." *

It is evident that neither the derivation of this word nor precision in language warrants its use to describe a prolonged period.

Thus, both the words *panic* and *crisis* should be used with reference to a brief period which may or may not be followed by a prolonged disturbance. They are usually employed indiscriminately. *Panic* is the favourite word of the street. *Crisis* is more commonly used in books. It would be difficult to find any dividing line in what has been written and said upon the subject in the use of these two words; yet there is a real distinction between them. The former refers more properly to a mental state; the latter to an actual, existing condition. Upon reflection a *panic* may disappear; but a *crisis* remains. It is irrational for a community to yield to a panic. It is equally irrational to attempt to ignore a crisis. When a crisis occurs, the alarm of a panic greatly aggravates it. On the distinction between the two, Professor Sumner says, in speaking of the crisis of 1857:

" A definite discrimination is intended here between the terms *crisis* and *panic*. When certain forces have been set in operation in the commercial

---

* Political Economy, book iii, chap. xii.

organization by antecedent acts or occurrences, their consequences must follow.

"They may combine in such a way or advance to such a pitch that a crisis is produced.

"A panic is properly psychological. It is a wave of emotion, apprehension, alarm.

"It is more or less irrational. It is superinduced upon the crisis, which is real and inevitable; but it exaggerates, conjures up possibilities, takes away courage and energy. It is not possible to preach down a crisis; it is a fact and is there; it must run its course, and be accounted with for all there is in it. The soberest man appreciates the facts the best. It is useless to preach confidence to him in the face of the facts which infuse suspicion and warning. A *panic* can be partly overcome by judicious reflection, by realization of the truth, and by measurement of facts." *

Mr. Hammond Chubb, in an article on the Bank Act and the Crisis of 1866, thus distinguishes a panic from a crisis:

"A crisis is caused by an insufficiency of capital for carrying on the undertakings which have been set on foot; a panic is the unreasoning fear of those who find themselves likely to be affected by such a condition of things." †

It should be added that a panic is not always a mere incident accompanying a crisis. It may occur as a prior independent event, and the spirit of alarm

---

* A History of Banking in all Nations, vol. i, p. 425.

† Journal of the Royal Statistical Society (London), vol. xxxv, p. 184.

which characterizes it may assume such proportions as to cause a crisis.

Depression.—The word *depression* is defined as—

" A state of dulness or inactivity." *

" The state of being lowered in force, activity, or intensity." †

" A diminution of prosperity, as of trade." ‡

A period of depression may be briefly defined as a protracted season in which the activities and profits of industry and trade fall materially below their normal level.

This term most satisfactorily describes the protracted and wide-reaching checks to advancing prosperity which affect the industrial and commercial world. In distinction from a *panic* or *crisis* it refers to a prolonged period. It is not a matter of days, but of years. During its continuance the discouraging situation must be recognised and calmly met. Recuperative forces must accomplish their work.

The following definitions, or statements, clearly express the distinction between a panic or crisis and a period of depression:

" A panic or crisis is usually short, sharp, and decisive in its results. A depression is a condition which has duration of time attending it." #

" There is an abuse of language when we speak of a *crisis* which has been going on for the last six

---

* Worcester. † New English Dictionary. ‡ Webster.
# Carroll D. Wright. Report on Modern Industrial Depressions, 1886, p. 15.

years. This seems to betray some confusion of ideas between depression of trade and an entirely different phenomenon, a crisis or panic in the city when merchants are in agony for the loan of money, and cannot get it." *

" A *crisis*, as the word indicates, is not, or ought not to be, only a transitory situation." †

The observance, in English speech, of the distinction contended for in this chapter, is taken for granted in a recent French publication, Le Dictionnaire du Commerce, etc., compiled by MM. Yves Guyot and A. Raffalovich.

In defining a crisis, M. Raffalovich says:

" It would not have the meaning given if applied to a prolonged state of languor, of atrophy, to a chronic, morbid condition, for which the English employ the word *depression*, while they reserve the expression *crisis* for sudden accidents, which frequently have a quality of panic." ‡

The distinction between a brief season of crisis and a considerable period of depression is recognised by many who nevertheless use the word crisis for both." #

The following quotations illustrate the different uses of the word. M. Émile de Laveleye says:

" This sharp period of the crisis is not of long

---

* Walter E. Smith. The Recent Depression of Trade, p. 15, Oxford Cobden Prize Essay for 1879.

† Maurice Block. Revue des Deux Mondes pour 1879, mars–avril, p. 433.

‡ Article, Crise.

See especially the description of two kinds of crises by Paul Leroy-Beaulieu, quoted herein, chap. iv, pp. 124–125.

duration. The panic ceases. Foreign capital comes in. Interest lowers. Industry, however, suffers for a much longer time." *

M. Courbon, a French senator, in his statement before a commission appointed by the French Chamber of Deputies, says:

"There are two distinct sorts of crises, the one temporary and the other persistent and profound."†

Max Wirth says: "Two kinds of crises are to be distinguished: Crises of the medium of circulation, and crises of capital" (" Krisen der Umlaufsmittel, und Krisen des Capitals ").‡

In addition to the foregoing, the words *crash* and *collapse* are frequently used as descriptive of the sudden breakdown which marks the advent of a crisis. The word *pressure*, used more frequently, perhaps, half a century ago than now, designates that condition of stringency in financial circles which threatens a crisis, though sometimes used as synonymous with crisis. #

Distinction between Depression and Poverty.— Before passing from the distinction between panics or crises and depressions, it should be distinctly

---

* Article, Crise, in La Grande Encyclopédie, vol. xiii, p. 381.

† Referred to in Carroll D. Wright's Report on Industrial Depressions, 1886, p. 39.

‡ Geschichte der Handelskrisen, 1890, p. 1.

"A pressure on the money market may be defined (as) a difficulty of getting money in the London market, either by way of discounting bills, or of loans upon Government securities."—J. W. Gilbart, Practical Treatise on Banking, vol. i, p. 96.

noted that depression is not the same as poverty, although the two may appear contemporaneously. Just as depression describes a condition of greater duration than a crisis, so poverty applies to a condition more prolonged than a depression, and one which is essentially permanent. Depression runs its course and disappears. Poverty remains. The study of periods of depression reveals the fact that there are alternate seasons of activity and dulness in trade and industry, but that these alternate seasons do not, in a series of years, prevent an increase of prosperity. Poverty describes a permanent loss or abatement of prosperity. Progressive and highly developed countries suffer from depression; unprogressive and decayed countries suffer from poverty.

Much has been written upon agricultural depression. In describing conditions existing in farming communities where production is rendered less profitable by the competition of other lands, the term depression cannot be considered as correctly describing the situation. When agricultural production or any industry in any locality becomes unprofitable, and continues increasingly so for a period of ten years or more, this permanently decreased profit can hardly be explained as a phenomenon of depression. It indicates that other localities, or other methods, have gained a superiority which gives them a permanent advantage. It is more nearly a condition of poverty. The long eras of scarcity and destitution, prevalent in earlier centuries, such as that in England at the time of the

Wars of the Roses, and in the preceding wars with France, or that in France for the greater part of the century preceding the Revolution of 1789,* display little in common with modern depressions. They were rather eras of poverty due to exhaustion by war, to misgovernment, or erroneous economic policies.

ADJECTIVES

The distinction between the adjectives † employed in this connection is not so satisfactory as that between the substantives mentioned. This is because the conditions which they respectively describe, in a greater degree, appear simultaneously, and the dividing line between them cannot be so clearly drawn.

Financial.—The adjective *financial* is defined as " Of, pertaining to, or relating to finance or money matters." ‡

By general usage this adjective relates to the agency of credit as well as to the use of money, and thus includes reference to the relation of debtor and creditor.

A crisis in its predominant features is financial. This is particularly true in view of the increasing importance of credit and credit instruments and the development of banking. While the condition of commerce and industry may afford the remote causes of the disturbance, it is, in its early manifes-

---

* For a graphic description of this last period, see Taine's Ancient Régime, book v. Translation by John Durand.

† For the use of the word "monetary," see p. 110.

‡ New English Dictionary.

tations, financial, because financial transactions furnish the means by which the large volume of industrial and commercial operations can be conducted.

The essential feature of a *panic* or *crisis* is the inability of many debtors to meet their obligations and an apprehension of the inability of many more. The storm centre is among the banks and financial institutions.* Not only is it financial in its early manifestations, but a panic or crisis may run its course without seriously involving trade or industry. This is especially true if, as sometimes occurs, the crisis is not followed by a period of depression. The activities of commerce and industry may continue unslackened during the disturbance which marks the advent of a crisis, but when the crisis has taken an unfavourable turn and left its wrecks behind, both must suffer. In a crisis, the ruinous fall in prices manifests itself in securities more than in commodities. It is more keenly felt at the Stock Exchange than at the Produce Exchange.

Industrial.—The adjective *industrial* is defined as—

" Pertaining to industry or its results, relating to or connected with productive industry or the manufacture of commodities."†

By recent usage the words *industry* and *industrial* are more and more applied to the whole of the mechanism for the production of wealth, not only in manufacture, but in the obtaining of raw ma-

---

* See the figures for the failures in 1893 and the two succeeding years, given in Chapter III, pp. 58–59.

Century Dictionary.

terial for manufacture.   They are also frequently
used with reference to production in agriculture.

Commercial.—The adjective *commercial* is defined as—

" Relating to commerce or traffic; mercantile;
trading." *

The adjective *commercial* and the substantive
commerce both refer to trade or to the exchange of
commodities.

Industry refers to the original production or
manufacture of commodities or articles of utility;
commerce to the successive steps by which they are
placed where needed or demanded.   Of the two,
industry, or the original *production*, would seem to
be the more important, and a single word or desig-
nation would be simpler; but industry and commerce describe operations which, though distinct,
are so intimately associated as to render their separate consideration impossible.   Improvements in
transportation, with equal progress in the transaction and management of the business of the merchant, have greatly increased production and consumption, because, except for these improvements,
a large share of that which is now annually consumed could not be brought within the reach of the
consumer. †   Industry and commerce must thus go
hand in hand, and each depends for its life upon the
maintenance of the other.   In the more extended

---

* Worcester.

† Mr. Mulhall estimates that in the fifty years prior to 1896
distributive energy increased three times faster than production proper.   Industries and Wealth of Nations, p. 5.

period known as a depression, the disturbance is industrial and commercial as well; the financial disturbance is subordinate. The adjectives *industrial* and *commercial* are therefore properly employed to modify the substantive depression, and the adjective *financial* in describing a panic or crisis.

SUMMARY

The word *crisis*, if employed with entire accuracy, describes a brief period of acute disturbance in the business world, the prevailing features of which are the breakdown of credit and prices and the destruction of confidence. It has especially to do with the relations of debtor and creditor. The word *panic* describes a different phase of the same general condition or situation, which is essentially mental or psychological. On different occasions, one or the other phase is the more prominent. The adjective *financial* is appropriately used with each of these.

The term *depression*, or *period of depression*, describes a disturbance having a much longer duration, and which cannot be designated as financial. It pertains rather to industry and commerce, and includes the whole field of production and exchange. It is properly described as *industrial* and *commercial*.

Accordingly, the terms employed herein will be *financial panic* or *crisis*, and *period of industrial* and *commercial depression*, or simply *depression*. The word *crisis* will be used as a general term to describe the briefer period, except in the description of events wherein the *panic* phase seems to have been more prominent.

2

CHAPTER II

Two Classes of Disturbances.—As already outlined, these disturbances are of two classes. One includes panics and crises, the other periods of depression. The first are of brief duration, the second more prolonged.

Relation between the Two.—A period of depression usually follows a crisis. A crisis usually precedes a period of depression. Each may, however, occur as an independent event. The following are illustrations:

The original Black Friday, December 6, 1745, was a day of panic as well as of crisis, caused by the progress of the army of the Pretender. There was a run on the Bank of England, for which the invading army had a special antagonism, because the bank had been regarded as a Whig institution. There was no ensuing depression. With the defeat of the Pretender, the crisis subsided and normal conditions were restored. This crisis was distinctly political as well as financial.*

---

* Every serious political disturbance or revolution is likely to be attended by a crisis. The resulting fall in prices is the

18

Black Friday, May 11, 1866, sometimes called Overend Friday, was the day of the failure of Overend, Gurney & Co., in London, one of the most notable failures of a financial institution up to that time. This failure led to a crisis, followed by a period of depression, which, in England at least, was severe.

Black Friday, September 24, 1869, was due to the operations of a speculative clique at New York, the members of which created a corner in gold. The onward movement in the industrial and commercial world was not checked.

Mr. Giffen says that the months of July and August, 1870, at the beginning of the Franco-Prussian War, as well as the close of the war in 1871, marked the occurrence of crises in England, but by reason of the unprecedented prosperity of the time no serious results followed.*

The recent crises in the United States in September, 1873, and May, 1893, were followed by periods of depression.

The name of crisis has been denied by some for those disturbances which were not followed by serious abatement of business activity. Doubtless

---

most noticeable in the securities of the Government affected or of institutions depending upon it. On February 23, 1848, the day before the abdication of King Louis Philippe, five-per-cent Government securities at Paris were quoted at 116.75; March 7, after the close of the Bourse, at 97.50; March 20, at 72. The stock of the Bank of France was quoted on February 23, at 3180; March 7, at 2400; March 20, at 1650.

* The Cost of the Franco-German War; Essays in Finance, First Series, 1880, pp. 60–64.

the panic phase was prominent in the instances cited, but, in classifying them, it is appropriate to judge them, not as they appear in retrospect, but according to the experience of contemporaries who were compelled to face the situation as it then existed. To them it was a crisis of a kind similar to those which are followed by prolonged depression. The great fluctuations and losses at the New York Stock Exchange in May, 1901, certainly caused a crisis which, if the general condition of business had not been sound, would have marked the beginning of a depression.

Whether a crisis will be succeeded by a period of depression is not altogether a question of the severity of the shock; much depends upon conditions existing at the time.

"As a rule," says Mr. John Mills, " panics do not destroy capital; they merely reveal the extent to which it has been previously destroyed by its betrayal into hopelessly unproductive works." *

A crisis will be followed by a depression if it occurs contemporaneously with an exhaustion of resources and undue expansion of credit, and indicates the existence of actual cause for distress as distinguished from mere fright, or the apprehension of an unfavourable event which does not occur, or a derangement of the circulating medium, the effects of which may be only temporary. Those crises which are not so followed resolve themselves into

---

* Article read before the Manchester Statistical Society, December 11, 1867, on Credit Cycles and the Origin of Commercial Panics.

mere temporary shocks, succeeded by prompt and almost complete recovery. They are little more than a clearing of the atmosphere. If a crisis is an independent fact, and has no sequence in the form of prolonged distress, the business world will right itself and go on as before, like a ship after a severe storm, when, although the waves are still high and the wind has not yet subsided, the mariner sees safety ahead. They are not without beneficial effect, because they check injudicious and extravagant enterprise and give warning of the danger of speculation.

Crises, when followed by periods of depression, are part of a series of events, and the calamities which ensue are much more serious. They are like the bursting of the thunder-cloud which precedes a storm. They are not only serious in themselves, but, in addition, bring clearly to view the instability of existing business conditions. These conditions may have existed for a long time, but have escaped general recognition until brought to the light by some notable event.

Depressions without Preceding Crises.—A depression may occur without a preceding panic or crisis. In this case, the transition from activity to dulness is more gradual, and not marked by the sudden change which manifests itself on the occurrence of a crisis; but usually some significant event precedes.

The signal for the commencement of the depression in England in 1890 was the embarrassment of the firm of Baring Brothers; but, as stated in Mr.

R. H. Inglis-Palgrave's Dictionary of Political
Economy:

"Even in London there was no panic except in
Capel Court." *

And in the same connection it is said:

"Since 1866 no crisis has occurred in England
worthy to be classed with the one in May of that
year, nor, in fact, with any of those occurring in
each of the decades preceding 1866; but industrial
and trade depression has several times been protracted and severe."

Depression in one country often follows a crisis
in another country or countries, with which it has
extended commercial relations. The year 1873
witnessed severe crises at Vienna, Berlin, and New
York, while none occurred at London or Paris; but
at the latter places the derived effect of disturbances elsewhere became manifest later.

The superior organization of business and the
co-operation of banking institutions in later years,
the greater quantity and mobility of capital, all
have had much to do in diminishing the force of
panics or crises. Superior means of communication and of information have contributed to the
same result.

It is not too much to say that crises are becoming relatively less prominent and depressions more
so. The severe convulsions characterized by panic
and partial suspension of business are much less
noticeable than formerly, but depressions have not

---

* Vol. i, p. 462.   Article entitled Crises, 1857, 1866, 1890.

lacked in duration or universality. Depressions not preceded by crises have distinctive phenomena. There is not that sudden fall in prices or immediate abatement of activity which occurs at the time of a crisis. Instead of a sudden change there is a slow reaction against the preceding expansion, attended at first by fluctuations in prices and activity. The general tendency is downward, but several successive years may be strikingly alike in the volume of business transacted and in comparative prosperity. This was well illustrated in the first half of the decade beginning in 1881. It is not without reason that there is difference of opinion regarding the time when a depression commenced. There was a crisis in France in 1882, but it was not of sufficient magnitude to explain the general depression which occurred later. There was a crisis in banking circles in New York in May, 1884. The years 1882 and 1883 showed abatement from 1881 in many branches of business, but the value and volume of foreign trade in the United Kingdom did not reach its maximum until 1883. In the United States the decline in the price of iron began in 1880, but there had been an exceptional advance in the demand for iron and steel. Production and consumption increased in many branches in the two following years, and were well sustained in 1883.

The consideration of this class of depressions assumes importance, because in the development of modern business it is becoming more and more the prevailing type.

Crises have occurred in the midst of a depression. These are naturally less severe because of the contraction of business operations at such a time, and because the liquidation incident to the depression has diminished the volume of transactions upon credit and the number of establishments which rest upon unstable foundations. The events following the failure of the City of Glasgow Bank, October 1, 1878, illustrate the occurrence of a crisis in the midst of a depression. This crisis is readily distinguished from others in that it occurred when liquidation was well advanced. Crises of this class can often be traced to flagrant neglect of requisite prudence in management, and are usually local rather than general in their extent.

The Periodicity of Crises

Crises and depressions have been regarded as successive stages of an extended period, to which the name *cycle* has been given, and which embraces all the varying conditions from the highest degree of prosperity to the lowest point of depression. The word cycle, with this general meaning, was used by Sir William Petty as early as the year 1662. In speaking of the proportion of the produce of land which should be retained as rent, he says, "The *medium* of seven years, or rather of so many years as makes up the cycle, within which Dearths and Plenties make their revolution, doth give the ordinary rent of the Land in Corn." *

The periodicity of crises and depressions has

---

* A Treatise of Taxes and Contributions, chap. iv, sec. 13, pp. 24–25.

been very generally recognised. On this point, Prof. Leone Levi says:

" Experience teaches us that seven fat-fleshed, well-favoured kine—years of plenty—are generally followed by other seven, poor and very lean, ill-favoured kine—years of famine. . . . As a matter of fact, there has ever been an alternation of prosperity and dulness in trade." *

As stated by him in another place, the regular course after a collapse is depression, activity, excitement, collapse again.

The most confident advocates of the theory of periodicity assign to these cycles a definite and nearly equal duration of ten to twelve years. According to Mr. John Mills, above referred to, this cycle is divided as follows: After each panic or crisis, the first three years will witness diminished trade, lack of employment, falling prices, a lowering rate of interest, and very considerable distress. Then there will be three years of active trade, slowly rising prices, fair employment, improving credit. Then will come three years of unduly excited trade, in which speculation will be rife, prices will rapidly rise, and an unusual number of new enterprises will be begun. The tenth year will be one of crisis, followed again by three years of depression.

These three successive stages or seasons, each of three years, are styled by Mr. Mills the Post-Panic Period, the Middle or Revival Period, and

* Introduction to Prize Essays of Goadby and Watt upon the Depression of Trade, pp. iii–iv.

the Speculative Period.   In speaking of their regular succession, he says:

" The instances are already too numerous, regular, and persistent to allow any foothold for a theory of fortuitous coincidence.   There is no region of scientific inquiry in which the idea of so distinct and prolonged a series occurring *by accident* would not at once be scouted." *

The financial history of England affords strong corroboration for this contention of Mr. Mills, for crises or depressions have occurred there substantially at intervals of ten years, to wit: in 1815, 1825–6, 1836–7, 1847, 1857, 1866, and, as is held by him in another article, and by others, in 1875, though this last depression really commenced at an earlier date.

Some writers ascribe these cycles to physical causes, notably to variations in spots upon the sun, and assert that these causes have manifested themselves in India and the East, whence their results have been transmitted to other parts of the world.   The famines and deficient harvests there have rendered the inhabitants unable to furnish, in the average quantity, agricultural produce in exchange for English manufactures.   Prof. W. S. Jevons has been regarded as the most prominent advocate of the sun-spot theory.†   His views upon

---

* Article above referred to read before the Manchester Statistical Society, December 11, 1867.

† Article on Solar Period and the Price of Corn, read at Bristol in 1875, Investigations in Currency and Finance, chap. vi, p. 194.   See also same work, chap. vii, p. 206 and chap. viii, p. 221.

sun-spots have been severely criticised; but, upon careful examination, it will appear that he did not assert their controlling influence with that positiveness which some of his critics have ascribed to him. Several writers, however, have gone so far as to ascribe to sun-spots the most potent agency in determining the quantity of agricultural products, and consequently conditions of prosperity from year to year.

Whether sun-spots affect harvests is a question of fact. Their periodicity may be regarded as established; their maxima in recent years occurred in 1848, 1860, 1870, 1881, and 1892.* It may also be conceded that there is a correspondence between their occurrence and the phenomena of terrestrial magnetism and aurora borealis. The opinions advanced to the effect that there is a correspondence between them and heat energy, rainfall, cyclones, quantity of atmospheric ozone, or visitations of Asiatic cholera cannot be accepted as established. Their influence in determining the scarcity or abundance of harvests cannot be conceded without further careful examination. The testimony is too conflicting and the data not sufficient to warrant admitting so much. On this subject, Prof. C. A. Young says:

"While it is not at all unlikely that investigation will result in establishing some real influence of sun-spots upon our terrestrial meteorology and

---

* See article Sun, by Prof. Simon Newcomb, in Johnson's Cyclopædia, vol. vii, p. 824. The interval between the maxima of sun-spots has been differently stated; 11.11 and 10.45 years are the periods having the largest number of supporters.

determining its laws, it is practically certain that this influence is extremely slight and so masked and veiled by other influences more powerful that it is extremely difficult to bring to light." *

Historically speaking, it must be said that no connection between sun-spots and prosperity has been established. It cannot be maintained that their influence in India has been very great, nor that the increase or decrease of trade with that country, so frequently referred to by those who have advocated this theory, is sufficiently important to account for the alternate ups and downs of business in the western hemisphere and Europe.† A vital objection to this theory is found in the different conditions existing in different agricultural countries. Some are benefited by less heat than that afforded in the average season and others by more. It is claimed for sun-spots that they coin-

---

* The Sun. Edition of 1895, p. 177.

† It is a singular fact that several of the writers who have given prominence to the influence of sun-spots, do not make it clear whether in their opinion they benefit or injure agricultural production.

The prevalent opinion since the investigations of Sir William Herschel in 1801 has been that they benefit harvests. (See Philosophical Transactions, 1801, vol. xci, pp. 265–318.) This opinion has, however, found numerous opponents. For a list of writers favouring or opposing the theory that sun-spots benefit harvests, see Bergmann's Geschichte der Nationalökonomischen Krisentheorien, pp. 249 et seq. Among its advocates are counted Norman Lockyer, the astronomer, and W. W. Hunter, statistician, of East India. Among those opposed are Prof. Richard A. Proctor, the astronomer, E. D. Archibald, the physicist, and Herman Fritz.

cide with a greater average of heat and less moisture. Thus they would benefit agricultural production in some localities and injure it in others. The corn crop of Kansas and other portions of the Southwest would have been better in the year 1901 with less heat and more moisture.

Others have ascribed changing conditions of prosperity to varying mental moods. Mr. Mills thought the regular recurrence of crises was due to the periodical destruction of belief and hope in the minds of merchants and bankers. To him panic is the destruction of a bundle of beliefs; crisis is not a matter of the purse, but of the mind.

The theory of a periodicity of crises, ridiculed by Prof. J. E. Thorold Rogers,* doubted by David A. Wells,† and accepted by Professor Nicholson,‡ but regarded by him as less noticeable than formerly, would have gained more general acceptance but for the variety of reasons given for it and the extreme and sometimes absurd views of many of its supporters.

But, however unsatisfactory the current explanations may be, the fact remains that in progressive countries the existence of a tendency to periodicity of crises, with the regular recurrence of a series of events consisting successively of crisis,# depression,

---

* Princeton Review, vol. lv, p. 223.

† Recent Economic Changes, p. 81.

‡ Political Economy, vol. ii, pp. 213–214.

The term "crisis," here and in other places, refers to the time of the change from activity to dulness, whether signalized by the actual occurrence of a crisis or not.

improvement, expansion, and a new crisis, is as well established as any tendency in the history of industry and trade. To ignore this fact would prevent an accurate analysis or understanding of the subject. The mistake lies in fixing a definite duration for the successive events of the cycle, and in failing to sufficiently recognise exceptional conditions of time, 'place, and social or economic development. Much depends upon the degree and rapidity of industrial advancement, the maintenance of social order, the presence or absence of sudden changes in fiscal policy, physical conditions, such as failure and abundance of crops, and upon the occurrence of business failures or other events which precipitate a crisis. These periodic disturbances will occur, but not with the regularity of the phases of the moon or with the uniform duration of the seasons of the year.

There is a distinct tendency towards the occurrence of a pressure or disturbance almost attaining the magnitude of a crisis at a time both preceding and succeeding the date of the crisis proper. In several instances the interval, both before and after, has been two years. This pressure usually occurs at the same season of the year as the crisis, and it is likely to occur more than once. This was illustrated by the revulsion in 1839, two years after the crisis of 1837; and again after the crisis of 1893, by the temporary improvement and later reaction in 1895–'96. The disturbance prior to a crisis was illustrated by the severe pressure in 1864 in England two years before the crisis of 1866. Before the crisis in the autumn of 1873 in the United States, there was a noticeable stringency in the money market in the autumn of the years 1871 and 1872. The same forerunner of disturbance appeared in the summer of 1856, prior to the crisis of 1857. In case the disturbance precedes the crisis, the failure to check the onward movement of activity and expansion is probably due to the strong impetus which it has gained. The occurrence of a distinct disturbance after the crisis proper may be ascribed to the fact that the liquidation which follows the crisis is not complete, and that an artificial activity is created without sufficient recognition of the depressed condition of business.

The existence of periodicity is more noticeable in countries like England and France, which, along with a high degree of development and large accumulations of available capital, have also reached a stage of greater uniformity in commercial and industrial operations. In these countries the accretions or losses of wealth in any one year bear a smaller proportion to existing wealth; nevertheless, they are slowly but surely affected by changing conditions at home and abroad. In England the tendency to a regular increase and decrease of activity is marked and striking. Periodicity is less noticeable in countries like the United States, where new fields for enterprise are constantly being opened and changes are more frequent. Alternations of prosperity and dulness are more sharply defined and more frequent, and the regularity in the recurrence of the different phases of the cycle is less perceptible.

PROBABLE DURATION OF THE SUCCESSIVE STAGES OF
THE CYCLE

The duration of crises varies. In 1873 the
failure of Jay Cooke & Co. occurred September
18th. The Stock Exchange was closed September
20th, and was not reopened until the 30th of the
same month. Clearing-House certificates were
issued. Currency commanded a varying premium
until November 1st. At that date—after six weeks
and two days—the crisis proper may be said to have
come to an end.

In England, in 1847, the extraordinary bank
rate of 8 per cent was maintained for twenty-eight
days; this was a year of high rates and numerous
changes; in 1857, the rate of 10 per cent for forty-
five days; in 1866, it continued at 10 per cent for
eighty-eight days. The time during which these
high rates of interest were maintained affords the
most correct indication of the duration of each of
these crises. M. Clément Juglar, who has given
much painstaking attention to this topic, says:

" The panic does not continue beyond six weeks
or two months; afterward comes the liquidation,
which continues for eighteen months or two
years." *

This season of liquidation, as he calls it, includes the earlier stage of a period of depression.

Generally speaking, the intervening period between the end of one crisis and the beginning of

* Maurice Block's Dictionnaire Général de la Politique, vol. i,
p. 592.

another has three distinct stages: first, the depression proper; second, a season beginning when diminishing activity has reached its lowest point, in which there is, after a brief stationary period, steady and healthy development; third, a season of rapid improvement, developing into overaction and speculation, after which comes a collapse. The duration of these successive seasons or periods has varied greatly. The usual length has been from two to five years for each. Of the three, the first, or period of depression, characterized by falling prices and progressively diminishing activity, has been longest, almost without exception. Indeed, in a majority of instances, it has continued longer than the two succeeding periods combined, namely, those styled by Mr. Mills the Middle or Revival and Speculative periods, during which improving conditions prevail.

If we accept the usual indications as a guide, the depression following the crisis of 1873 in the United States reached its lowest point in the year 1878, and in Great Britain—where the depression became severe later—in the year 1879. The depression after the crisis of 1893 in the United States was interrupted by a temporary revival, beginning in the autumn of 1895, which, however, disappeared in the following year, and the lowest point was not reached until June or July, 1897. The depression in several European countries, beginning earlier, in 1890 or 1891, gave way first to a stationary condition and then to gradual improvement at the end of 1894.

3

The Season of the Year at which Crises occur

Mr. Tooke, Mr. Langton, and others have mentioned the fact that crises usually occur in the autumn months. It is clear that production, whether in agriculture or in manufactures, reaches its maximum, or rather its completed results, in the autumn. This is due partly to the longer days and more favourable working weather of the warmer season, and partly to preparation for the larger demands of winter in the way of clothing, fuel, etc. Large advances of currency are required for the movement of the crops. Larger amounts of money are withheld from general circulation by those who do not make deposits in the banks. During the early autumn and the season succeeding, there are larger expenditures for future supplies. The greater demand for currency at this time is described as the "autumn drain." The quantity of agricultural production is uncertain, and the demand for all kinds of products may be out of harmony with the supply. Thus, disturbing conditions are likely to exist in the autumn.

In the fifty years from 1845 to 1894, inclusive, the Bank of England reserves showed a maximum in the month of June in fourteen years, and a minimum in October in thirteen years, the maximum and minimum appearing in these respective months much more frequently than in any other.*

* See an article by A. W. Flux, M. A., Manchester Statistical Journal, Session 1894–'95, p. 91.

Mr. Langton, in an article read before the Manchester Statistical Society, in December, 1857, illustrated by a chart the fluctuations of currency during a succession of years. In explaining it, he said:

" The first thing which will be noted on inspection of this chart is the quarterly fluctuation, exhibiting an almost invariable increase in the demand of the public upon the bank from the second week in each quarter up to the first in the following. . . .

" In the midst of other disturbances this wave may be traced in the magnitude of the operations of the third and fourth quarters, and the almost invariable lull in the second quarter of each year, the third quarter being generally marked by a rapid increase in the demand for accommodation at the bank. The culminating point of the movement, originating in the third quarter of the year, appears to be a moment favourable to the bursting of those periodical storms in which the commercial difficulties in the country find their crisis."

In some figures furnished by the Commercial and Financial Chronicle of New York, and published in a report of the Monetary Commission in 1898, attention is called to the large disbursements for payment of interest and dividends on railroad bonds and stocks in the United States in the months of January and July. Payments in these months, amounting in 1898 to $67,000,000 in each, are nearly twice as great as in April and October, the other months showing largest disbursements, and nearly five times as great as in the months of February and August.*

So great a fluctuation must necessarily cause a decided difference in the strain upon the banking resources of the country in different months of the year.

On the other hand, it should be stated that the usual signal for the appearance of a crisis is a conspicuous failure, or other convulsion, which causes wide-spread alarm and a more careful scrutiny of existing conditions. These failures do not occur in accordance with any general rules, or at any particular season, consequently it is difficult to generalize as to the season of the year when crises occur.†

Do Crises appear only in Highly Developed Countries?

It has frequently been stated that crises and depressions manifest themselves only in a highly civilized state of society, where commerce and industry flourish and there is enterprise and spirit. Also, that until within a comparatively short time they have not been recognised except in England, France, Belgium, the United States, Holland, and the Scandinavian countries, while more recently they have appeared in Austria, Germany, and Russia.

---

* Report of the Monetary Commission, University of Chicago Press, 1898, p. 310.

† For a statement by months of the comparative number of maximum and minimum prices on the New York Stock Exchange, see Chapter VI, p. 240.

It is no doubt true that crises occur where credit and enterprise are found. Nations which do not experience these visitations are not on that account to be congratulated, for their absence indicates a permanent state of stagnation. On the other hand, nations much less advanced than those mentioned have felt the influence of these disturbances. In 1873 and the succeeding years, the date of the most wide-spread and representative of all crises, Brazil, the Argentine Republic, and Peru, all experienced the distress which arises from falling prices, deficiency of employment, and the results of previous overaction. The disturbance in each of these countries followed an increase of trade relations with more advanced communities and large expenditures for public and private works. British Consular Reports of that time fully portray the situation there. The results were much the same as in more advanced nations, with a tendency to increased severity because of the absence of a diversity of resources. If the symptoms were less pronounced or the sufferings less acute, it was because the industrial organism was less complicated. A study of conditions in the Argentine Republic in 1890 affords one of the most valuable object lessons upon the subject of crises.*

It would thus seem that crises are incident to a state of progress and expansion rather than dependent upon the degree of advancement.

---

* See pp. 156–158.

Crises distinguished as Local or General

Crises and depressions are said to be local or general. That is, they may affect one nation or extend their influence over all nations having intimate commercial relations. They are becoming more and more general. This is due to obvious causes. First, the tendency to overaction and speculation is common to all progressive countries which have a system of credit. Hence, these forces work contemporaneously in all of them, and tend independently to cause the same results at approximately the same time. Second, the growth of commerce and of international credits tends more and more to create common interests and identical conditions among all commercial nations. The loss of one is in a very important sense the loss of all. A decrease of purchasing or consuming power in any nation must make its influence felt among the various nations with which it has trade relations. As Mr. Alfred Russell Wallace says:

"Much has been said as to the blessings of commerce among nations; it is, however, equally true that it causes the suffering of each to be felt by all. The ties of commerce unite nations alike for good and evil, and render the prosperity of each dependent upon the equal prosperity of all the rest. When this great truth is well understood, it may, perhaps, become the peace-maker of the world." *

While recognising that periods of depression are becoming more and more general, the fact should

* Bad Times, p. 83.

not be overlooked that there is a great degree of
inequality in the sufferings of different nations.   In
pointing out the coincident occurence of these dis-
asters in many countries, the tendency has been to
exaggerate this quality of universality.   A careful
analysis will show decided inequality, both in duration and in intensity; differences in date of commencement are also to be noticed.   This inequality
is traceable to the unequal severity in the country in
which the crisis originates as compared with others
to which it is conveyed later, and to the inferior
industrial organization and financial institutions of
some countries, and, as a consequence, unequal
capacity for withstanding the shock.

Degree of Severity in Different Countries

Frequent attention has been called to the fact
that France has suffered less from these visitations
than other nations.   This has been ascribed to the
exceptional frugality of her people, and to the
nature of land ownership in that country, viz., the
division into small farms, and the greater number
and proportion of landed proprietors.   While these
no doubt have their influence, there are other causes
of equal potency, among them a severe bankruptcy
law.   Whether by the educating forces of law and
established institutions, or by tradition, a high
standard of business honesty prevails in France.
The act of sons in toiling for years to pay the debts
of their fathers, and of notaries in paying for the
defalcations of one of their number, for the sake of
the profession, although without personal associa-

tions with him, indicates a standard of integrity and of compliance with business obligations which cannot be without influence upon the material prosperity of a people. It may be surprising that the nation whose soldiers are so noted for dash in war should furnish financiers and business men who are the embodiment of conservatism in their methods, but such is clearly the case. It should also be noticed that along with an almost stationary population, France shows much less fluctuation than other nations in the volume of trade and the quantity of production from year to year; and this makes business very stable and calculations more accurate. Fluctuations, such as sudden changes in prices or in the volume of production, are fruitful causes of crises. From these France is exceptionally free. The difference from year to year between the quantities of land devoted to the various kinds of agricultural production, as well as in the aggregate quantity of various manufactures, is exceedingly minute when we come to consider the extent of her agricultural territory and of her manufacturing industries.

The number of hectares in France under cultivation for wheat in 1885 was 6,956,765; in 1886, 6,956,167, a difference of only 598 hectares, or less than $\frac{1}{116}$ of one per cent. The difference in the number of hectares in 1881 and 1885 was even less —only 309.* The total values of domestic exports in the three years 1886, 1887, and 1888 were

* Statistical Abstract for Foreign Countries, 1885 to 1894–'95, p. 220.

respectively 3,248,800,000, 3,246,500,000, and 3,246,700,000 francs.* Taking 1887 as 100, the relative values for the three years named were respectively 100.07, 100, and 100.006. The quantity of pig-iron produced in 1893 was 2,003,000 tons; in 1895, 2,004,000 tons, or a difference of only 1,000 tons.†

Among the nations of Continental Europe, next to France, and on some occasions more than France, Belgium seems to have shown the greatest correspondence to conditions in the United States and the United Kingdom. Holland and Belgium stand at the forefront in the amount of foreign trade per capita. While the trade of Holland is much larger in proportion to population than that of Belgium, a greater share of the trade as well as of the manufactures of the latter country is made up of articles which are subject to decided fluctuations in price and activity—e. g., iron and steel, glass, stone, zinc, coal and coke.

It would seem that England is the country in which a spirit of adventure and speculation has done most to promote crises and depressions. The enormous waste of resources from enterprises, originating in that country, or supported there, cannot be explained by the greater wealth of her people, or the world-wide field which her commerce and colonization have opened up for the investment of capital. In addition to these influences, there has existed a spirit of boldness in enterprise, developing

---

* Statistical Abstract for Foreign Countries, 1885 to 1894–'95, p. 162. † Ibid., p. 316.

often into rashness, which has manifested itself in the multitude of promoters seeking capital, and even more strikingly in the great number of investors ready to furnish it.

It is probable that the United States furnishes an equal number of promoters of rash or absurd projects; but, whether because available capital has not been so abundant, or because investments are so numerous at home, where a greater degree of scrutiny is possible, these promoters have not found so large a number of gullible investors. A potent reason for these recurring seasons of speculation and rash enterprises in England has been the large accumulations of capital seeking investment. These are frequently so large as to require new fields of activity. It is the greater abundance of *disposable* wealth and its readier availability for investment, rather than the greater quantity, which distinguishes the English money market. Reliable historians give instances of companies formed and projects for the use of English capital which seem almost beyond belief. In speaking of the redundancy of capital existing towards the close of the seventeenth century, Lord Macaulay uses language thoroughly descriptive of conditions frequently recurring from that day to this:

" The natural effect of this state of things was that a crowd of projectors, ingenious and absurd, honest and knavish, employed themselves in devising new schemes for the employment of redundant capital. It was about the year 1688 that the word stock-jobber was first heard in London. In the short space of four years a crowd of companies, every one of which confidently held out to subscribers the hope of immense gains, sprang into existence. . . . Some of these companies took large mansions and printed their advertisements in gilded letters. Others, less ostentatious, were content with ink, and met at coffee-houses in the neighbourhood of the Royal Exchange. Jonathan's and Garraway's were in a constant ferment with brokers, buyers, sellers, meetings of directors, meetings of proprietors. Time bargains soon came into fashion. Extensive combinations were formed, and monstrous fables circulated, for the purpose of raising or depressing the price of shares. Our country witnessed for the first time those phenomena with which long experience has made us familiar. A mania of which the symptoms were essentially the same with those of the mania of 1720, of the mania of 1825, of the mania of 1845, seized the public mind. An impatience to be rich, a contempt for those slow but sure gains which are the proper reward of industry, patience, and thrift, spread through society. The spirit of the cogging dicers of Whitefriars took possession of the grave Senators of the City, Wardens of Trades, Deputies, Aldermen. It was much easier and much more lucrative to put forth a lying prospectus announcing a new stock, to persuade ignorant people that the dividends could not fall short of twenty per cent, and to part with five thousand pounds of this imaginary wealth for ten thousand solid guineas, than to load a ship with a well-chosen cargo for Virginia or the Levant. Every day some new bubble was puffed into existence, rose buoyant, shone bright, burst, and was forgotten." *

Some thirty years later, at the time of the South Sea Bubble, a new crop of preposterous schemes came to light. Among them were companies with the following titles:

" Wrecks to be Fished for on the Irish Coast; Insurance of Horses and Other Cattle (Two Millions); Insurance of Losses by Servants; To Make Salt Water Fresh; For Building Hospitals for Bastard Children; For Building of Ships against Pirates; For Making of Oil from Sun-flower Seeds; For Improving of Malt Liquors; For Recovery of Seamen's Wages; For Extracting of Silver from Lead; For the Transmuting of Quicksilver into a Malleable and Fine Metal; For Making of Iron with Pit Coal; For Importing a Number of Large Jack Asses from Spain; For Trading in Human Hair; For Fatting of Hogs; For a Wheel of Perpetual Motion. But the most strange of all, perhaps, was ' For an Undertaking which shall, in due time, be revealed.' Each subscriber was to pay down two guineas and hereafter to receive a share of one hundred, with a disclosure of the object; and so tempting was the offer that one thousand of these subscriptions were paid the same morning, with which the projector went off in the afternoon." †

The time preceding the crisis of December, 1825, witnessed great overaction in canal building and other improvements in the United Kingdom,

* History of England, chap. xix.
† Walter Bagehot, Lombard Street, ed. 1896, pp. 137–138.

also extravagant expansion of trade abroad, particularly with the South American Republics which had recently been freed from the Spanish yoke. The extravagances manifested in the two preceding centuries again appeared. Miss Martineau graphically describes the prevalent fever for sudden acquisition of wealth, often coupled with a less sordid desire to be identified with great and useful enterprises. In illustrating the recklessness displayed in some efforts for increase of foreign trade, she says:

" At Rio Janeiro more Manchester goods arrived in a few weeks than had been before required for twenty years; and merchandise—much of it perishable—was left exposed on the beach, among thieves and under variable weather, till the overcrowded warehouses could afford room for its stowage. It is positively declared that warming-pans from Birmingham were among the articles exposed under the burning sun of that sky; and that skates from Sheffield were offered for sale to a people who had never heard of ice. China and cut-glass were, in some places, pressed upon the natives, as preferable to cocoanut-shells and cow-horns, which had hitherto been their dishes and drinking-vessels." *

In his History of the Bank of England, Mr. Francis declares that in 1825 he saw the prospectus of a company to be formed for the draining of the Red Sea and the recovery of the gold and jewels left by Pharaoh and his army in the pursuit of the

* History of the Peace, vol. ii, p. 412.

Israelites. This, of course, was a burlesque, but a burlesque upon some of the projects of the time, which were scarcely less visionary.*

The explanation of these absurdities lies in the fact that this speculative disposition is an inevitable accompaniment of a spirit of enterprise and progress. A disposition which incites to delusive ventures of this kind is characteristic of an energetic people. This is proved by the organization, contemporaneously with these absurd projects, of companies for objects which proved useful and played an important part in the future development of England. Even at the time of the so-called South Sea Bubble, it is maintained that not more than ten per cent of the companies were for other than practicable purposes, and that the other ninety per cent proved successful and permanent.† Among the latter were companies for insurance, for fisheries, for trading with America, for improvement of harbours, for the manufacture of fabrics, and for the production of metals. At the time of the crisis of 1825, manufacturing and trade were increasing rapidly, and this increase was only temporarily checked by the events at the close of that year.

THE ARGUMENT THAT DEPRESSIONS BENEFIT A MAJORITY

A passing reference is due to the opinion of those who maintain that depressions are not after

---

* History of the Bank of England, 1847, vol. ii, p. 3.

† Eclectic Magazine, vol. xxviii, p. 473 ; reprinted from Hogg's Instructor.

all a calamity nor even disadvantageous. It is contended by some that a community is never more prosperous than when a number of persons are complaining of hard times. They argue that in so-called " flush times," when all kinds of business are active, prices will be high. This gives an advantage to the capitalist or employer. On the other hand, in dull times, prices will be low, and this gives an advantage to the wage-earner, because the purchasing power of his wages will be greater. A comparison has been made of the quantities and values of exports from the United Kingdom in the years 1871 and 1873. In the latter year, the quantities of many commodities exported were less than in 1871, but the aggregate values of nearly all were more. The increase in the rate of wages was altogether less than in prices. From this comparison the deduction is made that the profit of the increased price must have gone to the employer. In the succeeding depression wages decreased much less than prices.

The foundation for this contention is the inequality of the time requisite for the adjustment of wages and prices in changing conditions. It must be conceded that the rate of wages responds more slowly than prices to changes in activity.

The prices of manufactured commodities, especially, rise before wages adjust themselves to the change. This difference in the promptness of adjustment is even more marked in the comparative conditions of wholesale and retail trade. Retail prices fall much more slowly and rise somewhat more slowly than wholesale prices.

If these facts adequately described the whole situation in a depression, the view that an advantage accrues to a majority might be correct; but they do not. Lower prices and diminished profits occur simultaneously with diminished production and employment. Mills are closed and sales decrease. The changed conditions do not affect the manufacturer and wholesale merchant alone, but the whole field of industry and trade. It is not true that the interests of the employer and employee, or those of the wholesaler and retailer, lie in different directions. The prosperity of the whole community is the prosperity of every part. The serious and inevitable result for workingmen in every depression is that steady employment is more difficult to obtain, and many cannot find it at all. The retailer would be satisfied with the rate of profit current in a time of rising wholesale prices, if trade were brisk and no bad debts were to accumulate upon his books.

CHAPTER III

THE EVENTS PRECEDING THEM

A Crisis preceded by a Season of Activity.—
A financial crisis, with its usual sequence, a period
of industrial and commercial depression, is invariably preceded by a season of great activity marked
by much real or apparent prosperity. In many
instances this preceding activity has been so marked
as to awaken especial attention, and to call for congratulatory comments from those exceptionally
well qualified to forecast the future of business.

On July 6, 1825, the King's Speech, as read by
the Lord Chancellor, in referring to certain beneficial measures enacted by Parliament, contained
these words:

" . . . and his Majesty confidently trusts that
they will contribute to promote that general and
increasing prosperity on which his Majesty had the
happiness of congratulating you on the opening of
the present session, and which, by the blessing of
Providence, continues to pervade every part of his
kingdom." *

In February, 1825, a member of the Council,

* Hansard's Debates, vol. xiii, p. 1488.

in speaking of the material condition of the country, declared:

" The country was reaping, in honour and repose, all that had been sown in courage, constancy, and wisdom."

The crisis occurred in December of that year.

March 15, 1873, the London Economist, in its survey of the previous year, said:

" The industrial and commercial development of the whole of Germany and of Austria, Hungary, and the southeast of Europe, advances by strides which are most insufficiently understood among us. In the Austrian States the progress is astounding. The Vienna Government and Legislature are no longer the heavy and perpetual drag and discouragement on all new enterprises which they were a few years ago.　On the contrary, their spirit of practical and progressive reform sets an example to other nations.　All over the rich countries of the Danube capital and labour are vigorously at work in the discovering and turning to profit the amazing .resources which have been lying unheeded for centuries." *

The Bourse at Vienna was closed May 9, 1873, and a crisis of great severity occurred, followed by a depression of exceptional length.

On December 31, 1892, R. G. Dun & Company's Weekly Review of Trade said:

" The most prosperous year ever known in business closes to-day with strongly favourable indications for the future."

---

* London Economist, Supplement of March 15, 1873, p. 2.

In a book published early in 1893, giving, with additions, a translation of that portion of M. Clément Juglar's work on Crises which pertains to America, Mr. De Courcey W. Thom, the translator, after pointing out some disturbing features, says:

"But the fact that an analysis of the bank returns to the Comptroller of the Treasury * shows that available resources (capital, deposits, surplus, and undivided profits), as compared with demands (loans and discounts), are good and growing, considered in regard to the other signs indicating prosperity, justifies the prediction of the steady development of a prosperous period." †

The occurrence of the crisis, beginning in May, 1893, is well known.

Preceding Indications.—This preceding period is characterized by well-defined indications, some of which develop contemporaneously, but which, so far as they are distinct in time, occur in approximately the following order:

1. An increase in prices, first, of special commodities, then, in a less degree, of commodities generally, and later of real estate, both improved and unimproved.

2. Increased activity of established enterprises, and the formation of many new ones, especially those which provide for increased production or improved methods, such as factories and furnaces, railways and ships, all requiring the change of circulating to fixed capital.

---

* The word "Treasury" occurs in the original.
† A Brief History of Panics in the United States, p. 144.

3. An active demand for loans at slightly higher rates of interest.

4. The general employment of labour at increasing or well-sustained wages.

5. Increasing extravagance in private and public expenditure.

6. The development of a mania for speculation, attended by dishonest methods in business and the gullibility of many investors.

7. Lastly, a great expansion of discounts and loans, and a resulting rise in the rate of interest; also a material increase in wages, attended by frequent strikes and by difficulty in obtaining a sufficient number of labourers to meet the demand.*

Many of the above tendencies are indications of genuine prosperity. They are precursors of disaster only in case of overaction, when the equipment for the creation of certain classes of commodities, and their consequent production, is out of harmony with that for other classes, and speculation takes the place of more legitimate enterprise.

It should be especially borne in mind that in the events preceding a crisis, as well as in any season of growing prosperity, the increase of activity as well as of prices is far from equal in different lines. Higher prices will first be quoted in some particular commodity or commodities, and later in the rest. The increase of activity and price is usually most noticeable in articles the production of which can most readily be enlarged or diminished

---

* For a more detailed examination of the indications preceding a crisis, see Chapter VI.

by human volition, such as the so-called " industrial elements "—coal, iron and steel, or timber; or in articles required to supply some new demand of convenience or luxury. Food products, especially such as may be called the necessaries of life, vary much less in price. Their fluctuations depend much more upon natural causes, which are beyond human control, such as the quantity of rainfall and the degree of heat. Instances have not been lacking in periods preceding crises in which the prices of certain articles have declined.

The following figures giving export values in the United Kingdom, 1870–'73, and wholesale prices in the United States, 1897–'99, will illustrate the unequal rise:

United Kingdom. Export Values, Average for Each Year *

The prices of the first five items are given in shillings and decimals of shillings; the last two in pence.

	1870.	1871.	1872.	1873.	Increase, per cent, 1870 to 1873.
Coals, per ton........	9.64	9.80	15.83	20.90	116.8
Pig-iron, per ton....	59.18	61.08	100.85	124.65	110.6
Salt, per ton........	9.99	10.47	14.15	18.77	87.88
Wheat flour, per cwt.	16.31	16.51	17.48	18.97	16.3
Butter, per cwt.....	109.80	116.27	112.23	118.14	7.5
Cotton piece goods, per yard.........	3.55	3.33	3.51	3.45	† 2.8
White or plain woollen and worsted cloths, per yard...	35.17	37.52	41.19	41.00	16.57

* Statistical Abstract for the United Kingdom, 1868–'82, p. 110, for prices; the percentages in the last column are computed from the prices given.   † Decrease.

United States. Wholesale Prices *

Instead of average prices for the year, those for the month of July are given.

	July, 1897.	July, 1898.	July, 1899.	Increase, per cent, July, 1897, to July, 1899.
Steel billets, per ton............	$14.00	$14.75	$33.80	141.42
Bessemer pig-iron, per ton........	9.39	10.31	20.45	117.78
Wire nails, per 100 lbs............	1.35	1.36	2.70	100.
Steel rails, per ton	18.00	17.00	28.25	56.94
Hemlock boards, 1st qual., per M.	8.25	9.00	12.50	51.51
Pine boards, do...	45.00	45.00	51.00	13.33
Wool, Ohio fine fleece, per lb...	.477	.62¼	.633	32.7
Shawls of 42 oz...	3.55¾	3.60	3.60	1.19
Cotton, upland middling, per lb.	.07⅞	.06¼	.06⅛	22.22 †
Cotton thread, per spool..........	.0311¼	.0311¼	.0311¼	Same price
Wheat flour, per bbl.............	4.65	5.35	4.50	3.22 †
Granulated sugar, per lb........	.0447	.0509	.0521	16.55

In the period preceding a crisis, fixed capital in factories, furnaces, ships, and railroads will increase in greater proportion than food, clothing, and the consumable goods which are the necessaries of life.

A period of prosperity is thus a necessary prelude to every crisis or period of depression. It

---

* Bulletin of the Department of Labor for March, 1900, article on Wholesale Prices, by Roland P. Falkner, Ph. D. The percentages are computed from the prices given.

† Decrease.

furnishes the impetus for many undertakings which are improvident, and the excuse for luxury and extravagant expenditure. These are the fruitful sources of disturbance.

It should be noticed that the high prices and activity which precede a crisis usually pass the zenith some months or even a year or two before the crisis occurs. Probably also there will be fluctuations in prices and in the demands for commodities sufficient to give warning. In later years there is a distinct tendency towards a longer interval between the date of the maximum of prices and the occurrence of the crisis.

It will be interesting to trace the prices of iron prior to several crises.

Prior to the crisis of December, 1825, in Great Britain, the price of iron reached its maximum in the first quarter of that year.*

Before the crisis of 1836–'37, manufactured iron in Great Britain reached its maximum price in the second and third quarters of 1836, and attained its maximum production, up to that time, in the year 1836.†

Prior to the crises of April and October, 1847, in Great Britain, manufactured iron reached its maximum price in the third quarter of 1845, but there was a great increase of production, which reached its maximum in 1847. Scotch pig-iron reached its maximum price in the second and third

---

* Tooke's History of Prices, vol. ii, p. 406.

† Chart, giving a History of the Iron Trade, by W. G. Fossick.

quarters of 1845.* The reason for the high price was evidently the exceptional demand for new construction. †

Prior to the crisis of September, 1873, in the United States, railway construction reached its maximum in the year 1871. Pig-iron attained the highest price in the month of September, 1872. ‡

The crisis of 1857 in both countries, and that of 1866 in Great Britain, seem to have occurred with less warning. In both these cases, it is evident that the prominence of the failures which occurred hastened liquidation.

Whether the crisis begins contemporaneously with the decline in activity and prices, or is delayed for a time, depends upon a variety of circumstances, particularly the presence or absence of alarming failures or other events which destroy confidence; the strength of banks and credit institutions, and their ability to carry the existing enterprises which depend upon borrowing; the development of new demands by increased consumption, etc.

---

* See Fossick's Chart.

† There was a panicky condition in 1845. The main distinction between the two years was that 1845 was marked by a great number of enterprises projected and an accumulation of capital for their completion, much of which remained on deposit. The year 1847 was characterized by expenditures for the completion of many of these projects.

‡ More complete details bearing upon the course of prices prior to a crisis are given in Chapter VI.

The Phenomena of Crises and Periods of Depression

The usual signal for the beginning of a crisis is a conspicuous banking or mercantile failure, or the exposure of some fraudulent enterprise which attracts wide-spread attention. This is immediately followed by universal alarm in financial circles. Money is hoarded. Credit is refused. The established order of affairs, in which a very large share of business transactions is conducted in reliance upon credit, and which depends for its continuance upon the maintenance of confidence, is suddenly overturned.

There is a " run " upon banks, frequently resulting in the suspension of cash payments. The holder of securities and commodities is unable to dispose of them, except at a ruinous sacrifice. The change which occurs in the relations between buyer and seller, and lender and borrower, is not adequately described by saying there is a ruinous fall in prices and an unusual rise in the rate of interest. There is rather an abrupt cessation of normal transactions between them. There is a disposition to buy nothing and to do nothing until the storm passes over.

There is little satisfaction in studying the prices which prevail during a panic or crisis. Sales are made under such exceptional circumstances, and are marked by such fitful changes from day to day, that they afford no reliable information regarding actual values. Frequent and unexpected failures are sure to occur. After the first shock of alarm has spent its force, the prevailing features are uncertainty and a vague suspicion of instability from which none are free.

The end of the crisis comes after the shock has spent its force and when the true situation is understood. If there are no deep-seated causes for the disturbance, prosperous times will continue as before, though with a considerable degree of abatement. If such causes do exist, a period of depression ensues.

There is no clearly defined boundary line which marks the transition from a crisis to a period of depression, but distinct conditions predominate. During the crisis the embarrassment of banks and bankers is the most prominent feature, because their obligations are payable on demand, and they feel more promptly and more keenly the effect of the change in conditions. As the liquidation incident to the depression progresses, the embarrassment of merchants and manufacturers becomes relatively more prominent. The following figures illustrate this, and tend also to show that a crisis, as distinguished from a depression, is predominantly financial.

Aggregate liabilities of bankers and banking institutions in the United States failing in 1893 and the two succeeding years:

1893 (year of crisis)............................		$170,295,698
1894 (year of depression)............	$13,969,950	
1895 (" ")............	22,764,000	
Average for the years 1894 and 1895.............		18,366,975
Excess in 1893 (year of crisis) over average for 1894		
and 1895 (years of depression)................		$151,928,723
or 827 per cent.		

Aggregate liabilities of all others, including merchants and manufacturers:

1893 (year of crisis).............................. $231,704,322
1894 (year of depression)............ $135,030,050
1895 ("   "   )............   136,236,000
Average for the years 1894 and 1895............   135,633,025
Excess in 1893 over average for 1894 and 1895.... $96,071,297

Excess of liabilities from failures of merchants, manufacturers, and others in 1893, year of crisis, over average for two ensuing years of depression, slightly less than 71 per cent.*

It thus appears that the percentage of excess of liabilities in the crisis year over the average for the two succeeding years of depression was nearly twelve times as great (827 to 71) in banking failures as in mercantile, manufacturing, and all other failures.

A comparison of the different classes of failures in England in 1866, the date of the last actual crisis there, with the two succeeding years of depression, 1867 and 1868, shows a still greater preponderance of banking failures in the crisis year.† The comparison in both cases would be even more impressive if, instead of giving the figures for the years in which the crises occurred, it were confined to the weeks or months which marked their actual duration.

A period of depression presents some of the features of a crisis. Numerous failures occur as

---

* The figures giving the amount of liabilities have been furnished by the editor of Bradstreet's.

† For list of failures, with liabilities, see Record of Failures and Liquidations, by Richard Seyd, pp. 489 *et seq.*

before; but during the crisis the characteristic feature is the inability to obtain credit, or realize by sales, irrespective of the standing of the borrowers, or the value of that which they have for sale. At a later time failures are due to actual shrinkage of values, and to probable inability of borrowers to pay. The whole level of prices is lowered as compared with what it was before the crisis; and thus the whole machinery, not only of credit, but also of industry and trade, is thrown out of gear. There is stagnation in trade and in manufacturing. Wages are lower and men are thrown out of employment. The shrinkage of values continues. Money is not invested in purchases, or in any form of enterprise, because buyers and investors are not sure that prices have reached their lowest level. It is not invested in loans, partly because those who are most competent to transact business, or engage in industry, fear to begin new undertakings with borrowed capital, or develop those already established, partly because lenders are distrustful of obtaining again what they lend. As a consequence money is idle, and as the depression continues, rates of interest become lower, not so much because of abundance of money, as because only selected risks are accepted, and new enterprises are not commenced.

The conditions during a depression are the converse of those preceding a crisis. The latter characterize the ascending plane which precedes; the former, the descending plane which follows. The vital inquiry in the time of every depression is to ascertain when the worst has been reached. The turning-point is marked by no sudden shock like that which characterized the crisis. It comes gradually and quietly, and shows the working of recuperative forces, which are sure to triumph.

An examination of statistics shows that the actual visible decrease of activity in enterprise and employment, during a period of depression, is much less than is popularly supposed. The investigations made by Mr. Carroll D. Wright, Commissioner of Labor, in framing his Report of 1886, indicate that the decrease in the number of establishments in operation in this country during the year ending July 1, 1885, was only $7\frac{1}{2}$ per cent as an average, or 5 per cent absolutely idle, and an additional 5 per cent idle part of the time. The decrease in the number of men employed in agriculture, trade, and transportation, mechanical and mining industries, and manufactures was the same.* It is probable that the actual percentage was somewhat larger, and it should be remembered that this depression, at least in the United States, was not of the severest type. Its seriousness, however, will seem more impressive when we realize that this percentage indicated the non-employment of a million persons.

The number of railway employees of all classes, in the service of the railways of the United States, fell off from 873,602 in 1893 to 779,608 in 1894,

---

* Industrial Depressions, 1886, pp. 65–66.

or 10.75 per cent; the number per mile of railways fell from 515 in 1893 to 444 in 1894, or 13.78 per cent.*   In Great Britain in 1879, the worst year of the depression occurring after 1873, the percentage of unemployed in certain representative trades reached a very high figure.   The trades-union statistics of the United Kingdom show that of the Iron Founders' Society, 22.3 per cent were out of employment; of the Amalgamated Society of Engineers, 13.3 per cent; of the Amalgamated Society of Carpenters and Joiners, 7.6.†

It is important to recognise that the percentages showing a decrease in employment do not at all indicate the extent of the derangement.   The changes wrought are analogous to the increase or decrease of price in case of scarcity or surplus in the supply of necessary commodities.   Mr. Tooke, in his History of Prices, estimates that formerly a deficiency of one-sixth to one-third in the English harvest resulted in a rise of 100 to 200 per cent in the price of grain. ‡   So, on the other hand, the price of a surplus controls the price of the whole product.

The examination of the phenomena of depressions is not complete without recognition of the great increase in the equipment for production

---

* For number of employees, see Statistics of Railways of the United States for 1898, p. 40, issued by the Interstate-Commerce Commission.

† Statistical Tables and Reports on Trade Unions, 1893, pp. 78–80.   See Chapter V, pp. 137–141, below.

‡ History of Prices, vol. i, pp. 12–13.

which precedes them. This increase makes itself felt in the greater supplies which sooner or later will be available to meet the increasing demands of consumption. Upon further examination it will also appear that its influence is one of the most important factors in causing that inequality of activity and employment which is observed in comparing alternate seasons of prosperity and depression.

CHAPTER IV

CAUSES OF CRISES AND DEPRESSIONS *

THE student who would seek to explain the causes of crises and depressions must approach the subject with extreme caution. After extended examination, many have reached the conclusion that the discovery of definite and uniform causes is impossible. The degree of uncertainty, however, does not differ from that which is apparent in similar lines of investigation; for, while it is especially noteworthy in seeking the causes of crises, the difficulty of reaching definite results in any branch of economic or financial investigation has been conceded by many whose ability has been most generally recognised. To quote again from Professor Cairnes:

"An economic law expresses, not the order in which phenomena occur, but a tendency which they obey ; . . . therefore, when applied to external events, it is true only in the absence of disturbing causes, and consequently represents a hypothetical, not a positive truth." †

---

* See the selection of opinions given in Appendix A.

† The Character and Logical Method of Political Economy, p. 107.

If there has been a failure to reach satisfactory explanations of the causes of crises and depressions, it has not been due to the absence of interest, or to the lack of suggestions. When these disturbances occur, committees of Congress or of Parliament are appointed to investigate. These committees take testimony and collect voluminous information from many sources. In all the testimony there is an evident exaggeration of the efficiency of laws and of governmental action in remedying the difficulty. In the meantime, individual effort guided by intelligence and prudence and co-operating with forces which are invariably, though almost unconsciously at work, solves the difficulty.

Different Theories as to Cause.—In the report of Mr. Carroll D. Wright, heretofore referred to, nearly five pages are filled with alleged causes, suggested to agents of the Bureau of Labor or to committees of Congress. Among them are these:

" Withholding franchise from women."

" Want of training of girls for future duties."

" Faulty laws relative to the guardianship of children."

" The custom of issuing free railroad passes."

" High telegraph rates."

" The use of tobacco." *

In referring to the existing depression in 1878, Mr. Jevons says:

" It is curious to notice the variety of explanations offered by commercial writers concerning the cause of the present state of trade. Foreign com-

---

* Industrial Depressions, pp. 61–63 and 76–78.

5

petition, beer-drinking, over-production, trades-unionism, war, peace, want of gold, superabundance of silver, Lord Beaconsfield, Sir Stafford Northcote, their extravagant expenditure, the Government policy, the Glasgow Bank. directors, Mr. Edison and the electric light, are a few of the happy and consistent suggestions continually made to explain the present disastrous collapse of industry and credit." *

Dismissing explanations entirely frivolous, that treatment of the subject will be most valuable which distinguishes between substantial causes and those influences which are merely aggravating or incidental features.

At the very beginning, we may eliminate from the list of responsible causes, different economic or fiscal regulations established by custom or governmental policy. We are enabled to do this by the recognition of uncontested facts. Crises and depressions have occurred almost contemporaneously in different countries, under every prevalent system of banking; in monarchies and republics; in countries having free trade alike with those maintaining revenue or protective tariffs; in those having only metallic money, and in those having metallic and paper money; in such as have irredeemable paper money, and in those having paper money redeemable in coin; in such as have gold as the standard alike with those having silver; also, in countries having gold and silver with a fixed ratio between them. They have likewise occurred at different

* Investigations in Currency and Finance, p. 221.

times in the same country, under all the various regulations adopted.

The degree of intensity, of course, will be very much increased by mistaken policies relating to banking, tariff, or currency. Nor can it be denied that the permanent prosperity of a country depends largely upon correct policies in the particulars named. But crises and depressions are essentially temporary derangements of the existing order of things. That order may be good or bad, and one of the most frequent causes of crises has been a too hasty or radical change in established policies.

Among the theories most strongly advocated, or containing the largest degree of truth, may be enumerated:

1. Lack of confidence.

2. The abuse or undue extension of credit, either by excessive bank credits or by inflated issues of currency.

3. The readjustment of conditions made necessary by inevitable changes in values or prices.

4. A general fall in prices.

5. General changes in prices occasioned by changes in the monetary unit.

6. Contraction of the circulating medium or insufficient volume of money.

7. Over-production or under-consumption, the disturbing effect of which many writers maintain has been greatly intensified by the so-called modern revolution in production and distribution, which, as they allege, has resulted in a general increase of supply out of proportion to demand. It is also

asserted that this revolution renders recent depressions exceptional in their nature—more lasting and severe.

8. Psychological tendencies; the mental and moral disposition of mankind.

It is intended later to consider each of these in order.

The Responsible Cause.—In seeking the responsible cause, it is submitted:

1. Some of the above influences may create a derangement which will tend directly to cause a panic or crisis, and indirectly to cause the more serious and permanent condition known as a depression.

Depression may be greatly intensified by some or all of these influences.

2. The central fact in all depressions, as well as in those crises which are followed by depressions, is the condition of capital. These disturbances are due to derangements in its condition which, for the most part, assume the form of waste or excessive loss of capital, or its absorption, to an exceptional degree, in enterprises not immediately remunerative. In some form or other this waste, excessive loss, or absorption, is the ultimate or real cause. A somewhat similar idea is expressed by those who say that crises and depressions are due to misdirection of productive energy.

The alleged causes enumerated may be the proximate or apparent causes, or they may aggravate the disturbance. They may also, when carefully analyzed, prove to be mere descriptions of the manner in which capital is wasted, or of the means for its waste; but to the general causes above named, these disturbances may be traced, however much their operations may be obscured. The numerous crises without ensuing depressions are much more difficult to explain. They are preceded by a variety of causes, and sudden events which cannot be foreseen have much to do with their occurrence. The only satisfactory investigation which can be made is of the crises followed by depressions, or of depressions proper.

Elementary Definitions: Wealth, Land, Labour, Capital.—For a thorough understanding of this subject it is necessary to review a few elementary definitions.

WEALTH comprises all things which are alike useful, limited in supply, and transferable. All wealth is produced from, or created by, land, labour, or capital.

LAND includes every form of nature in earth, seas, or air, together with the natural forces which may be set at work. It is the source of our so-called " raw materials."

LABOUR includes physical strength and exertion, and the mental qualities which furnish them with method and ingenuity.

CAPITAL, technically defined, is wealth withheld from immediate consumption for the purpose of producing wealth in the future. It includes food, clothing, and fuel for support of those engaged in the production of wealth, necessary seed for planting, raw material for the finished products of manufactures; or, if we look at the subject from the standpoint of the employer or capitalist, money for wages and the purchase of supplies. These may be included under the term circulating capital. There is also fixed capital, which includes tools, machines, factories, buildings occupied or used by those engaged in productive employment, improvements upon land, likewise ships and railways with all their equipment.*

Nations are rich or poor, not in proportion to the abundance of land or natural resources which they possess, but according as they have an abundance or lack of capital.

The efficiency of productive energy in creating wealth increases with increased capital in a far greater proportion than the increase of capital. The form of statement is adopted by some, that while capital increases in an arithmetical ratio wealth increases in a geometrical ratio.

In the creation of the world's wealth, land is an invariable quantity.† Its productiveness cannot be augmented except by the application of capital and labour to derive or extract wealth from it.

---

* The term capital is used here in its most comprehensive sense. Adam Smith and others have maintained that supplies in the possession of consumers are not capital. Whether they are or not is rather a question for academic discussion than of importance in the determination of this problem. For a summary of opinions on this point, see Hobson's Evolution of Modern Capitalism, pp. 209 *et seq.*

† While, by legal definition, land includes the buildings and improvements upon it, by economic definition, all buildings and improvements are designated as capital.

The creation of wealth upon any considerable scale requires the co-operation of labour and capital. To use a comparison of Prof. Thorold Rogers, they are like the two blades of a pair of scissors. The results which can be secured by labour without capital are practically invariable. The efficiency of labour cannot be increased without the tools which capital furnishes. Adam Smith and others have contended that the increased skill and dexterity which labourers have acquired are the result, or rather a part, of capital. Certain it is that without the assistance which capital affords in making a division of labour possible, and in stimulating improved methods of production, labour could gain no material increase in efficiency. Capital, on the other hand, with the co-operation of labour, and land to work upon, is capable of indefinite increase. Upon its expansion all expansion of wealth depends.

Fundamental Propositions concerning Capital. —John Stuart Mill, in his chapter entitled " Fundamental Propositions respecting Capital," says:

" The first of these propositions is, that industry is limited by capital. . . . To employ labour in a manufacture is to invest capital. . . . This implies that industry cannot be employed to any greater extent than there is capital to invest. . . .

" There can be no more industry than is supplied with materials to work up and food to eat. . . .

" While on the one hand industry is limited by capital, so on the other every increase of capital gives, or is capable of giving, additional employ-

ment to industry, and this without assignable
limit. . . .

" Every addition to capital gives to labour either
additional employment or additional remunera-
tion." *

On the same subject, Adam Smith says:

" Every increase or diminution of capital, therefore, naturally tends to increase or diminish the real
quantity of industry, the number of productive
hands, and consequently the exchangeable value of
the annual produce of the land and labour of the
country, the real wealth and revenue of all its
inhabitants."†

Forms of Derangement of Capital.—The derangement in the condition of capital which causes
depressions manifests itself in a variety of ways.
All these tend to produce, directly or indirectly,
waste or exceptional loss, permanent or temporary.
In some forms this waste or loss is obvious enough.
In others it is not. It is controlled by human will
in some cases. In others it is not. The different
forms in which this derangement manifests itself
may be grouped in three divisions:

I. Direct loss or waste, such as results from private or public extravagance, from the investment of
capital in undertakings which fail, or from natural
causes, such as pestilence, the violence of the elements, or unfavourable weather.

II. Indirect loss or waste, such as results from

---

* Principles of Political Economy, book i, chap. v, sections
1 and 3.

† Wealth of Nations, book ii, chap. iii.

a lack of equilibrium between different classes or lines of production, manifesting itself in a glut of some commodities contemporaneously with a scarcity of others.

III. Most important, the inevitable changes which characterize modern industrial and commercial progress. These changes may be grouped under two subdivisions:

1. Changes resulting in the absorption of exceptionally large amounts of capital in enterprises the completion of which requires a considerable time, or which, when completed, are not immediately profitable, such as canals, railroads, large factories, and extensive public and private works of every kind. This class of investments of capital shows its effect in the disturbance of the normal relation between expenditures for remote production and those for production for early use, and has its basis in that preparation for additional supplies to meet the demands of increasing consumption which is characteristic of a progressive society.

2. Changes in methods of production occasioned by invention, improved machinery and methods, requiring the substitution of new appliances and equipment for old; also changes caused by the development of new fields. All these involve the loss of much of the capital theretofore invested, and are attended by serious derangement in the employment of labour.

The causes mentioned in each of the three divisions all act and react upon each other and operate concurrently in producing disturbances.

Incidental Features.—Incidental to the increased activity which manifests itself in a progressive era are the tendencies to overaction, and to engage in an unusual number of unprofitable undertakings; also the speculation and fraud which find an inviting field in a time of expansion. Often these incidental features seem to assume greater prominence than the principal facts of the situation. It is also true that the absence of equilibrium between different classes of production, mentioned in the second division, is very much intensified by the unequal progress of improvements in different lines of production. For example, improvements in manufactures have been much greater than in agriculture.

Each of the groups described may be considered more in detail.

I. Direct Loss or Waste of Capital

1. One of the most obvious losses of capital proceeds from extravagance in private or public expenditure. The aggregate earnings or accumulations of society must, in a succession of years, exceed the expenses or the quantity consumed. Otherwise progress and improved conditions would be impossible; even a stationary condition could barely be maintained. But, particularly in times of prosperity, the tendency is towards a steady increase of expense or consumption. A people adjust their wants and expenditures to a certain scale. This scale is not likely to be lowered, unless some serious warning is given. This fact shows the

effect of a general anticipation that the future will be as prosperous, or more so, than the past. The natural growth of human wants often results in general extravagance in habits of living, and the consumption by many, if not by all, of more than their share of the contemporaneous additions to the stock of useful things, and trenches upon prior accumulations. Thus, the capital needed to make provision for future supplies is impaired. Extravagance in public expenditure brings the same result.

2. Another form of direct loss or waste is the sinking of capital in improvident or unsuccessful enterprises, such as mines which yield no return, or railroads and other undertakings of considerable magnitude which, after the expenditure of large amounts, are not completed, or which, when completed, are found to be altogether unprofitable.

3. Similar in effect to extravagance and improvident enterprises are the losses due to certain natural causes, such as droughts or cyclones. These destructive forces diminish the supply of the necessaries of life, especially of food. The quantity which producers of these commodities, who are also consumers of other commodities, can offer in exchange is lessened, and the sum total of all commodities is diminished. If, for illustration, the total ordinary consumption or expenditure of the average consumer be estimated at 70 per cent for necessaries, 20 per cent for conveniences, and 10 per cent for luxuries, and a drought, or other natural cause, diminishes the supply of food, the

consumer must devote a larger percentage of his
expenditure to the purchase of necessaries, and will
have a smaller percentage remaining for conveniences and luxuries, the demand for which is
accordingly lessened. On the other hand, the farmer receives no more for his products, for what he
gains by increased price is offset by the decrease of
the quantity which he has for sale. Thus the
whole course of trade is injuriously affected. The
effect of food scarcity is nowhere more keenly felt
than in manufacturing communities. Operatives
find that the cost of living increases, and the manufacturer finds that he must sell to a diminished
market.

The loss occasioned by war, whether in the
form of actual waste or destruction, or by the withdrawal of productive labourers, is another way in
which capital is wasted. Some reasons will hereafter be given why war does not have the immediate
influence in causing depressions or crises which
would be anticipated. All these are forms in which
capital is directly lost or wasted.

II. INDIRECT LOSS OR WASTE. DISTURBANCE OF EQUILIBRIUM

While the causes already mentioned are sufficiently evident, there is a form of waste more productive of crisis which is not so obvious. Therein
lies one of the chief causes of these recurring disturbances. It is the lack of harmony between supply and demand in the production of certain classes
of commodities. Attention has already been called

to the unequal rise in the prices of various articles in the time preceding a crisis.*   It has frequently been noticed that periods of depression are characterized by the existence of a glut of many articles side by side with unusual scarcity of others, and by reason of the unusual supply of some commodities a popular impression exists that a main feature of the situation is the general abundance of all.   At such times attention is called to the fact that warehouses are filled to overflowing with articles, ordinarily commanding a ready sale, for which no customers can be found.   A brief examination will show that the absence of customers is not the result of general abundance.   A customer is one who has other useful articles to exchange for the contents of the warehouses, or who has money derived from the sale of such other articles.   If the things in the warehouses have any utility, there must be some one who desires them.   At least there are those who would take them as a gift.   The obstacle in the way of disposing of them is not the absence of demand, but the absence of effective demand, which is based upon a desire for the article and the possession of some equivalent to be given for it. The possession of a useful commodity is the basis of demand for another commodity in exchange.   If a commodity which any one possesses does not meet an existing want felt by one who has an equivalent, no exchange is possible.

Evidently much of the difficulty in the maintenance of an equilibrium between products arises

* Chapter III, pp. 52–54.

from the failure of producers to place themselves sufficiently in accord with consumers, and from their tardiness in keeping pace with constant changes of fashion and taste.

There is a well-defined limit to the efficiency of productive energy. If an undue share of this energy is devoted to some special kind of production, it must be to the detriment or decrease of some other kind of production. In the one there will be an excess and in the other a deficiency of supply. It has been said that production and consumption should keep pace like two wheels of the same vehicle. If all production could be exactly proportioned to demand or consumption there would be few disturbances. On this subject Max Wirth, in his excellent work on Crises, says:

"If production in the single branches could be adjusted as accurately as the branches of work in a watch factory, where, to every 1,000 cases, just 1,000 springs, 1,000 faces, etc., are ordered, and where the separate pieces ordered in indefinite numbers exactly fit to each other, there never would be any over-production, never could a crisis originate. Such systematic order is, however, impossible in a business world, where millions work on their own hook, and each one according to his own notions. There is always more or less of a gorge in one branch by the side of insufficient supply in another. But the more the abyss between demand and supply widens, and the more prices sink or fall, the sooner an extraordinary shaking-up of business is possible, the nearer the danger of a crisis approaches." *

As he states, in the very nature of the case, this exact equilibrium between supply and demand is impossible. The stimulus of competition and of unusual profits is sure to direct the attention of producers to some favourite commodity, and impel them to provide excessive quantities for the market. The extent of the demand for any article is uncertain and speculative. It will vary with natural causes, such as conditions of weather, also with the caprices of buyers. The demand for woollens will decrease in a mild winter; a change of fashion, or a variation in temperature from the normal average, may render the best-made garment almost valueless.

Again, the adjustment of demand to supply is a problem of such complication that accurate calculation is impossible. With the increasing division of labour and increase of commercial relations, the field is so large that it is impossible to make exact computations of probable consumption. It involves a world-wide survey. He who comes nearest to a comprehensive view is most likely to gain success.

The influence of direct loss or waste in causing depression, as described in the first division above, has been very generally recognised. The influence of an absence of equilibrium between different classes of products, as mentioned in

* Geschichte der Handelskrisen, 1883, introduction, p. 5.

the second division, has also received due attention.*

In more recent times, with the great increase of industry and commerce, the causes mentioned in the first two divisions tend to become less effective in creating depressions, while those included in the third division tend to increased effectiveness. Lavish expenditures to gratify private and public extravagance tend to right themselves, and cannot long interfere with the prosperous course of trade. Nations recover from the devastation of war, and from the effects of a scarcity of agricultural products.

Scarcity of food in the olden times caused impoverishment. The extent of the suffering arising from scarcity or famine is now greatly lessened by the wide area from which food supplies may be drawn, and the great variety of products from different climes, also by the accumulation, not alone of capital, but of capital in the form of food supplies.

The third form of derangement or loss due to preparation for the future, and to the progress of commerce and industry, has received occasional reference, but does not seem to have been elaborately analyzed.† This will be considered at some length.

---

* One of the clearest statements of the effects of lack of equilibrium in producing crises is contained in the Journal des Économistes for 1858, vol. xvii, p. 166, in an article by Ambroise Clément. This article seems to have attracted less notice than its merits warrant.

† See, in Appendix A, opinion of Professor Jevons, and the quotation from an article in the Bankers' Magazine (London), vol. xviii, p. 5.

III. The Inevitable Changes resulting from Modern Industrial and Commercial Progress

First Subdivision: Absorption of Capital, the Utilization of which is Postponed.—In considering this subject, the essential fact is the great difference of activity in successive periods in the creation of increased facilities and improvements. If careful examination be given to the period preceding each depression, it will be noticed that it was characterized by improvements on a large scale, by extensive preparations for an increase in production or distribution. In one era, the building of canals was a leading feature; in another, the building of railways or ships; in another, the opening up of great areas of agricultural territory; in another, the building of numerous factories and the increase of facilities for manufacturing. The occasion for undertakings of so considerable magnitude is the expectation of obtaining commodities more cheaply, or an actual or probable increase of the demands of consumption, and the opinion of investors that in supplying these demands large profits can be realized. Often extensive enterprises are commenced because an unusual surplus of capital seeks investment, or because construction is rendered cheap by low prices. The substitution of canals for transportation by beasts of burden, and of railways for canals, afforded a most attractive prospect for expenditure of capital. The accomplishment of any process of manufacture by machinery, which has been performed by manual labour, is sure to enlist the inter-

6

est of investors. At such a time labour is generally employed. The increased demand for divers
materials causes a rapid increase in their prices.
This increase by repercussion affects all prices,
though in a less degree. At the beginning of
this period the equipment to supply the increased
demand for many things is entirely inadequate,
and labour and capital are utilized to add to it.
Later, the increased equipment provides a supply
in excess of the demand, and there is a notable
fall in prices. In providing the increased supply,
available capital, if not exhausted, is greatly diminished, and the favourable results, accruing later
in the form of a general increase of production and
consumption, are deferred for a considerable time.
The forms in which there is an exceptional absorption of capital in the different countries are well
defined. In the United Kingdom, where the territory for the construction of railways is, for the
most part, occupied, there has not been since 1847
a notable activity in railway building prior to a
depression. The extent of the absorption of capital in investments, at home and abroad, the results
of which are deferred, is well indicated by the statistics of capital created and issued, which include
loans to municipal and private corporations and
subscriptions for new companies.

Figures are published annually giving not only
the amount of applications, but actual money calls.
The nominal share capital of joint-stock companies,
registering under the Act of 1862, affords a similar
indication, though less significant. The very con-

siderable fluctuations in these two items are shown by the following figures: *

Year.	Capital created and issued.	Actual money calls on same.	Nominal capital of joint-stock companies registered.
	(In 1000s	of pounds	sterling.)
1870	92,250	80,000	38,252
1873	154,700	....	152,056
1874	....	110,550	....
1876	43,200	....	48,314
1877	....	38,600	....
1881	189,400	115,250	....
1882	....	....	254,744
1885	77,972	77,875	119,222
1888	....	....	353,781
1889	207,037	167,804	....
1893	49,141	41,953	96,654
1896	....	....	309,532
1897	157,299	....	....
1898	....	101,201	....

From these figures it appears that the amount of capital created and issued in 1873 was more than three times as great as in 1876; more than twice as great in 1881 as in 1885, and more than four times as great in 1889 as in 1893. Nominal share capital shows similar fluctuations, and closely corresponds to the changing movement in capital created and issued.

The most common form for the absorption of capital, as well as the most correct barometer of activity in the United States from 1848 to 1890 was railway building, which, in each case, reached a maximum some months, or years, before the occur-

* For a complete statement by years (1870–1900) see Appendix B, p. 342.

rence of the crisis or the beginning of the depression. Prior to the crisis of 1857, the maximum construction was in 1856. Prior to that of 1873, it was in 1871. Prior to that of 1884, it was in 1882.

The following figures give the number of miles of railway construction in certain years: *

1854.....	1,360	1869.....	4,615	1880.....	6,706
1855.....	1,654	1870.....	6,078	1881.....	9,846
1856.....	3,642	1871.....	7,379	1882.....	11,569
1857.....	2,487	1872.....	5,878	1883.....	6,745
1858.....	2,465	1873.....	4,097	1884.....	3,923
1859.....	1,821	1874.....	2,117	1885.....	3,023
1867.....	2,249	1875.....	1,711		
1868.....	2,979	1879.....	4,809		

The diagram on the opposite page shows the increase in each year from 1854 to 1900.

After railway building has reached its maximum, construction follows on a very large scale in docks, warehouses, rolling-stock of railways and other facilities for transportation. These improvements are accompanied by extensive building operations. These continue until prices become prohibitive, or there is a decrease of demand for enlarged facilities. Railway building in the United States tends to the greatest activity in years when the prices of material are at the highest figures. This is illustrated by comparing the amount of expenditure for railway construction and the prices of materials. The table on page 86, taken from Poor's Manual of the Railroads, shows by periods of five years the cost of those constructed for twenty years, from 1864 to 1883, inclusive.

* Statistical Abstract of the United States for 1900, p. 374.

0 10 20 30 40 50 60 70 80 90 100 110 120 130 140

1854
5
6
7
8
9
1860
1
2
3
4
5
6
7
8
9
1870
1
2
3
4
5
6
7
8
9
1880
1
2
3
4
5
6
7
8
9
1890
1
2
3
4
5
6
7
8
9
1900

Annual railway construction.

Period.	Cost of construction.	Increase or decrease, period to period.
1864 to 1868........	$271,310,000	....
1869 to 1873........	841,260,000	Increase 210 per cent.
1874 to 1878........	356,940,000	Decrease 57 "
1879 to 1883........	1,194,540,000	Increase 234 "

The following statement of railway construction and the prices of steel rails for the cycles including the crises of 1873, 1884, and 1893 will illustrate the same tendency:

1867 to 1878, inclusive. Prices of steel rails, barring a rise in 1872 and 1873, fell from an average price of $166 per ton during the year 1867 to an average price of $42.25 in 1878. The average price by years, during the twelve years named, was $100.70, or approximately $100 per ton. During seven of these years, or 1867 to 1873 inclusive, the price was above the average; in five years, or 1874 to 1878 inclusive, it was below. The number of miles built in the five years when the price was below the average was 11,479; during the seven years when the price was above the average, 33,275.*

1879 to 1885, inclusive. In 1879 prices of steel rails rose to an average of $48.25 per ton, reached a maximum average of $67.50 in 1880, and then fell to a minimum average of $28.50 in 1885. During this period of seven years the average price by years was $46.05. During four of these

---

* Gold commanded a varying premium during the years from 1867 to 1878 inclusive, but the significance of the figures given is not materially changed by an allowance for this premium.

years, or 1879 to 1882 inclusive, the price was above the average; in three years, or 1883 to 1885 inclusive, it was below. The number of miles built in three years when prices were below the average was 13,691; in the four years when the price was above the average, 32,930.

1886 to 1898, inclusive. In 1886 the price rose again to an average of $34.50 per ton, and, after fluctuations, fell to a minimum average of $17.62 in 1898. During this period of thirteen years the average price of steel rails was $27.93. During nine of these years, or 1886 to 1893 inclusive, and 1896, the price was above the average; in four years, or 1894 and 1895, 1897 and 1898, it was below. The number of miles built in the four years when rails were below the average price was 7,582; the number of miles in the nine years when the price was above the average was 50,902.*

The effect of this larger cost in years of high prices is worthy of careful attention. The railways constructed when prices are high must compete with other transportation routes constructed at a lower cost; or, if not compelled to compete with other routes, must prove profitable or unprofitable according to the relation between income and cost.

---

* See Mileage of Railway Construction, Statistical Abstract of the United States for 1900, p. 374. Average Prices of Steel Rails by Years, same, p. 429; also, Iron and Steel and Allied Industries in all Countries, by James M. Swank, 1897, p. 41.

Until 1877 more iron rails than steel were used in construction, but the general course of prices was the same for both. There was a greater rise in iron rails in 1872 and 1873, years of extensive railway building.

The numerous foreclosures and reorganizations which followed the building of railways in each of these periods were not altogether due to construction in advance of demands. Scarcely any of them were abandoned. Nearly all of them are in operation to-day, and prove useful additions to the transportation facilities of the country; but they were constructed at a cost very much in excess of that upon which their net income would bring a profitable return.

To summarize in a few words the argument that depressions are caused by unusual expenditures of capital for prospective demands, it may be said:

Production has for its aim the affording of supplies for consumption. It may be for the purpose of supplying such consumption as will meet demands which are well established, and approximately uniform from year to year, nearby consumption, or it may be for remote consumption. It may look either to increase of commodities already in use or to altogether new commodities.

In production for the satisfaction of these two kinds of wants, there is a marked difference in the time intervening before the results of the expenditure of capital and labour can be realized. As has been already stated, in considering the maintenance of equilibrium in the production of different kinds of commodities, the amount of production is limited by capital. If a larger share of it is applied to production for anticipated wants, or in preparation for future consumption, there must be a corresponding decrease in the production of that required for present wants. It conveys a correct understanding of the effect of expenditure for remote consumption to say, in the language of trade, that it requires a longer time to bring the goods to market.

Effect of Absorption of Capital upon Foreign Trade.—The effect of undue absorption of capital for future uses in producing depressions has been well illustrated in the United States and similar countries by the relation between exports and imports. In the period of expansion preceding a depression, imports will be very large, and will bear an unusually large proportion to exports. With the beginning of the depression, or soon after, there will be a decided change. In any country where available capital has been exhausted in developing new fields, or in preparing for increased production, exports will show a great increase as compared with imports. It is probable that both the quantity and value of imports will decline. The exports will command a lower price than formerly, but will greatly increase in quantity, and so great will be the increase in quantity that the aggregate value will probably increase also. The decrease in imports is due to diminished consuming or purchasing power, caused by the exhaustion of capital. The same diminished consuming power tends to increase exports, because a smaller proportion of the domestic product is consumed at home than formerly, and consequently a larger proportion is sent abroad. There is also necessity for increased exportation to meet the obligations incurred abroad during the preceding expansion. Later, however, an even more important factor in increasing exports arises from the fact that the increased equipment, made possible by the utilization of so much capital in providing improved or enlarged facilities, begins to make its influence felt, and renders the production of many commodities cheaper than in other countries, and thus makes exportation possible where otherwise it would not be.

The following trade statistics in the United States illustrate this: *

Years ending June 30th.	Exports.	Imports.	Percentage, Exports to Imports.
(In millions	and tenths	of millions	of dollars.)
1875 (year of depression)	513.4	533.0	96
1876 (" ")	540.3	460.7	117
1877 (" ")	602.4	451.3	133
1878	694.8	437.0	158
1879	710.4	445.7	159
1880	835.6	667.9	125
1881	902.3	642.6	140
1882	750.5	724.6	103

The years 1875, 1876, and 1877 were years of depression. The next two years, 1878 and 1879, witnessed the change to activity. The years 1880, 1881, and 1882 were years of activity. It will be noticed that an adverse balance of trade of almost

* To the same effect, see statistics as to exports and imports for the Argentine Republic, p. 157; also for Austria, p. 202. The subject of the varying proportion between exports and imports is more fully considered in Chapters V and VI. The relation between exports and imports is given more detailed consideration in Chapter V.

twenty millions in 1875 was changed to a favourable balance of two hundred and sixty-five millions in 1879, or a difference of two hundred and eighty-five millions. In the earlier portion of the period the principal factor in increasing the exports was diminished consuming power; in the later portion, increased producing power.

In the normal course of events, the increase of exportation will continue for a considerable time after the close of the depression, although the proportion to imports will not be so large. The same force which increased production and exports before is still effective. This increase of exports will continue until increased activity at home increases demand and prices, and diminishes exportation. In 1880 and 1881, respectively, the exports from the United States were valued at $835,000,000 and $902,000,000, showing the continuance of the increase; but with enlarging home demands, imports for these two years showed a much larger percentage of increase. In 1882, the culminating year up to that time of railway building and many other forms of activity, exports fell off $152,000,-000, while imports increased $82,000,000.*

Second Subdivision: Results of Invention and Improved Methods of Production.—Closely associated with the factors enumerated in the former subdivision, and equally promotive of depressions, are the substitution of new methods, the results of invention, improved utilization of capital, and

---

* It should be stated that the inferior crops of 1881 account for a considerable share of this decrease of exports.

the opening up of new fields. It is impossible to depart from the established conditions, even in the direction of decided general improvement, without entailing loss and bringing serious distress to many persons. There is not merely a temporary wrench; many investors lose their capital, and many workmen lose their employment. No statistics can be obtained to measure the loss by the absolute dismantling or diminished efficiency of manufacturing plants made necessary by the competition of improved machinery; but this loss is very large, and is most keenly felt in countries where increase in wealth is greatest. There is the substitution of machinery for skilled or unskilled labour, and the substitution of new and superior mechanism for machines formerly in use. The invention of single machines often multiplies tenfold the producing power of an individual. Mr. Carroll D. Wright cites certain improvements in the manufacture of boots and shoes: " Goodyear's sewing-machine for turned shoes with one man will sew 250 pairs in one day. It would require eight men working by hand to sew the same number. By the use of King's heel-shaver or trimmer, one man will trim 300 pairs of shoes a day where it formerly took three men to do the same. One man with the McKay machine can handle 300 pairs of shoes per day, while without the machine he could handle but five pairs in the same time." *

In many departments of industry, equal and even greater advances have been made. It must

* Industrial Depressions, 1886, p. 82.

be noted, however, that the displacement of labour by machinery is very unequal in different kinds of production.

The statistics of coal mining in the United Kingdom show, on comparison of 1883 with 1897, that the number of coal miners increased by a larger percentage than the output of coal. In 1883 there were 514,933 coal miners employed, while in 1897 there were 695,213. In 1883 there were mined 163,737,000 tons, while in 1897 there were mined 202,119,000 tons. The increase in coal mined was 23.44 per cent, while the increase in the number of coal miners was 35.01 per cent.*

In the consideration of the influence of machinery and labour-saving devices, two opposing errors have obtained wide acceptation:

First, that labour-saving devices are an evil.

Second, that they confer an immediate and unmixed benefit.

It is a grave error to suppose that the increased productive power which multiplies the quantity of available commodities can be an evil, because there

---

* Fifth Annual Abstract of Labour Statistics, 1899, pp. 64, 81.

It should be noted that in the statistics for 1897, persons employed in private branch railways and tramways and in washing and coking of coal were included, while in 1883 they were not. This would diminish the difference somewhat. The number so employed is not separately given for 1897, but in 1892 was 19,342. This decrease in the quantity of coal mined in proportion to the number of men employed has not occurred in the United States, because mechanical inventions and machinery have been more generally used.

is still an illimitable demand for more, and every increase of supply contributes to the satisfaction of human wants. On the other hand, the entire or partial destruction of the capital formerly used to supply demands, which under improved methods are otherwise supplied, and the displacement of labour, cause a derangement not unlike that occasioned by absolute waste or destruction.

The opening up of new fields in agriculture and for the obtaining of raw material has the same general effect as the improvements accomplished by invention. The increase of available agricultural lands contemporaneously with railway building in 1873, and prior thereto, rendered large areas of land much less valuable. The value of many residence lots in cities has been diminished in the same manner by the development of street and suburban railways.

Effects of Progress as viewed from the Standpoint of Consumption.—The effect of progress in promoting depression may be viewed from the standpoint of increased consumption as well as from that of improved methods of production. The most progressive peoples are eager to obtain the best of everything available. There is an increased demand for and a disposition to use as ordinary conveniences of life, things which formerly were either regarded as luxuries or had been unknown, such as gas in the place of candles, and electric lighting as a partial substitute for gas. In the same category may be classed a number of modern improvements in sanitary conditions, whether secured by public enterprise, as municipal sewers, or by private initiative, as in the more careful construction of dwellings; also in the location of houses with regard to air, light, and the prospect afforded. Improved methods of transit have made available for residence much larger areas in the neighbourhood of cities. The disposition to secure the benefit of these advantages is by no means to be decried. The lower death-rate and better standard of health, as well as the greater degree of enjoyment and higher prevalent standard of taste which result from them, must be a benefit from an economic as well as from a social standpoint; but the changes wrought by these improvements in the standard of living cause a much more rapid exhaustion of capital and bring a slower return than would occur in a less progressive society.

Alike in kind is that derangement in the condition of capital which arises from the substitution of one article for another, when the change does not result in so great an advance as in the substitution of gas for candles. In response to the modern demand for the very best instruments and appliances, these changes are constantly taking place. We may instance the substitution of wire nails for cut nails. There was in existence an equipment which was ample for supplying the latter, but the former were regarded as preferable. A new equipment was provided for wire nails, which in less than twenty years practically supplanted the cut nail. Thus, in the history of the period, we have double capital invested for the purpose of supplying nails.

Everywhere in the most progressive countries there is manifest the destruction or abandonment of the old and the adoption of the new. That which is regarded as perfect in one decade is thrown aside as worthless in the next. An industrial revolution is constantly in progress. If unprogressive countries do not experience depressions, it is because there is no such industrial movement or commercial growth. They do not pass through eras distinguished by preparation for increase of production, nor do their inhabitants enjoy that great increase of commodities and facilities which is gained by more progressive peoples.

INCIDENTAL FEATURES

Tendency to Exceptional Overaction.—Side by side with the destruction which inevitably accompanies an improving condition is the tendency to overdo in those things which are new. Upon analysis it will appear that this tendency is quite different from a speculative disposition. It is due to the ever constant desire to accomplish the greatest results with the least labour and in the readiest way. The disposition to enter new and fertile territory, and by overaction there, to promote crisis and depression has frequently been noticed. The same temptation to overaction in exploiting valuable inventions operates with still greater force.

Speculation and Fraud.—The large profits afforded by successful enterprises and those which give new or additional facilities stimulate speculation; speculation stimulates fraud. These find a fruitful field for their operations in the inflated prices and the multitude of projects which precede every crisis. But, though they may precipitate crises, they are not the ultimate cause either of the extravagances of the time or of the collapse which follows. Speculation is rife in a time of rising prices. Rising prices proceed from an increase of demand out of proportion to supply, so that speculation in an article has its basis in increased demand for that article. Increased demand is characteristic of an energetic and progressive people.

DISTINCTIVE QUALITY OF RECENT DEPRESSIONS

It thus appears that in their distinctive quality recent depressions are a necessary incident of that progress which is characteristic of modern civilization. They are part of a *transition period* from a lower to a higher plane of production and consumption, and are preliminary to the enjoyment, on that higher plane, of a greater quantity and variety of the necessaries, conveniences, and luxuries of life.

This period of transition may be roughly divided into three shorter periods. The first is characterized by the employment of labour and the expenditure of unusual amounts of capital in preparation for increased or improved production. This is followed by the second period, which is a season

7

of readjustment to new conditions in which there is a great disparity in the supply of numerous commodities and facilities and the demand for them. The prices of many kinds of property decrease on account of oversupply due to increased equipment for production, improved methods, or the competition of new fields. This readjustment is accompanied by serious loss to those whose capital has been rendered useless or whose labour has been displaced. This is the period of depression. In the third period a readjustment to the changed conditions is accomplished and the benefits accruing therefrom are secured.

Different Theories as to the Causes of Crises and Depressions

It will now be profitable to consider in order the alleged causes of crises and depressions which have been most strenuously supported, and to examine the elements of truth or error contained in each.

Lack of Confidence.—The effect of lack of confidence in causing panics or crises cannot be overlooked. It cannot be measured by any rule, or explained in accordance with any economic principle, yet its influence must be recognised. The effect of a great failure, or of an exposure of fraud in the management of a prominent corporation or banking institution, is paralyzing upon business. Liquidation is hastened and credit for the most commendable enterprises is refused. But we must not accept the popular impression, prevalent in many quarters, that this is the sole source of the difficulty, a view especially favoured by speculators and by all those who hope for gain from rising prices. One thing is certain: in times of excessive expansion, there is too much confidence; in times of depression, too little. Unfortunately, an excess of confidence was our undoing. The men who promoted the calamity were full of energy and hope. Confidence is a quality of the mind. Its possession is essential for the utilization of opportunities which present themselves and for the maintenance of that degree of activity which is appropriate under existing conditions, but it cannot create wealth.

In its influence upon prosperity, the effect of confidence is analogous to that of proper economic policy or the security of property. Each is essential for the maintenance of prosperity, but they cannot create it. Their absence destroys, but their presence can only be effective when co-operating with other forces. No great progress is possible when they are lacking.

As a destructive force, the influence of an absence of confidence is very great. But unless confidence is rational and rests upon solid foundations, it injures more than it benefits. Its possession may stimulate enterprise, but however much we may admire enterprise, it is out of place when prudence should hold sway. In case there is a genuine depression, to blame men for lack of confidence is to blame them because they prefer to act in recogni-

tion of the existing situation rather than in ignorance of it. The vital error of this theory is the
idea that business operations should be conducted
in reliance upon conjecture rather than upon fact.

*The Abuse or Undue Extension of Credit, either
by Excessive Bank Credits or by Inflated Issues of
Currency.*—In the consideration of this problem it
should be said that confidence is a quality of one
who engages in commerce or industry. Credit is
confidence reposed in one so engaged.

This theory is supported by the admitted fact
that crises occur most frequently where credit is
most in use. Credit, like confidence, is in the first
instance a matter of belief. It is belief attended
by action. This belief may be well founded or
baseless. The indebtedness which one may safely
incur is measured by the convertible value of his
property. Credit is dangerous when out of proportion to available or convertible capital. If
prices fall, or enterprises fail, the convertible value
of the property of debtors must greatly diminish,
and many of them are unable to meet their obligations. As a result, a crisis is probable.

Rightly analyzed, however, credit is a means
employed in connection with other and more potent
forces. It determines the magnitude rather than
the nature of undertakings. In every advanced
society there is a speculative or extravagant tendency, more or less active according to the apparent
prosperity of the time, and the opportunities
afforded for obtaining capital for investment.
Credit is one means of obtaining control of capital,

and thus promoting enterprise. Many pages have been written in support of the position that credit creates capital, or that it is itself capital. It is sufficient to say that it greatly facilitates the use of capital and stimulates production. It insures the constant employment of labour and the continuance of the machinery of production. It enables undertakings requiring a long time before they can afford results, to proceed side by side with those which bring prompt return. By its use the manufacturer and the merchant increase their stocks, and all those engaging in business can greatly enlarge their field of operations. In the transaction of business, credit marks the third stage of development, as follows:

1. Simple barter, in which he who owned an article of value could dispose of it only in exchange for something of value owned by another who desired the article owned by him.

2. The use of money having universal value, and affording at the same time a standard of value and a medium of exchange. By its use he who owns an article of value can exchange it for money, irrespective of the possession by the buyer of any specific commodity which the seller desires.

3. The use of credit, by which the owner parts with his wealth for the promise of future payment, and for no immediate equivalent, but in reliance upon the ability and honesty of the borrower. Just as the use of money, as compared with barter, diminished the difficulties of trade, so the use of credit greatly facilitates operations, as compared

with a situation in which money alone is used. Credit enables the borrower to do what otherwise only the actual owner of capital could do.

The general result of the use of credit is to provide for enterprises by a greater number of persons, on a much larger scale, and with greater convenience. Thus, the difference between the conditions which arise from an extended or a limited use of credit is rather one of magnitude than otherwise. The same general tendencies would be at work in either case.

If we consider, it will be seen that the cause of the abuse of credit is a spirit of speculation created under the influence of successful operations and large accumulations of capital, or an attempt to keep alive unprofitable enterprises, or the indulgence in extravagance and waste somewhere. Banks having the power to issue bills do not issue them, and thereby expand credit, unless there is a demand for larger credit, unless the spirit of speculation and expansion is already rife. Lenders do not lend money, nor do wholesale dealers grant credit, except in response to demands upon them. They but fall in line with their surroundings, and yield to influences powerfully at work. Bankers are frequently blamed as the responsible cause of crises. No doubt many of them at the time of a convulsion, and in the days preceding or succeeding it, are at fault, some for too great conservatism, others for too great liberality in the granting of discounts. Their critics find fault with them alike for bringing on the crisis by granting loans too freely, and for making it severe by refusing them. In these crises they are largely controlled by their environment; they do not create conditions. They but reflect the good or bad times, which come without their behest, and the existence of which they must recognise.

Under the head of abuse of credit we may include another explanation of crises, namely, inflation of the currency. This is not independent of abuse of credit. Both lead to the same thing, because an increase in the volume of the circulating medium increases the opportunity for the expansion of credit.*

As affecting crises, inflation of the currency stimulates the speculative fever and promotes unprofitable enterprises. It is particularly true that, if irredeemable paper money is issued in any considerable quantity, prices are sure to rise. An unnatural rise in prices is the most fruitful parent of injudicious investment. Investors do not stop to think that while an article may bring many more dollars than before, the dollar has not the same purchasing power. The result of inflation was never better illustrated than in the period during and after the late Civil War. An increase in nominal values was caused by the large increase of paper money. This created a desire for new and, in

* A distinction should, of course, be made between inflation proper and an enlargement of the currency in response to the demands of increasing business, or to take the place of that which has been withdrawn from active circulation in time of panic. An increase at such time is not inflation.

many cases, useless undertakings. In the eight
years from 1866 to 1873 inclusive, a greater
mileage of railways was built than from the completion of the first railway in the United States in
1830 to the end of 1865. Many of these were
commenced after the premium on gold had fallen,
and prices were more nearly normal; but the buoyant spirit of enterprise, which had been stimulated
by rising prices and unusual profits, still continued,
and resulted in the severest crisis this country ever
experienced.

*The Readjustment to New Conditions because of
Inevitable Changes in Values or Prices; a General
Fall in Prices; Changes in the Monetary Unit.*—
Under this head may be included the theory of
those who regard a depression as merely the result
of a general fall in prices, and of those who ascribe
the difficulty to changes in the monetary unit.

Business engagements consist in obligations to
do or furnish something in the future, the price or
value of which is fixed by a standard existing in the
present. Industrial operations are conducted in
dependence, in a general way, upon the maintenance
of a certain level of prices. It is maintained that
crises are due to the fact that these obligations must
be performed at a time when the range of prices
is so different from that prevailing when the com-
pensation was fixed or contract made, that one
of the parties must lose. It will readily appear
that if there is a considerable change in prices, such
derangement might ensue as to cause a crisis, and
the effects of the change would protrude them-

selves into the future, so as to aggravate a depression.

The beginning of a crisis is little more than the sudden development of wide-spread inability to meet obligations. If the convertible property of debtors should fall in price, the ability to pay would be greatly diminished. In actual experience, this theory, more than either of the two preceding, would seem to give the immediate cause of the difficulty, and on some occasions the sufficient cause, so far as the mere crisis phase is concerned. But, if the disturbance is prolonged, the real difficulty is deeper. It should not be forgotten that for every seller there is a buyer; for every borrower there is a lender. That which one loses by a change in prices the other gains. It is a well-known fact that in all our great manufacturing centres, after a season of low prices, numerous mechanics and artisans withdraw money from savings-banks, and, taking advantage of the situation, purchase or build houses for themselves. It is also well known that a low price of raw materials is frequently the ground for investment in industrial undertakings, which are needed and will be profitable, and which would not have been commenced in a time of high prices.

The general economic condition of a nation is not changed by a rise or fall of prices, because prices merely measure the value of property. So far as such rise or fall is concerned, there would remain the same quantity of things useful as before. If there is less of national wealth it is not due to fall of prices, but to some other cause.

A legislature, for the benefit of debtors, might pass laws staying the collection of debts, or a despot might declare that fifty pieces of money should be regarded as equal to one hundred in payment of obligations theretofore made; but neither of these measures would cure a depression. They might relieve debtors and injure creditors, but could not set the wheels of industry in motion.

It is true that a change in prices, by causing the bankruptcy of many persons and the discouragement of others, removes many useful members from active participation in trade or industry, and, as a practical fact, the discouraging effect upon business of a steady fall in prices cannot be exaggerated. It destroys the accuracy of all calculations and dissipates hopes of profit. It falls with peculiar weight upon those who are relying on credit. At times, however, such a fall should rather be regarded as a salutary warning of the dangers of overaction, and of the necessity of adaptation to new conditions. Every progressive era must be characterized by especial danger to those who embark in business in reliance upon credit, because the tendency of invention and modern development is to create a lower price level; and in spite of temporary alternations of rise and fall, this general tendency must always be at work.

Speculators may hold commodities, hoping to gain from a rise of prices. Merchants and manufacturers may suffer losses from a fall in prices. This fall may threaten or cause a crisis, and, as a result, wide-spread liquidation and bankruptcy may

occur.   These are the visible signs of crises, but
behind them the real causes appear.   Either the
resources of buyers have been diminished by waste
or locked up in something not immediately remunerative, so that the effective demand for commodities is lessened; or the development of improved methods, or of new fields for the production
of the commodities, is such that the cost of producing them is diminished.*

A fall in prices causes only a transfer of wealth
from one individual to another.   Between the
mere transfer of wealth and its loss there is a vital
difference.   As upon all other branches of this
inquiry, a surprising difference of opinion has developed concerning the comparative effect in producing depressions, of money lost in speculation
and actual loss of capital.   To illustrate, let us
contrast two transactions:

1. The sum of $10,000,000 is paid to a mine-
owner for a mine which proves to be worthless,
and nothing is expended for its development.   The
money has simply changed hands from buyer to
seller, without the transfer of any equivalent.

2. The sum of $10,000,000 is actually expended
in labour and materials for the development of a
mine.   No mineral is obtained, and the mine proves
to be worthless, so that the capital expended upon
it is wasted.   In the first case there is only a transfer of money from one person to another, while
in the second not only does the investor pay out

---

* See first and second subdivisions, under Division III, pp.
81 and 91 of this chapter.

his money, but it is wasted.   It will be noticed that in the second case there is an absolute destruction of wealth, while in the first there is none.   Which transaction tends the more to produce depression?

All will agree that the second has such tendency.   As to the first, some contend that, equally with the second, it tends to produce depression; while others maintain that it has no such tendency at all.

The latter view would be correct, if we considered only general principles and disregarded certain traits of human nature.   A mere transfer of property from one person to another cannot be so injurious as the absolute destruction of wealth.   But we cannot overlook the evils which may spring from such transactions as those illustrated by the first example.   It is a common saying that no man retains what he steals, or judiciously invests what he gains by sudden speculation or unexpected windfall.   Not only will the loser by such a bargain become a smaller consumer, and, under the influence of discouragement, a poorer producer; but the gainer will inevitably expend his money in extravagance, or he will engage in similar transactions, in the hope of further multiplying his gains without participation in legitimate business.   The distinction between the two cases illustrated attracts less attention, because in every period of excessive activity, numerous instances of both appear contemporaneously. At such a time, not only will there be injudicious and wasteful enterprise leading to actual loss of capital, but also a spirit of speculation, under the influence of which much property changes hands at absurd prices.

An important fact apparently supporting the theory that a crisis is caused by speculation, is the large quantity of property, both real and personal, which is held in expectation of a rise in price. There is no present demand for such property at the prices asked. When a crisis occurs these values prove entirely fictitious, and sales can only be made at much lower figures. This results in serious loss and a necessity for readjustment according to the actual situation.

The Contraction of the Circulating Medium or an Insufficient Volume of Money.—The two may be considered together. These expressions, as commonly employed, seem to refer not to metallic money, the quantity of which is not a matter of arbitrary control, but rather to credit or paper money, whether issued by the government or by banks. No doubt serious disturbance and loss would be caused by a sudden or arbitrary contraction in the volume of outstanding paper money. Prices would fall. It would be difficult to maintain the existing lines of credit. But a distinction should be made between that decrease or contraction which proceeds from arbitrary regulation and that which results from conditions of trade or from a panic which causes hoarding. That system of note issues is most perfect which provides for all situations, including not only ordinary demands, but also the exceptional cases of sudden shrinkage. It is hardly probable that under rational management material contraction of the currency would be attempted, except to correct inflation in a time of depreciated paper money, or to substitute a better form of currency to take the place of that which is withdrawn. * Monetary panics, so called, have occurred of which the distinctive feature is an unusual scarcity of money. They may happen when the relations between demand and supply seem to be normal and the essential conditions of prosperity exist; but, by reason of some sudden shock, money is withdrawn from circulation. For such emergencies provision should be made, but it is not a question of the quantity of outstanding paper currency. At such a time there would be a great shrinkage in the quantity of available money whatever the amount ordinarily in circulation. Temporary increase of currency at such a time, if properly guarded, will, no doubt, be helpful. If the state of industry is a healthy one, the danger will soon pass away; money will circulate again and normal conditions return. If conditions are not prosperous, then the scarcity of money is not the real cause of the disturbance. In either event, the temporary scarcity is an effect and not a cause, though it must be conceded that when the distress has been caused by other influences, the scarcity of money greatly intensifies it.

It would be difficult to find a crisis traceable to insufficient volume of paper money. Examination of statistics will show that crises occur rather when there is an unusual amount of credit money in circulation, and sometimes when there is an exceptional supply of metallic money. In the year 1837, in the United States, there was not only the greatest aggregate amount of paper money in circulation up to that time, but also the greatest quantity per capita. The year 1857 also shows the greatest aggregate amount of paper money in circulation up to that year, and, with the exception of one year, the greatest quantity per capita; in 1873 and 1893 the amount also surpassed all previous years, and in per capita was near to the maximum. Yet these four years were years of severe crises. Even more notable is the unusually large proportion of paper money to specie in crisis years.*

Volumes have been written upon this subject, more particularly with reference to questions of coinage of silver and the currency. It is contended that prices are determined by the relation between the volume of money (some include all kinds of money, others, metallic or basic money only) and the total quantity of commodities. Consequently it is maintained that as the volume of money diminishes, prices decrease and financial loss and crises occur. This expresses only a part of the truth. As affording a rule to follow, it is a grave error, for it entirely overlooks another factor— namely, the efficiency of money. The efficiency of money depends upon its rapidity of circulation, and the extent to which substitutes are employed to take its place. The facts upon this point as regards prices are very well expressed by John Stuart Mill:

* See Muhleman's Monetary Systems of the World, pp. 128– 130, 135, 140.

" The proposition respecting the dependence of general prices upon the quantity of money in circulation must be understood as applying only to a state of things in which money—that is, gold or silver—is the exclusive instrument of exchange, and actually passes from hand to hand at every purchase, credit in any of its shapes being unknown. When credit comes into play as a means of purchasing, distinct from money in hand, the connection between prices and the amount of the circulating medium is much less direct and intimate, and such connection as does exist no longer admits of so simple a mode of expression." *

Mr. Tooke, the author of the standard work on prices, also says:

" There is not, so far as I have been able to discover, any single commodity in the whole range of articles embraced in the most extensive list of prices, the variations of which do not admit of being distinctly accounted for by circumstances peculiar to it . . .† Circumstances do frequently operate with such force as to reduce prices in the face of an expanding currency, and to advance prices when the currency is diminishing. In point of fact, the expansion is frequently rather an effect than a cause of enhanced prices."

Again, the volume of money in use or circulation does not depend upon the amount issued. Publish a rumour some morning that a leading bank is in a shaky condition, and before sunset there will be

---

* Political Economy, book iii, chap. viii, sec. 4.
† History of Prices, vol. ii, p. 349.

a contraction of available currency greater than any law-making power or finance minister ever accomplished in the same time.

It requires little consideration to recognise that, given a certain quantity of money, there may be two conditions: one, that of universal distrust, when money is kept out of circulation; another, that of general confidence, when borrowers are trusted and money is readily obtained.   In the latter event a certain quantity of money may be sufficient to transact the business of a community or a country; in the former, a far greater quantity will not supply the demand.

Attention has already been called to the occurrence of crises in years when there was an unusual quantity of money in circulation.   It is also true that an insufficient volume of money is not the cause of extended seasons of distress.   This is conclusively proved by a well-established fact.   In all depressions prices go down while money is accumulating in banks and rates of interest are going down, so that at the worst of every depression we have a great abundance of money and low rates of interest side by side with low prices.   Low rates were quoted at New York in 1878, in 1886, and 1897, and at London the lowest rates prevailed in 1859, 1868, 1879, 1885, and 1895, all severe or severest years of depression.

On the other hand, there are not lacking notable instances in which an exceptional abundance of money has been a moving cause of depression. This has been true, not only of paper money, but

8

of gold and silver money, and also of capital which they represent. The great increase of money in Germany due to the payment of the French indemnity is one illustration of this. Enterprises were undertaken which at other times would have been impossible, and in private as well as public expenditures there was an era of extravagance. Half in humour and half in earnest, a German comic newspaper said: " Let us have another war; let us be beaten and pay an indemnity and then we shall be prosperous again." It would, however, be far from correct to say that this great indemnity was not a benefit to Germany. Much of it was wasted, no doubt; but a much larger share was expended in enterprises ultimately very beneficial, but the benefits of which were long deferred. The ground for the unfavourable comparison with France was that in the latter country the war had caused an earlier liquidation, and there was an absence of those extensive projects and investments which were possible in Germany.

The mining of large quantities of gold or the sudden development of some new source of wealth has the same tendency to bring expansion in enterprise, together with a general increase of all kinds of expenses, and to cause the locking up of large quantities of capital in projects not promptly remunerative. The Boston Board of Trade, in a report made in April, 1858, upon the events of 1857–'58, mentioned as an important fact in causing the depression, " the discovery of the rich and extensive gold mines of California, by which many

hundred millions of gold have been rapidly added
to the currency of the world."

✳ The tendency of large accessions or accumulations of capital to cause disturbance is well expressed by Mr. Bagehot:

✳" At intervals . . . the blind capital of a country is particularly large and craving; it seeks for
some one to devour it, and there is ' plethora '; it
finds some one, and there is ' speculation '; it is devoured, and there is ' panic.' " ✳

Thus, paradoxical as it may seem, the starting-
point for crises and depressions may be found in
abundance rather than in scarcity, whether of
money or of capital.

✳ *Over-production   or   Under-consumption.* — In
support of this theory it is said that every crisis or
depression is marked by a glut of supplies in the
market, by the inability to dispose of stocks of merchandise or to transfer convertible property of any
kind at fair prices.   Increased production in itself,
however great, cannot be a misfortune or cause a
crisis.   It is a benefit until the time, impossible of
anticipation, when all shall have secured as much
as they want.   Human wants are of infinite
variety, and the strongest desire is for abundance.
Modern invention, improved facilities for transportation, better methods in the transaction of business
and in the utilization of capital, all tend towards
securing greater abundance.   These must be a

* Essay on Edward Gibbon, vol. ii of Collected Works, p. 2.
For the whole quotation of which the above is a part, see Appendix A, pp. 311–312.

benefit, because they increase the supply of the necessities and comforts of life. The gradual progress from our first parents, clothed in nature's garb, to the elaborately gowned women and well-dressed men of the present day, is due to increased productive power, especially in the manufacture of fabrics suitable for clothing. In brief, general over-production is impossible. But if by the term " over-production " is meant disproportionate production of some things; that the machinery of production is out of harmony, making too much of this and not enough of that, a condition is described that may be a cause of depression. It is not, however, a correct use of terms to call that condition " over-production." It is merely the absence of equilibrium between different kinds of production already mentioned.

That upon which greatest stress is laid by those who ascribe. crises and depressions to over-production is the adoption of labour-saving machinery, the improvements and inventions which help to create abundance and greatly increase the aggregate supplies of the human race. These must, in the long run, be a benefit, for we do not work for the sake of working, but for the sake of the things that we produce by work, and the larger the number of things we produce and the easier the work, the better our condition.

But there is a constantly recurring necessity for adjustment to new conditions. Some economists tell us remorselessly that those who have learned a trade must, when machinery begins to do the

work they have done, learn another trade, or turn
their attention to other employment.   But this is
not so easy, particularly if a man has reached middle life, so that he cannot easily learn another trade,
or if other lines of employment are already more
than full.   Likewise, if a man has built a factory,
and invested in it all his capital, and improved
machinery makes his investment useless, it is little
consolation to him to tell him he must change to
something else; he has his all in that factory.*

There is between the old conditions and the
establishment of the new a time of transition in
which numerous interests must suffer.   In the long
run, it must be admitted that great benefit is conferred.   The human race is richer, but for a multitude of individuals the loss is serious; and so many
are involved that, often in the midst of great abundance, depression may exist.

Especial prominence has been given by the supporters of the theory of over-production to the so-
called modern revolution in production and distribution, which, in recent years, it is maintained, has

---

* "In some books on political economy the removal of capital from one employment to another is spoken of lightly, as if
it were an easy process.   No delusion can be greater.   Such
changes can, of course, be made in some kinds of business without very serious loss.   A banker, whose fixed plant consists of
a few chairs and tables, may, if he has been prudent, wind up
his affairs and invest his capital elsewhere.   But a manufacturer or farmer, with money sunk in all sorts of ways, cannot
sell his plant without heavy loss, except in very peculiar times
and under extraordinary circumstances."—William Fowler,
M. P., Contemporary Review, vol. xlvii, p. 538.

multiplied the necessaries and conveniences of life more rapidly than the demand. It is asserted that this revolution has rendered recent depressions exceptional in their nature, more lasting and severe. Among those holding this opinion may be mentioned the late Mr. David A. Wells. He placed special stress upon the increased machinery of production and distribution, and called attention to the fact that the great depression of a little more than a quarter of a century ago began soon after the opening of the Suez Canal, contemporaneously with which appeared exceptional improvements in the machinery and economy of distribution of such products as wheat, rice, wool, and meats; or in increased sources of supply, as in copper, tin, nickel, silver, and quinine.

He quotes M. Georges de Laveleye, who maintains that the industrial activity of the greater part of the past century was devoted to fully equipping the civilized countries of the world with economic tools, and that the work of the future must necessarily be that of repair and replacement, rather than of new construction, and adds:

" A more important inference, and one that fully harmonizes with the existing situation, is, that the equipment having at last been made ready, the work of using it, for production, has in turn begun, and for the first time the world has become saturated, in recent years, with the results of these modern improvements." *

---

* Contemporary Review, vol. lii, pp. 291–292.   Recent Economic Changes, p. 63.

Mr. Wells also says:

" All investigators seem to be agreed that the depression of industry, in recent years, has been experienced with the greatest severity in those countries where machinery has been most largely adopted; the least, or almost not at all, in those countries and occupations where hand labour and its products have not been materially interfered with or supplanted . . . as in China, Turkey, Mexico." *

In another article he states that the years 1879, 1880, 1881 for the United States were years of abundant crops and great foreign demand, and are generally acknowledged to have been prosperous; while the years 1882, 1883, 1884 are regarded as having been years of extreme depression and reaction, *yet the movement of railroad freights greatly increased during the latter period.*†

In further support of this contention he states elsewhere that side by side with facts as to the destruction by loss of capital in worthless enterprises, conversion of circulating capital into fixed, and extravagant consumption, should be placed the fact that statistics not only fail to reveal the existence of any great degree of scarcity, but, on the contrary, prove that those countries in which depression has been, and is most severely felt, are the very ones in which desirable commodities of every description—railroads, ships, houses, live-stock, food, clothing, fuel and luxuries—have year by year been accumulating with

---

* Contemporary Review, vol. lii, p. 293.

† Ibid., p. 385.   Recent Economic Changes, p. 82.

the greatest rapidity and offered for use and consumption at rates unprecedented for cheapness. If lack of capital by destruction or perversion had been the cause, the rate of profit on the use of capital would have been higher. But the fact is that the rate of profit on even the most promising kinds of capital, during recent years, has been everywhere exceptionally low.*

In the above paragraphs Mr. Wells states very forcibly the theory which now has so many advocates, namely, that production has recently outstripped consumption, or that the world has become " saturated " with the results of these modern improvements. On careful analysis it will appear that his views as to the cause of depressions are in the same line with those advocated in this chapter, though he does not give sufficient recognition to several important particulars. It is especially erroneous to regard the industrial and commercial movement as having reached a development such that further advancement must stop. It is not correct to say that the civilized countries of the world have become fully equipped with economic tools, and that the work of the future must necessarily be that of repair and replacement rather than of new construction. The tendency to abandon the existing equipment and supersede it with new construction was never more pronounced than now. An impression was prevalent in the least prosperous years of recent decades that the days of great activity would not return again; that a partial

---

* Popular Science Monthly, vol. xxxi, pp. 303–304.

paralysis had fallen upon industry and trade from which they could not recover. The prosperity which has followed each depression, notably that of the last few years, has dispelled this impression. The conditions which led to the opinion that the industrial movement had reached a standstill have been succeeded in each case by greater activity than ever before existed. Mr. Wells also failed to recognise the very great increase of consumption in recent years contemporaneously with increased production. In view of this increase, the apparently excessive quantity of available commodities in a time of depression cannot be regarded as indicating overproduction by a mere comparison with the quantity in previous years. Prof. Richmond Mayo-Smith, in his recent work on Statistics and Economics, has

Annual Consumption Per Capita in Different Countries in Different Years *

	1862.	1880.	Increase, per cent.
Meat, France..............	25.9 kilos	33 kilos	27.41
	1868.	1890.	
Meat, England............	100.5 kilos	124.5 kilos	23.88
	1871-'75.	1891-'95.	
Tea, Germany.............	.02 kilos	.05 kilos	150.00
Petroleum, Germany.......	3.75 kilos	14·82 kilos	295.2
	1871.	1896.	
Flour, United Kingdom	150 lbs.	257 lbs.	71.33
Tea, " "	3.91 lbs.	5.77 lbs.	47.57
Eggs, " "	12.6	40	217.46
Butter and margarine, "	4.7 lbs.	11.1 lbs.	136.17
Cocoa, "	.23 lbs.	.62 lbs.	169.56
Bacon and ham, "	3.4 lbs.	15.9 lbs.	367.64
Refined sugar, "	5.28 lbs.	41.53 lbs.	686.55

* Statistics and Economics, part ii, pp. 40, 41, 46, 47.

collected data showing the great increase of the consumption of certain articles in recent years.

The table on page 121, giving selections from his work, will illustrate this.

The above list, with the exception of petroleum, is made up of food products. In manufactured articles the average increase of consumption is much greater. In the quantity of cotton used in manufacture the increase in Germany in the twenty years from 1871–'75 to 1891–'95 was from 2.84 to 4.95 kilograms per capita,* or 74.3 per cent.

In the Statistical Abstract of the United States, it appears that in this country in the twenty years from 1875 to 1895 the increase in cotton used in manufacture was even greater, or from 11.9 to 22.75 pounds per capita,† or 91.1 per cent. The increase in the world's production of pig-iron— which may be taken as the approximate consumption—from 1875 to 1895 was from 13,675,000 tons to 28,871,000 tons,‡ or 111.12 per cent. Most remarkable of all increases of staple products in any country is that of crude steel in the United States, the production of which, in the twenty years last mentioned, increased from 389,799 to 6,114,834 tons,# or 1,468.71 per cent.

Again, Mr. Wells omits to recognise the greater tendency to failure of equilibrium between vari-

---

* Statistics and Economics, part ii, p. 46.

† Statistical Abstract of the United States, 1900, introductory leaf.

‡ Iron and Steel and Allied Industries of all Countries, 1897, by James M. Swank, p. 14.   # Ibid., p. 15.

ous kinds of production which invariably manifests itself in a time of rapid growth, and the more frequent changes in taste and fashion occurring at such a time. This failure of equilibrium explains the abundance of desirable commodities existing during the time of the depression in the late decade to which he refers. It may be conceded that the depression has been most pronounced in countries where machinery has been most largely adopted, a result largely traceable to the increase of manufactured products as compared with that of agricultural products. It may be that all classes of useful articles increased in that period, but they increased in very unequal proportions, and this lack of equilibrium was a leading feature of the depression. The depression must continue until there is a readjustment of production, and equilibrium under new conditions is attained.

As regards Mr. Wells's statement that if lack of capital by destruction or perversion had been the cause, the rate of profit on the use of capital would have been higher, while in fact it is lower, this condition presents nothing difficult of explanation. It is sufficient to say that there are two ways in which capital is employed: one is in the maintenance of the ordinary existing volume of trade and industry for present consumption, the other is in the formation or promotion of new enterprises or new construction. The latter often creates the more active demand for capital, but in a time of depression this latter demand is greatly diminished, if not entirely suspended, as a result of which much capital is for a time idle; money, its representative, accumulates in banks, and profits become lower.

The eminent French economist, M. Paul Leroy-Beaulieu, gives qualified support to the theory of general over-production. He divides crises into two classes, one of which he styles *commercial* or *financial*, the other, *general economic* (*économiques générales*).

In his Treatise on Political Economy he says:

" Crises are a momentary derangement of the economic gear, due to the fact that, for various causes, the market for important categories of products suddenly becomes considerably restricted, and this, by repercussion, hinders the sale of all.

" It is in the circulation, frequently also, but not always, in the apparatus of credit, that crises begin to manifest themselves, but they have their principal roots in production and consumption, in the lack of actual equilibrium between the one and the other.

" Economic crises are of two kinds, very diverse and very distinct: . . .

" 1. Crises called commercial and financial. These are periods of depression and embarrassment succeeding periods of excitement which arouse the imagination of producers and cause abuses of credit.

" 2. The second class of crises, which has been less studied, is that of general economic crises, which have their root in very great changes, frequently in great progress accomplished in production. These crises may become severe without any abuse of credit, without any slackening of public confidence. They are the crises which are much the most intense and prolonged." *

In further description of the distinction between the two kinds of crises, he says:

" The former occur with frequent periodicity almost every decade, and last a short time. The latter occur at longer intervals, and more irregularly, but continue longer." †

General economic crises, he avers, result from " great and sudden progress in production," although he concedes the general principle that, if we have in view a very long time, there cannot be " a universal and definite excess of production for the whole human race. This universal excess would manifest itself only when the human race, abundantly provided with the commodities essential for its existence, and with those intended for its enjoyment, should prefer an increase of leisure to a new increase of consumption." ‡

When " great and sudden progress in production " brings on a general economic crisis, it becomes " necessary that there should be new adaptations to meet this sudden progress, and these adaptations require time and extraordinary effort. It is like a crisis of birth or acclimation. . . . It is advisable to revise attentively all conditions of production." #

Extended quotations have been made from the writings of M. Leroy-Beaulieu, because he states so

---

* Traité d'Économie Politique, vol. iv, p. 406.
† Ibid., p. 409.   ‡ Ibid., p. 450.   # Ibid., p. 451.

clearly the necessity for time as a factor in educating consumers to appreciate the value of new commodities, and in inducing those changes of habit and taste which are necessary to prevent an accumulation of products. At times there seems to be a sort of inertia in disposing of essential and very desirable commodities, so great as to give plausibility to the contention of those who maintain that over-production is a positive fact. Their whole argument may be summarized by saying that the world more readily adopts innovations in production than in consumption. Improvements in production proceed from the more progressive, while increased consumption must proceed from a larger number who adopt changes more slowly. This slowness in making use of new or increased supplies is very unequal in different countries, though its effect is apparent everywhere; but this does not constitute general over-production. It rather describes a situation, in which there is a temporary absence of adjustment between different lines of production. There has never been a time when a scarcity of some articles of consumption was not a noticeable fact. To say that general over-production is possible is to allege that the human race can create more than it can use, and that men love to toil rather than to enjoy, deductions contradicted by all experience.

Along with statistics which are alleged to show over-production, we have the undoubted fact that a large share not only of the human race as a whole, but of those who dwell in the most advanced

countries, earnestly desire—in many cases suffer
for—the very commodities of which it is alleged
there is a superabundance, and, further, they are
able and willing to do their part in producing other
things craved by those whose commodities they desire. It may be conceded that habit and slowness in
adopting changes increase the difficulty of harmo-
nizing production and consumption in all their varied
lines—a problem incapable of exact solution—but
they do not explain the general nature of the difficulty which would exist in spite of the influence of
habit and did exist and cause keen distress before the
explanation of excess of production was thought of.

It has been argued by some of the supporters
of the theory under consideration that if lack of
equilibrium were a cause of depression, there would
be a fall in the price of some articles and a rise in
the price of others. To this it is a sufficient answer to say that, in times of depression, diminished activity and the greater supplies furnished
by the increased equipment for production, tend to
diminish all prices. The absence of equilibrium
is conclusively proved by the admitted fact that
there is a notably unequal fall in the prices of
different commodities, just as there is an unequal
rise preceding a depression.*

As regards the argument that recent depressions are much more severe and of a distinct type,
it has already been stated that crises have become
less prominent and depressions more so. The contrast between the years of greatest and least ac-

---

* See Chapter III, pp. 52–54.

tivity is not so marked. The duration of the depressions is usually longer and the recovery more gradual than formerly, but in their essential character they are the same as in the years preceding the opening of the Suez Canal in 1869, an event to which many writers refer as contemporaneous with great advances in production and distribution. If, with increase of credit and the greater rapidity with which improvements are made, destructive forces have increased, recuperative forces have increased also.

On the occasion of earlier disturbances, the unusual severity of the depressions and the exceptional developments preceding them have been given a prominence as great as that ascribed to the period following the opening of the Suez Canal. In a carefully prepared work by a Swedish writer, Professor Bergfalk, published at Upsala in 1859, the author, with much detail, points out the exceptional conditions existing in the period from 1848 to 1857. He gives the following as the co-operating causes which led to the crisis of 1857:

1. The wonderful extension of the modern system of communication by steamship lines, railroads, and electric telegraph lines.

2. The abolition of the English Navigation Act in the year 1849, and the changes directly or indirectly caused by this in other countries; also the removal of certain prohibitions and restrictions upon exports and imports.

3. The strong tendencies in most branches of industry to grow and expand on a large scale.

4. The discovery of rich gold mines in California and Australia.

5. The abolition of the last remnants of the feudal system in German and English laws.

6. The political movements of the year 1848, which gave to European capital a direction partly from Europe to the United States, and partly from state loans to industrial enterprises.

7. The war in the East, which partly in itself and partly in connection with the failure of the crops in Western Europe, caused a revolution in the industrial world, inseparable from every war, and an increase in the commerce between Western Europe and the Levant.

8. The liberation of the mouth of the Danube from Russian dominion.*

These changes certainly make a showing worthy to be compared with the more distinctively industrial advance prior to 1873.

The greater part of the past century may be characterized as an era of awakening, a time of constant advancement, in which progressive forces were at work. Unfortunately, these forces caused the era to be strewn with many wrecks, misfortunes which, if rightly considered, must be seen to be inseparable from the benefits which have been gained.

Psychological Tendencies; the Mental and Moral Disposition of Mankind.—It must be conceded that after full consideration is given to general economic

---

* Bidrag till Handelskrisernas Historia, Prof. P. E. Bergfalk, pp. 33–34.

9

laws, many of the phenomena of crises remain capable of explanation only as the result of various characteristics of human nature, which cannot be classified according to any established rule, and seem to be more or less capricious, such as the tendency of men to move in a mass; the disposition to alternate moods of hope and discouragement, of trust and distrust; to excessive action and inaction by turns.

In view of the influence of these various characteristics, it has been deemed sufficient explanation by some to say that the cause of crises rests in the mental and moral disposition of mankind. In an important sense this is true of everything in human affairs. Great changes in political or economic conditions occur only in response to some powerful tendency in human nature. But in order to make progress in investigation, it is necessary to examine and analyze the specific lines in which mental and moral forces work, and to seek to give them, as far as possible, definite and concrete form, conceding the influence they must exert.

No human trait is more marked than the love of acquisition, and in this love of acquisition will be found, in its various workings, the source not alone of many benefits and great progress, but also a contributing cause of all the phases of our business and industrial life. Prompted by the desire for accumulation, human activity, like forces in the physical world, is along the line of least resistance. In other words, a man seeks to ob-

tain wealth in the easiest and quickest way. If
he can obtain by speculation larger amounts or
quicker accumulations than by the usual plodding
way, he is likely to become a speculator. Thus
we shall have abnormal buying. We shall have
new enterprises for which there is no call; the
abandonment of the work of the producer for the
business of the broker or the promoter. The result is, that business is overdone or incompetently
managed, credit is abused and, if this movement is
wide-spread, financial collapse will ensue. Other
well-known traits are the fondness for pleasure and
display, and the extravagance which they engender.
These tend to bring waste. Another characteristic
is the desire to perform work with the least labour
and the greatest profit. This leads to invention
and improvements in production and in the methods
of transacting business. This characteristic, salutary as it is, nevertheless causes disturbances, local
and temporary, but promotive at times of industrial
depression.

The admitted fact to which attention is called
by the advocates of this theory, is the ready disposition of investors to furnish capital for undertakings in a time of activity, and the disposition to
withhold it in a season of dulness. While it must
be conceded that the varying moods of individuals
have much to do in increasing activity and inten-
sifying dulness, these moods only explain a part
of the changing movement. 'Every period of activity arises from unusual opportunities for profit.
At such a time, mines have been discovered or

profitable fields have been opened, promising transportation lines are being constructed, or increasing
demands for consumption afford an opening for
new construction. Investments bring a large return. When all these have been exploited and the
exaggerated returns which were obtained at the beginning of the activity have ceased, contrary conditions follow. Profits are small and results are
uncertain. That men should invest in one season
and refrain from investing in another indicates
nothing capricious. They simply act in accordance
with ordinary rules of conduct. The disposition
to invest when large profits can be realized is not
unlike that in a period when there is a special demand for men of a particular trade or profession.
This causes numerous persons to enter that trade
or profession. In either case the ordinary laws of
supply and demand govern human action.

Military Armaments and Liquor Traffic.—
Much has been said in works of this character upon
the burden of military armaments and the great
amounts expended for drink. Commercial and
industrial disturbances have been traced to these
causes. While these no doubt have their evil side,
it must be remembered that we have to deal with
existing conditions. These two forms of expenditure have existed for centuries. The established
course of affairs has adapted itself to them so that
only by very considerable increase in the waste
incident to military organization or in the expense
for drink can we find a cause of periods of depression.

Having reviewed the alleged causes of crises and depressions, it will be profitable to consider some incidental facts pertaining to them.

Crises Severe because Unexpected.—Crises have their most serious effects because they are unexpected.   A recognised decrease of capital or wealth may continue for a long time and yet no crisis occur.   As stated by Prof. Bonamy Price:

" Crisis is not merely another word for poverty.   If the diminution of wealth is met by wise curtailment of speculation, even in its legitimate form, property may dwindle, but the convulsions peculiar to a crisis will not be developed." *

And again the same author says:

" It is not the magnitude of the loss alone which constitutes a crisis.   A bad harvest in England is a loss of £30,000,000; that is, you have got to buy or purchase £30,000,000 of capital twice over.   But it does not generate a financial storm. The same is true of war.   Nothing destroys like war.   Again, take the cotton famine in England. It was a terrific loss of money.   The poor men had no wages; all the vast apparatus of capital was earning nothing."†   The calamities were anticipated.

Overaction is contemporaneous with the lack of attention to the results which must follow it. The manufacturer or merchant proceeds in a season of activity with a groundless confidence that the activity is normal and that it will continue.   It is

* North British Review, vol. liii, p. 472.
† Bankers' Magazine (New York), vol. xxix, p. 362.

this groundless confidence which impels him to strain his credit and increase his production or his holdings. In the language of Hecate to the witches in the play of Macbeth: " And you all know security is mortals' chiefest enemy."

This fact affords a reason why war and famine may not be attended by crises. Their results are foreseen and provided for. There are, of course, other factors involved in time of war. The emergency of the situation and the spirit of patriotism give a stimulus to industry.

The Results of Waste or Derangement Postponed.—It is also true that the destruction of wealth, as by the waste of war or improvident enterprise, and the derangement caused by the locking up of capital in preparation for future consumption, do not show their results in crisis or depression until some time has elapsed. At such times all available savings are expended, and such support as can be gained from the influx of capital from abroad by foreign loans, withdrawal of investments or otherwise, is fully utilized. After the exhaustion occasioned by war, there is, for a time, great activity in providing supplies, which have been rendered scarce by extraordinary demands. As a result, during war or a period of unusual enterprise, and for a time thereafter, the true situation is obscured by exceptional activity, by the fact that labour is generally employed, prices are high and rising, and speculation is rife. A similar activity after the destruction of great quantities of property by fire or flood, has led to the delusion that a season of restoration, following one of these visitations, is one of prosperity.   The after-effect, in either case, is not unlike the experience of a spendthrift, who wastes his substance in excessive expenditure, enjoying the time, but soon awakes to the fact that his sources of support are gone.

CHAPTER V

In order to understand the characteristic features of depressions, it will be profitable to consider first, in retrospect—that is, by an examination of conditions in past years—what are the general indications of prosperity or depression.

In the next chapter certain indications will be considered with a view to forecasting the probable approach of crises or depressions.

There is a considerable difference of opinion concerning the time when depressions have actually existed, or, at least, have reached their severest stage. This difference of opinion is attributable to the habit of accepting the opinion of persons familiar only with one particular branch of business; to the undue prominence ascribed to the range of prices, or to some single department of statistics; also to an impression that these periods are exactly contemporaneous everywhere, although it is evident that, if the disturbance or revival started in one country, or countries, and its influence was transferred to others, there must be an interval between the date of commencement in the respective countries. The best results will be obtained by an examination of a considerable number of indications and by tracing their concurrence with admitted seasons of prosperity and depression.

Among the indications most frequently considered in this connection are the employment of labour; trade with foreign countries, including the general as well as the varying proportion between exports and imports; the amount of revenue collected, particularly excise or internal revenue taxes; the volume of bank clearances; agricultural production; the production, consumption, and prices of certain staple articles of manufacture, notably iron and steel, which are required to provide for enlarged or improved facilities; railway tonnage and earnings; business failures; certain social statistics. Each of these will be considered in order.

The Employment of Labour

The employment of labour affords a most valuable indication. When those who seek work can readily find it, it is evident that the fixed capital of a country is not idle, and that its circulating capital is ample for present needs. As those who labour for hire constitute so large a share of the consuming community, the steady employment of the labouring classes will greatly enlarge the market for commodities, and thus prevent, or tend to prevent, that accumulation of products which is a feature of every depression. Production is larger also the more general the employment of labour.

The maximum of employment is reached prior

to the crisis or the beginning of the depression, usually in the preceding year; the minimum of employment is usually reached in the year which is marked by other indications as the severest one of the depression. The more general employment in the year preceding a depression goes to confirm the opinion that the greatest degree of prosperity is reached some time before the breaking out of the crisis or commencement of the depression.

It is noticeable also that in a time of depression production does not decrease in an equal ratio with employment. This is another important proof of the fact to which attention has already been called, that in these periods an important feature is the improvement in methods of production, under which, with a less amount of labour, an equal or larger product may be obtained.

An examination of statistics leads to the conclusion that this indication, the employment or non-employment of labour, shows most reliably the presence or absence of prosperity. That it is not more generally accepted is due to the fact that our statistics are so meagre, and that we are unable to make comparisons for an extended period; but, so far as figures are available, they show that the proportion of employment points out in a most striking manner the degree of prosperity in trade and industry.

Mr. George H. Wood, in the Journal of the Royal Statistical Society for 1899,* gives a col-

* Journal of the Royal Statistical Society, vol. lxii, pp. 639–666.

lection of statistics of non-employment in the United Kingdom for nearly forty years, collated from the Annual Statistical Tables and Reports on Trade Unions, and the later publication known as the Annual Abstract of Labour Statistics, official documents compiled by the Labour Department of the Board of Trade. He lays particular stress upon the percentage of unemployed in each year. These statistics comprise only the unemployed members of certain trade unions, including machinists, carpenters and joiners, tailors, iron, steel, tin, and blast furnace workers, shipwrights, blacksmiths, etc.; but as these unions include nearly all the workers in certain occupations, and comprise those which experience the greatest fluctuations in employment, his figures can be taken as showing the condition of employment in those branches which fluctuate most with changing conditions of activity.

The diagram on page 140, derived from Mr. Wood's tables and from the later annual issues of the Abstract of Labour Statistics, shows the upward and downward movement in the percentage of employment from 1860 to 1900.*

---

* See Table III, pp. 645–646, of the above article; also the Seventh Annual Abstract of Labour Statistics, 1900, p. 76.

The percentages indicated by the black line are taken from the Annual Statistical Tables and Reports on Trade Unions; those indicated by the dotted line, after 1886, are from the Annual Statistical Abstracts of the Labour Department. The difference between them is only slight.

See also exact percentages given in Appendix B, p. 329. The percentage of employed is given instead of percentage of

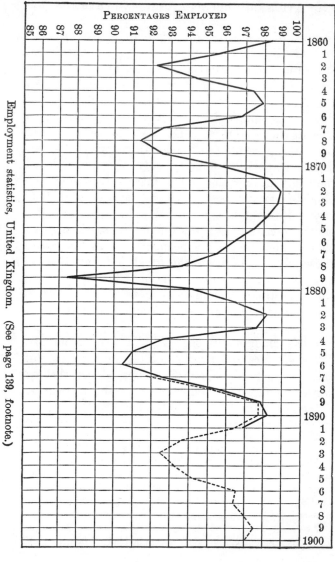

PERCENTAGES EMPLOYED

Employment statistics, United Kingdom. (See page 139, footnote.)

Other statistics giving the unemployed in a more limited number of occupations prior to 1860 are presented in the tables in the Fourth and Fifth Reports on Trade Unions.*

This diagram, with reports pertaining to the years prior to 1860, shows that the highest percentages of employment in the United Kingdom, where statistics cover the longest period and are most complete, occurred in the years 1856, 1865, 1872, 1882, 1890, and 1899, years preceding respectively the depressions or crises occurring or beginning in 1857, 1866, and 1873, and the periods of diminished activity beginning in 1883 and 1891. It will be noticed that employment in 1900 shows a decrease from 1899, thus pointing to 1900 as the year of a change to diminished activity. Whether 1900 shall prove a more prosperous year than 1901 and the succeeding years is a question which the future must determine. The lowest percentages were reached in 1858, 1868, 1879, 1886, and 1893,† the worst years of the respective depressions. Of these years, 1879 was the worst. It showed the largest proportion of unemployed in almost all branches for which statistics are available, and may be called the *annus pessimus* of English labour. This shows also the exceptional severity of the depression occurring between 1870 and 1880.

---

non-employed. The percentage for each year is given in the diagram at the line designating that year.

* For statistics prior to 1860, see especially Statistical Tables and Report on Trade Unions, Fifth Report (1893); also Appendix B, p. 329.

† There may be a question between 1893 and later years.

In the United States statistics as to non-employment are not available for so long a period, and no general figures for the whole country have been collected. Several States have collected data. Most of the reports upon the subject, however, place more stress upon the number employed than upon the percentage of employment. In order to give the greatest value to statistics stating the number engaged in any particular occupation, it is important to include a survey of the whole field of employment. An increase in the number employed in any trade may arise from an increase in population, or from an increase in production in some particular line, and thus be the result of changes from one occupation to another, so that it is difficult to derive correct inferences regarding the general condition of labour from the number employed in any particular branch of production. These statistics, however, are of very considerable value. In the State of Pennsylvania figures are available for a period of eight years, from 1892 to 1899 inclusive, of the average number of persons employed in 354 establishments engaged in divers industries, including manufactures of iron and steel, glass, shipbuilding, locomotives and engines, as well as certain textile manufactures. These figures point to the year 1894 as the least prosperous in the last decade. They also tend to confirm the statement already made that there was a revival of industry in the year 1895, which was not sustained in the following year.*

* Chapter II, p. 33.

The following statement gives the number employed each year: *

Years.	Number of establishments considered.	Total number of persons employed.
1892..................	354	136,882
1893..................	"	122,278
1894..................	"	109,383
1895..................	"	127,361
1896..................	"	118,092
1897..................	"	121,281
1898..................	"	137,985
1899..................	"	154,422

The following diagram more clearly indicates the comparative number employed each year:

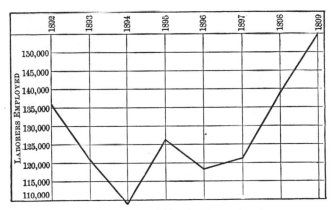

Employment statistics in Pennsylvania.

---

* Annual Report of the Secretary of Internal Affairs, State of Pennsylvania, for 1899, part iii, p. 258.

In the Twenty-fourth Annual Report of the Bureau of Statistics of Labor of the State of Massachusetts, pp. 128–129, the

FOREIGN TRADE: THE GENERAL RELATION BETWEEN
EXPORTS AND IMPORTS AND THE VARYING RELA-
TION BETWEEN THEM

In trade statistics, the increase or decrease in the
aggregate value of both exports and imports—that
is, the total foreign trade—has marked most accurately the varying degree of activity from year to
year. An increase in the total value of exports and
imports indicates a large volume of trade due to exportation or importation, or both. In the United
Kingdom in the decade ending in 1870 the maximum
value of imports and exports per capita was in the
year 1866. In the following decade the maximum
was in 1873. From 1867 up to that date there had
been an increase each year, which was exceptionally
large in 1871 and 1872. The minimum following
was in the year 1879, there being a steady decline,
with the exception of the year 1877, in each year
after 1873. In the following decade the maximum
was in the years 1882 and 1883; then a decline

---

percentage of unemployed is given for five years, from 1889 to
1893, as follows:

Year.	Percentage unemployed.	Year.	Percentage unemployed.
1889	1.44	1892	1.65
1890	2.30	1893	8.51
1891	.91		

These figures sharply contrast conditions in 1893 with those
of the four preceding years.

For statistics of the number employed in New York, Pennsylvania, Massachusetts, and Wisconsin, in certain years, see
Appendix B, pp. 330–331.

until the minimum was reached in the year 1886, from which time there was a gradual increase until and including 1889 and 1890; then a decline until and including 1894; then an increase which continued until and including 1900.* In the United States in the decade beginning in 1870 the maximum value of exports and imports per capita was in 1873, the minimum in the year 1876. There had been a gradual increase beginning in 1868 and lasting until and including 1873; then there was a decline. In the decade beginning in 1880 the maximum was in the year 1881, with a very large volume of trade in the preceding and two succeeding years; the minimum in the year 1886. In the following decade the maximum was in the year 1892, and the minimum in the year 1895, since which time there has been a general increase, though for the most part in exports.†

The accompanying diagram illustrates the rise and fall in the total of exports and imports of several leading countries.

As the aggregate foreign trade of the United States is, in proportion to wealth and population, much less than that of the United Kingdom, Holland, Belgium, France, or Germany, it is presumably a less accurate indicator of the presence or absence of prosperity.

It is frequently said that the volume or quantity of exports and imports furnishes a more accu-

---

* See Appendix B, p. 332, for detailed per capita figures.

† Ibid. The fiscal years ending June 30th are intended. ¦

10

rate barometer of conditions than their values. Quantity should, of course, be carefully considered, and especially the quantities of different kinds of exports and imports. Presumably, a large importation of raw material for manufacture gives better promise for the future than an importation of finished products. But, in the first place, it is manifestly impossible to derive inferences from a comparison of quantities of the manifold articles exported and imported from year to year, in view of their great variety and unequal utility. It should also be noted, as regards the comparative accuracy of inferences derived from quantity and value, that in progressive countries the standard of living is constantly rising. Articles formerly regarded as luxuries come to be regarded as things of convenience, and things of convenience come to be considered as necessaries. Not only is the number of consumers increasing, but the average consumption of each individual is increasing. An increase in the volume of exports and imports accordingly indicates an improved standard of living, but as regards employment, profits of trade, and readiness in disposing of products, the value affords an indication worthy of equal if not greater consideration. This is especially true if a comparison be made of successive years.

General Relation between Exports and Imports; the Balance of Trade.—It would be outside the scope of a book of this kind to enter upon an extended discussion of the balance of trade or the relation between exports and imports. It will be sufficient to state briefly some of the general rules respecting the proportion between them. Above all, it is necessary to make a careful examination of the situation in each particular country. A creditor country receives tribute from interest or profits on investments abroad. The United Kingdom, Holland, France, Belgium, and Germany are creditor nations. Some countries also receive the earnings of shipping, or the carrying trade, to which may be added commissions, profits from international commerce, and exchange on money transmitted in the settlement of balances. From all these sources Great Britain derives a very large income. In 1899, Mr. Giffen estimates the annual amount received by Great Britain from interest and profits on investments abroad at about £90,-000,000; from commissions on trade at £18,000,-000; from shipping engaged in international trade, over £70,000,000; in all, approximately, £178,000,-000 per annum.* In 1898, the excess of imports of merchandise over exports was £176,530,714, an amount very nearly the same as the aggregate of income and earnings mentioned. Norway also furnishes an illustration of the income derived from the carrying trade. All these countries naturally have an excess of imports; and an adverse balance of trade as shown by computed valuations does not show an absence of prosperity.

It is evident that for another reason a mere balance of the computed value of exports and

---

* See Journal of the Royal Statistical Society, vol. lxii, pp. 8–12, and 35.

imports is not a safe guide by which to judge of the prosperity of a country. There is no uniform standard in making valuations. Different countries have different standards. The same country may have one rule for the valuation of exports and another for imports. In some countries, as in the United States, the values of imports are computed as of the place of exportation, using as a basis invoices made out by the exporters; in others they are fixed at the place of importation by trained experts. In some countries freight charges are not included in the value of imports; in others they are. They are, of course, not included in exports. In addition to different rules regarding the place of valuation, there are different rules as to date. Some countries fix the value of imports as of the date of importation, while others value them according to the prices of the preceding year or years.

There is no uniformity in the different countries in the classification of the different kinds of exports and imports. Germany, France, and Switzerland have three classes—food, raw materials, and manufactured articles. Other countries have a larger number of classes. This increases the confusion. But the most serious difficulty arises from the lack of uniformity of methods in the valuation of exports and imports in the same country. Differences arise, not only from dissimilar methods of valuation, but from the unequal accuracy exercised in the valuation of the exports and imports. Presumably, imports are more carefully valued than exports, because, in most countries, tariff regulations make this necessary. It is intended that imports should be carefully appraised according to their actual value, either at the place of exportation or that of importation, while exports may be valued according to estimates of the merchants or shippers exporting them, without careful revision.*

For these reasons, the computed balance of exports over imports in any country cannot be accepted as showing the real balance in either the actual value or cost of the two.

It has been frequently asserted that in the United States the computed excess in the value of exports over imports in recent years is greater than the real balance. Mr. Edward Atkinson, as the result of a computation in April, 1901, furnishes some figures which would indicate that the computed balance is less rather than greater. He takes as a basis of comparison our average computed value of exports and imports in the trade with European countries for the fiscal years ending June 30, 1898 and 1899, respectively, and compares them with the valuation of imports and exports made in the respective European countries for the calendar year 1898. These figures show that our valuations of imports from Europe are

---

* See an article on The Comparability of Trade Statistics of Various Countries, by Sir A. E. Bateman, C. M. G., Publications American Statistical Association, New Series, vol. iii, p. 533, 1893; also a paper presented by him at the International Statistical Institute at Christiania in September, 1899.

16.2 per cent greater than those made in the countries of export, while the foreign valuations of our exports to Europe are 37.5 per cent greater than those given in our computations, as follows:

	Exports.	Imports.
Foreign valuations, 1898......	$1,279,617,183	$265,046,080
Home valuations (average of 1897-'98 and 1898-'99)........	930,175,318	307,990,327
Excess, foreign valuation......	$349,441,865	
Excess......................	37.5%	
Excess, home valuation......................		$42,944,247
Excess.......................................		16.2%

This method of comparison, while perhaps the best available, cannot give accurate results for several reasons. First, the computations in the European countries are by calendar years, while in the United States they are for years ending June 30th. Second, the freight charges are omitted in this country; some European countries omit and others include freight charges on their imports. Third, the time required for shipment necessarily makes exact comparison impossible. What is shipped from one country in the latter part of 1898 would be counted as an import in another country in 1899. Of course no comparison can make allowance for those differences in value which are based on different degrees of utility in the respective countries of export and import.

The first ground of uncertainty is removed by the use of the computations given in the December numbers of the Monthly Summary of Commerce and Finance issued by the Bureau of Statistics of the Treasury Department. These computations give the values of exports to and imports from the various countries by calendar years. It is possible to make a comparison of these values as given by the Treasury Department with those made by the countries from which they are imported or to which they are exported. In Appendix B of this book a computation is given showing the home and foreign values of exports and imports in the trade with the United Kingdom, Germany, and France for the four calendar years 1896 to 1899.*

While, as already stated, these figures can give no exact results, they would seem to show that the real balance in our favour is actually greater than that computed by the Treasury Department. Our valuations of exports to the United Kingdom for each of the four years named were less than theirs. The excess of their valuations varied from 9.2 per cent in 1896 to 14.4 per cent in 1899. This excess is, however, explained in part by their different* system of computation, which includes freight charges in the value of their imports. On the other hand, imports from the United Kingdom show their valuations also to be greater than ours, ranging from 15.8 per cent more in 1896 to 24.7 per cent in 1898. Trade statistics of France show their valuations of exports from this country to that to be greater than ours, while our valuations of their exports are considerably more. Valuations of our imports from Germany come nearest to

---

* See Appendix B, pp. 334–335.

a coincidence in amounts.   Exports to that country are valued there at a higher price, while imports from Germany in three of the four years were valued at a higher figure in this country.   In none of the four years was the difference in our valuation of imports more than 3.6 per cent—the excess in 1897—while in 1899 their valuation was 0.2 per cent more.   The total aggregate of exports to all of these countries for the years mentioned shows their valuation of our exports to be 15.7 per cent more than ours, while our valuation of imports from them is 1.9 per cent less.

A further fact should be considered.   In comparing the aggregate value of exports and imports in all countries furnishing trade statistics, the computed value of imports in any year largely exceeds that of exports.   In some figures prepared in 1880, Neumann-Spallart pointed out the large excess in a series of years.   The excess in the quoted value of imports for the preceding decade was approximately $1,000,000,000 per annum.   Mr. C. A. Harris, in R. H. Inglis-Palgrave's Dictionary of Political Economy, under the title "Imports and Exports," gives these computed values in detail for 1890: The excess for that year in the valuation of imports into the European countries was approximately £209,000,000; into Asia, £1,000,000; into Australia, £2,000,000; into North and South America, £7,000,000.   The excess in the valuation of exports from Africa was something over £2,000,000.   These created an aggregate excess in the value of imports of that year, for the countries for which statistics are available, of about £217,000,000.*

The difference between the values in the countries of exportation and those of importation, so far as it can be traced, is made up of carrying charges, exchange paid to bankers, and the profits of merchants and shippers engaged in international trade. It is a question whether the total amounts so paid explain the whole difference in the computed values. After making full allowance for these expenses we are compelled to fall back upon a principle which is of the very essence of all commerce—viz., the superior utility of commodities in the countries into which they are imported. Thus, the difference between the aggregate value of imports and exports, as computed at the custom house, must be considered in connection with so many other facts and circumstances that it is not independently a significant indication of prosperous times or the contrary.

The Varying Proportion between Exports and Imports.—The question remains whether an increase of exports or of imports is the better indication of prosperity. It is safe to say that an increase of imports affords the more conclusive indication of an increase in the consuming or purchasing power of a people. But this increase may arise from increase of wealth, and consequent command over the products of other countries, or from overaction and extravagant expenditure. In the former case it is a favourable indication, in the

* Dictionary of Political Economy, vol. ii, pp. 364–365.

latter it is not.   This question cannot be answered without consideration of the situation of each country.   Creditor nations manifest tendencies quite the opposite from those apparent in debtor nations. A still more important distinction is that between new and developing countries and those which are older and already more highly developed.

The Varying Proportion in New and Developing Countries.—A general tendency may be stated which applies to new and developing countries, particularly in those which obtain credit from other countries, as follows: imports will show an abnormal increase in the period prior to a depression. During the depression exports will be much in excess of the normal proportion.   Upon examination it will appear that this is clearly in accordance with rules which are easily understood.

The need of material for development, as in railways, buildings, etc., causes large importations in a time of activity.   These importations decline when the season of greatest activity has passed. Thus, large importations made for the development of a new country are naturally indications of prosperity.   This indication fails, however, when overaction begins, or undue preparation has been made for future production.   The progress made in the development of newly opened fields seldom stops short of excess.   In so far as it is wholesome it will give preparation for larger production in the future, but during the time of preparation for this larger production there will be excessive expenditures and extravagance.

In the study of importations into this country the indications which belong both to a debtor country and to a rapidly developing country have appeared. While the United States is not a debtor country as formerly, great quantities of material for construction and large quantities of money for investment were formerly sent hither. This tended to increase importations.

As regards exports from a debtor or developing country, the factors which influence increase or decrease have already been pointed out, namely: * First, after a crisis there is large exportation, even at low prices, by reason of the existing depletion and the diminished credit from wealthier countries. Second, in growing countries like the United States, the improved equipment, secured by the absorption of capital for increased production, soon causes a further increase of exportation. Increase of exports from the first of these causes points towards mere reparation, while that from the second points towards an enlarged proportion of the world's production and trade.

Exceptional conditions in the United States occasion greater and more irregular fluctuations than in other countries in the proportion between exports and imports. Among them is the great difference in harvests and in prices of agricultural produce.

Under the stimulus of great fluctuations in values, speculation is more prevalent, and this has its influence upon the course of foreign trade. To

* See Chapter IV, pp. 89 *et seq.*

a greater extent than in any other country industrial activity is increased or diminished by the changing demands for new construction characteristic of a developing country in which there are great opportunities. In the past, the period of greatest activity, as well as of apparent prosperity, has occurred after the time when exports bore the largest proportion to the total foreign trade. In this season of greater activity, the proportion of imports has increased while that of exports has declined. 1899 and 1900 were more active and prosperous years than 1898, but the proportion of exports to imports decreased materially in the two later years.*

After the crisis of 1873, the maximum proportion of exports was reached in the year ending June 30, 1879; yet the two or three succeeding years show much greater activity as well as prosperity. After the crisis of 1884, the year 1885 showed the maximum proportion of exports until the unusual agricultural exports of 1892. The years succeeding 1885, at least 1887 to 1892, showed a much greater degree of activity.

The varying proportion of exports and imports, as well the sharp decline in imports after the commencement of a depression, is well illustrated by an examination of the foreign trade of the Argentine Republic in the time preceding and succeeding the collapse of 1890. The change is especially noticeable in the year 1891. The fluctuation in the aggregate of exports and imports is

---

* See Chapter VIII, p. 302.

Argentine Republic

All exports and imports are given, as well as imports of iron and manufactures thereof, and imports for construction of railways, telegraph lines, etc., in thousands of pesos (gold). In the third column the percentage of exports to imports is given for each year. In the fourth and fifth columns the percentage of exports and imports is given, using the average for the nine years as a basis of 100. The percentage of imports of iron and manufactures thereof and of material for railways, etc., is given on the same basis in columns seven and nine.

Year.	1 All exports.	2 All imports.	3 Percentage of exports to imports.	4 Percentage of exports based on average.	5 Percentage of imports based on average.	6 Imports of iron and manufactures thereof.	7 Per cent based on average.	8 Imports of material for railways, etc.	9 Per cent based on average.
1886...	69,835	95,409	73.1	70.5	86.2	12,292	91.6	5,102	40.7
1887...	84,422	117,352	71.9	85.3	106.0	14,359	107.0	5,039	40.2
1888...	100,112	128,412	77.9	101.1	116.0	17,643	131.5	15,472	123.5
1889...	122,815	164,570	74.6	124.1	148.7	24,727	184.3	24,173	193.1
1890...	100,819	142,241	70.8	101.9	128.5	9,566	71.3	36,273	289.7
1891...	103,219	67,208	153.5	104.3	60.7	4,508	33.6	17,869	142.7
1892...	113,370	91,481	123.9	114.5	82.6	10,339	77.0	3,545	28.3
1893...	94,090	96,224	97.7	95.1	86.9	13,057	97.3	3,279	26.1
1894...	101,688	92,789	109.5	102.7	83.8	14,251	106.2	1,913	15.2

very great, but greater still in imports of iron and manufactures thereof, and greatest in imports of material for construction of railways and telegraphs. It will be noticed that the aggregate of imports was twice as great in 1890 as in 1891, though exports were larger in the latter year. Imports of iron were more than five times as great in 1889 as in 1891. Imports of railway and kindred material were nearly twenty times as great in 1890 as in 1894, though the total of exports was larger in the latter year.

The figures on page 157 portray the situation.* The diagram opposite traces the movement shown by the figures in columns 1, 2, 6, and 8, of the table on the preceding page.

The Varying Proportion in Creditor Countries or those of Matured Development.—It has been maintained by high authority that tendencies in a creditor country are the reverse of those in debtor countries; that in a time of prosperity, exports maintain more than the average proportion to imports, while, in a time of depression, imports increase more than exports. On principle, strong arguments can be made for this contention. A creditor country grants large credits to other countries, and in a time of prosperity these credits are largely for commodities exported either from the country affording the credit or from another of the group of creditor countries. In addition to money

---

* See also exports and imports for Austria-Hungary, 1866 to 1876, Chapter VI, p. 202, and for the United States, 1875 to 1879, Chapter IV, p. 90.

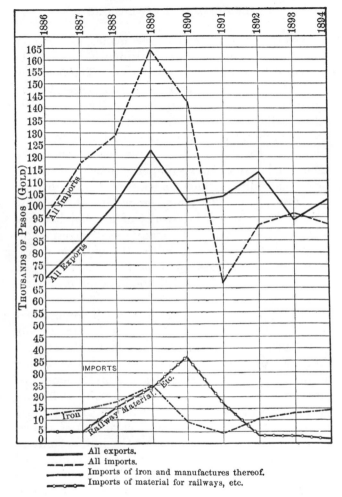

1886	1887	1888	1889	1890	1891	1892	1893	1894

THOUSANDS OF PESOS (GOLD)

All Imports

All Exports

IMPORTS

Iron

Railway Material, Etc.

——————— All exports.
— — — — — All imports.
——————— Imports of iron and manufactures thereof.
—o—o—o— Imports of material for railways, etc.

Comparison of exports and imports in the Argentine Republic.

loaned, large investments are made, particularly for improvements, the material for which is largely obtained from the creditor country. The tendency to increased value of exports is emphasized by the greater increase in the prices of these materials than in those of other commodities.

Another argument in the same line is found in the fact that the creditor countries manufacture more, and have greater supplies of articles of luxury and commodities which find a readier sale in time of prosperity. The abundant wealth of the New World is expended for works of art and luxuries obtained in the Old. To many the strongest argument for this contention will be the apparent necessity for an increase of exports from developed countries to correspond with the increase of imports into developing countries.

In support of the argument that with diminished activity the proportion of imports in creditor or developed countries increases, it may be said that in a time of depression credit is extended to debtor countries in a diminished degree; investments are decreased or suspended; there is a consequent decrease in exports. Another factor of almost equal importance is the low price of commodities prevalent in time of depression. Creditor countries have abundant resources, and take advantage of these low prices and import largely.

An examination of trade statistics shows that in a time of exceptional activity there is some tendency to an increase in the proportion of exports from creditor or developed countries to debtor or developing countries, but this tendency is by no means universal. The great increase of exports from the United Kingdom during several years prior to the crisis of 1873 has been referred to in support of this theory; but exports at that time were, no doubt, very much increased by the disturbances arising from the Franco-Prussian War, which not only caused a large demand for supplies from the two countries at war, but also afforded other countries opportunities for trade which they had formerly supplied. Before accepting this opinion several important facts must be considered.

First. The trade of creditor or developed countries shows much less fluctuation than that of new or developing countries, and the increase of exports from European creditor countries is rather in trade with each other than with debtor countries. For instance, in the year 1889 exports from France increased over the preceding year more than at any time in a period of thirty years, showing an increase of 505,000,000 francs; but of this increase 253,000,000, or more than one-half, was in exports to the United Kingdom, Belgium, and Switzerland.*

There is a tendency towards a contemporaneous increase or decrease of exports and imports between these creditor countries.

Second. Increased demand for the products of creditor countries is not contemporaneous in all the debtor countries. This is partly because their resources for supplies in exchange are not so varied.

---

* Tableau Décennal du Commerce, 1887 à 1896, pp. cxlvi and cxlvii.

Some export only food and raw materials, the supply of which varies with sunshine, moisture, and other natural causes which are not uniform everywhere. The year 1889 witnessed an increase of exports from the United Kingdom to Canada, Cuba, and most of the South American states, but diminished exports to Australia, China, and Japan. The same increase to some debtor countries and a decrease to others was apparent in 1873 as compared with 1872.

From a survey of the whole situation it would appear that, if an increase of wealth gives an impetus to larger purchases and extravagant expenditure in the newer and less developed countries, the same influences are alike effective in the older and more wealthy countries.

INCOME TAXES, EXCISE OR INTERNAL REVENUE TAXES

Income taxes collected, which are based upon the income returned, furnish an indication of the prosperity of the wealthier portion of the population. In the United Kingdom the value of these statistics has been very much diminished by frequent changes in the rate. Only three years show a decrease in the amount collected as compared with preceding years in which the rates were the same, viz.: the year ending April 5, 1867, when the rate was fourpence per pound; the year ending April 5, 1876, when the rate was twopence, and the year ending April 5, 1893, when the rate was sixpence. It is needless to say that each of these years was one of diminished prosperity. The property returned for income tax would seem to furnish a more correct indication, as it is independent of changes in the rate. The significance of the figures included in these returns must, however, depend upon the accuracy of assessment. They indicate prosperity in the years 1870 to 1874; in a less degree from 1880 to 1883; also in 1889 and 1890 and from 1897 to date.*

Amount of taxes collected on beer, tobacco, and spirits shows the condition of a larger portion of the public. Internal revenue taxes are intended to be imposed either upon luxuries or upon other articles of voluntary use. They furnish a valuable indication of the purchasing power of a community for purposes of consumption, and hence of its prosperity.

The statistics of Germany giving the quantity of beer brewed from 1884 to 1898 show decreases in only two years—viz., 1885–'86 and 1894–'95. Increases were most notable in the years 1886–'87, 1887–'88, 1889–'90, 1895–'96, and 1897–'98. These may be taken as respectively years of depression and prosperity.

In the United States it is difficult to derive conclusions from the changing amount of collections of internal revenue, by reason of the frequent changes made in rates and in the articles taxed. The collections per capita upon articles on which taxes have been permanently maintained—spirits,

---

* See Appendix B, p. 336.

tobacco, and fermented liquors—show low figures for the six years from June 30, 1873, to June 30, 1879; the lowest collections were reached in the last two years. Then come four years of large collections, from June 30, 1879, to June 30, 1883, at which time material changes were made in rates and articles taxed. Then followed four years, from June 30, 1883, to June 30, 1887, in which total collections were small or diminishing, the year of lowest collections being that ending June 30, 1885. Then succeed six years of rising, or higher collections, ending June 30, 1893; after which there are four years of decreased collections, ending June 30, 1897; after which time there was a uniform and considerable rise, until the reductions in 1901.

The quantity of fermented liquors upon which taxes were paid during the same period shows a very great increase. A diminished quantity, however, was reported in the years ending respectively June 30, 1874, 1875, 1877, 1894, and 1897. There was also a decrease in the year ending June 30, 1899; but this resulted from the large increase in the tax provided for in the Revenue Law of 1898.

Internal revenue taxe respond more promptly to changing conditions tl ın duties upon imports, though neither will chaɪ ;e in exact accordance with the increase or decrease of prosperity. Imported articles are contracted for in anticipation of future demands. The volume of orders is largely determined by conditions existing at the time when the orders are given, and in reliance upon the probable continuance or increase of the

demand indicated at that time. If a crisis inter-
venes and renders these anticipations incorrect,
nevertheless most of the orders are filled. Internal revenue taxes increase or decrease more nearly
in accordance with existing conditions, because the
element of distance and the necessity for ordering
in considerable quantities do not play so large a
part.

The production of articles upon which internal
revenue taxes are levied, however, is not likely to
diminish immediately in proportion to decreased
prosperity. Any considerable decrease of consumption involves some modification of the habits
of the people. The increased demand for the
articles taxed, developed in time of improvement,
shows tardiness in responding to existing conditions
when a depression begins.* A similar slowness to
increase consumption would seem to have its effect
at the close of a depression.†

BANK CLEARANCES

Large bank clearances denote large trade and
frequent transfers. Clearances furnish excellent
indications of the volume of transactions. Their
amount is increased by high prices, whether of commodities or securities. A large volume is favour-

---

* For statistics as to internal revenue taxes, see Appendix
B, p. 336; also Statistical Abstract of the United States for
1900, frontispiece and p. 30; also Report of the Commissioner
of Internal Revenue for 1900, pp. 431–442.

† Note especially the figures giving per capita tax for 1878
and 1879, 1887 and 1888, and 1897, in Appendix B, p. 336.

able because it shows the ability of sellers to find ready buyers, and an active money market; but its value as an indication is diminished by the different degrees in which settlements by bank clearances are established, and by the different relations at various times between speculation and more legitimate trade.

At the New York Clearing-House the maximum amount of clearances for the first seven years of its existence, from 1854 to 1860 inclusive, and for the four following decades respectively, was reached in 1857, 1869, 1873 and 1880,* 1881, and 1899. The minimum years for the same periods were 1858, 1861, 1876, 1885, and 1894.

It is difficult to frame general inferences from the course of clearances at the New York Clearing-House, but several striking facts appear. First, a steady and continuing increase in the most notable periods of prosperity, as from 1878 to 1881 inclusive, and from 1897 to 1899. There was also a steady increase from 1870 to and including 1873. Second, a notable falling off in the year following a financial crisis, illustrated by the small volume of clearances in 1858, 1874, 1885, and 1894. The amount of the falling off from the previous year may be taken as some measure of the severity of the crisis. The percentage of decrease was greatest in 1857–'58 and least in 1884–'85. Third, an increase in clearances would seem to precede a general improvement in business. To illus-

---

* Both 1873 and 1880 are given for this decade because the amount in each year was notably in excess of the amounts for the intervening years.

trate: a steady increase commenced in 1895, though permanent improvement did not begin until later.

The London Bankers' Clearing-House shows a much more uniform upward and downward movement in the volume of clearances. As in New York, it would appear that the beginning of an increase precedes a general revival of business.

From 1868 to 1900 the maximum amounts cleared were in the years 1873, 1881, 1890, and 1899; the minimum amounts, succeeding the maximum years named, in 1879, 1885, and 1894. For the most part, there was a steady increase and decrease between the highest and lowest years.*

The diagram on page 168 shows the bank clearances from 1854 to 1900 for New York and from 1868 to 1900 for London.

Transactions on the Stock Exchange furnish an indication of the activity of the time. On the New York Stock Exchange these were especially large in 1881, 1882, 1898, 1899, and 1900. In the last twenty years the smallest volume was in 1894.†

---

* For statistics of the New York Clearing-House, see the Statistical Abstract of the United States for 1900, p. 61; also a work on Clearing-Houses, by James G. Cannon, p. 203, giving a table issued by the New York Clearing-House. For statistics of the London Bankers' Clearing-House, see Statistical Abstract for the United Kingdom for 1868 to 1882, p. 154; same for 1884 to 1898, p. 225. See also Appendix B, p. 337.

† See Appendix B, p. 337, for approximate value of shares sold, 1881 to 1900. The figures are from the Commercial and Financial Chronicle, January 12, 1901.

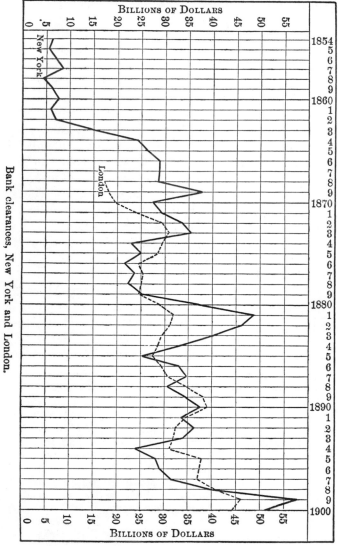

Bank clearances, New York and London.

Production and Prices of Certain Staple Commodities

In considering indications of prosperity, products may be divided into two classes: first, those largely beyond human control, which are dependent upon conditions of weather, etc.; and, second, those for the most part within human control, such as manufactured products.

The First Class, Illustrated by Agricultural Products.—As has been already stated, the volume and price of agricultural products exert a material influence upon prosperity. The demand for the necessities of life will not slacken, although supply is limited. Higher prices for wheat and corn bring disadvantage to consumers and do not bring a corresponding advantage to producers, because the high price is caused by smaller production, so that both producer and consumer suffer. The depressing effect of a failure of crops is especially felt in those countries which depend chiefly upon agriculture and have little diversity in their products. Conditions of crops, however, are so closely watched, and the effects of a large or small yield are so thoroughly measured, that they influence business conditions less than would be anticipated. Scarcity in one country is frequently contemporaneous with a surplus in another, and with improved means of communication the effect of a deficient crop in any one country is minimized. Abundant supplies of wheat are shipped from Puget Sound to Liverpool and Hamburg and frozen meat from

New Zealand to London. Prices, however, show a much greater fluctuation than would seem to be justified by inequalities in supply.* The striking changes from year to year in the price of wheat illustrate, though less than formerly, the principle enunciated by Mr. Tooke and others, that the value of the surplus determines the price of the whole, and that a small fraction of decrease increases the price altogether out of proportion to the deficiency of supply. The effect of war in creating unusual demands or cutting off sources of supply is similar to that of scarcity.

The Second Class, Illustrated by Iron and Steel. —The production, consumption, and prices of iron and steel afford more valuable indications than other commodities. They furnish a test of the extent of construction in a country, and particularly of the preparation for increased production.

Attention has already been called to the existence of an interval between maximum prices and the succeeding crisis, and to the tendency towards a longer interval in later years. Prices of iron and steel especially illustrate these tendencies. Production does not diminish so early as prices. It often continues at a maximum until the very beginning of the depression, and sometimes until later. These facts are easily explained. Enterprise in response to larger demands first exerts itself in the building of railroads or factories, the object of which is to increase production and the means for

---

* For figures of wheat production and prices, see Appendix B, p. 345.

exchange of products. The increased demand causes an increase in the equipment for production. After a time further capital is not available for these purposes. The sources from which it can be obtained are more and more becoming exhausted, and prices have so risen as to make the expense of further construction almost prohibitory. By this time the equipment for the production of iron and kindred articles has come to exceed the requirements of consumption, and a necessary fall in prices results, partly due to increased production and partly to the decreased demand; but the equipment is in existence, and, influenced by a variety of motives, the manufacturer continues production after demand has diminished and prices have gone down. He hopes that prices will recover, or that he may hold the field to the exclusion of competitors, or he is actuated by a natural reluctance to shut down his plant. Statistics of consumption are much less reliable than those pertaining to production. It is more difficult to make an enumeration of the various quantities retained by foundry-men and by other consumers than to enumerate the production at furnaces and mills. Naturally, consumption slackens before production, and in this fact is found one of the reasons for a fall in prices. At the end of a depression, consumption increases more rapidly than production. This furnishes a basis for a rise in price. It is hardly necessary to state that fluctuations in prices are far greater than in production and consumption. In the following chapter figures relating to prices and production of iron and steel will be given more in detail, to show their bearing upon the approach of depressions. By an examination of statistics of iron and steel in past years, it is easy to discover a correspondence between conditions of the trade and conditions of prosperity or depression. The production of pig-iron, which may be regarded as the best barometer of the iron and steel trades, reached a maximum in the United States, Great Britain, Germany, Belgium, Austria-Hungary, Russia, and Sweden in the years 1872 and 1873; * again in the years 1882, 1883, and 1884; and again in the years 1889 and 1890. In all of these countries there was a diminished product after 1873, so that the large output of that time was not equalled until 1879 in the United States, 1880 in Great Britain and Germany, 1881 in Austria-Hungary, and 1882 in Belgium. In all these countries there was a steady and continuing increase in 1880 and 1881. The minimum production in the intervening years occurred in the United States and Germany in 1876, in Great Britain in 1874 and 1879, in France and Austria-Hungary in 1877, and in Belgium in 1879. Following the maximum of 1882, 1883, and 1884, the minimum for that decade was reached in the United States in 1885; in Great Britain, Germany, and Belgium in 1886, and in Austria in 1887. Following the maximum of 1890, there were four years of diminished production, but be-

---

* The production was greatest in 1872 in Great Britain, Belgium, and Russia; in the other countries in 1873. The total production in all countries was greatest in 1873.

ginning with 1895, when the world's production equalled that of 1890, there has been a steady increase.* The following diagram shows the world's production of pig-iron by years:

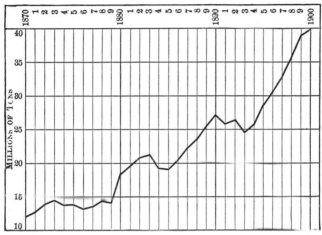

The world's production of pig-iron.

RAILWAY TONNAGE AND EARNINGS

Railway tonnage shows from year to year a steadier and more rapid increase than production

---

* Iron and Steel and Allied Industries in all Countries, by James M. Swank, Washington, 1897, pp. 13, 14, 70, 75, 78, and 88. See especially statistics of the world's production, p. 14. The figures giving the production of pig-iron tend to show that in the United States the depression following 1873 commenced and came to a close earlier than in most European countries, while the contrary is true of the depression of the last decade. For statistics concerning the production and consumption of pig-iron, see Appendix B, p. 340.

and consumption. Along with increase of population and a greater increase in the value of the average annual consumption of each individual, there is a still greater increase in the average weight of that which each individual consumes and in the average distance of the localities from which commodities are obtained. The growth of transportation is shown by the constant extension of railway and steamship lines and by facilities for handling increased tonnage without proportionate increase of expense.

Not only do tonnage and earnings respond to changing degrees of activity in trade, but investments in railways make up so large a share of the invested capital of a country that an increase or decrease in earnings has an important effect upon the conditions of the time. A comparison of the different kinds of traffic in the United States and the United Kingdom affords interesting information of the different conditions in the two countries, attributable especially to differences in the density of population, comparative amount of freight carried by land and water and the greater degree in which freight in the United States consists of raw material. A larger proportion of earnings in the United Kingdom is from passenger traffic, which in the United States afforded 22.16 per cent of total earnings in 1899, but in the United Kingdom over 40 per cent. In the past twenty years earnings from passenger traffic have increased more rapidly in the United Kingdom, while in the United States the increase is greater from freight traffic. Statistics of ton mileage in the United Kingdom are not available, though it is probable that there, as well as in the United States, the ton mileage, or average number of miles each ton of freight is carried, has increased somewhat more rapidly than the number of tons carried. In the United States much more than in the United Kingdom there has been an almost uniform decrease in the cost and charges for carrying freight. The charges in the United States are about 60 per cent of those in vogue twenty years ago. The figures show the progress in transportation and its importance as a factor in modern business development.

The years in which railway receipts show a falling off from previous years in the United Kingdom are 1858, 1878, 1879, 1884, 1885, 1886, and 1893. The decrease in 1893 is largest, that in 1879 comes next. The year 1879 is the only year in which there is a decrease in the number of passengers carried. Statistics of the number of tons of freight carried are available only since 1870. These show a falling off, as compared with the previous year, in 1874, 1878, 1884, 1885, 1886, 1892, and 1893.* In the United States, statistics of railway receipts are available from 1871; those of tonnage and the number of passengers carried, from 1882.†

---

* See Statistical Abstract for the United Kingdom, 1858–1872, p. 121. Same, for 1868–1882, pp. 138, 139. Same, for 1883–1897, pp. 210, 211. See also Whitaker's Almanac for 1901, p. 732.

† See Statistical Abstract of the United States for 1900, pp. 377–379.

The only years in which a decrease in the quantity of freight carried is apparent are 1884 and 1894. The number of passengers carried decreased in 1883, 1894, 1895, and 1897. Decreases in gross earnings occurred in 1874, 1875, 1876, 1877, 1884, 1885, and 1894.* The volume of railway traffic frequently shows features apparently exceptional, viz.: the falling off in tonnage is delayed for a considerable time after the depression begins, while an increase precedes the recovery in business. In addition to the influence due to the greater increase in transportation than in production, there are other reasons for these apparent exceptions. First, for delay in the decrease in volume; production at the mill or on the farm goes before transportation. The farmer plants his crops and the manufacturer makes provision for the output of his wares before he knows that he must dispose of them at a diminished price, perhaps at a loss. He must, nevertheless, send them to market. The accumulation of produce or merchandise, which is the result of over-production, is carried away after the full shock of the disturbance has been felt. Second, in the season preceding a revival, although the general range of prices is still low, a very large product is sent to market to be sold. Railroads obtain the benefit in tonnage and earnings. As illustrations, it may be stated that railway tonnage in the United Kingdom was less in the year 1878 than in 1879,

---

* Although 1884 shows a slight decrease in freight carried, the ton mileage (or tonnage multiplied by the number of miles carried) is greater.

which was less prosperous, and greater in 1891 and 1892 than in 1890, a more prosperous year. It was greater in the United States in the crisis year 1893 than in 1892, and in 1885 commenced to show a large increase, though prior to a general improvement of business.*

BANKRUPTCIES

In this country the greatest number of bankruptcies and insolvencies, as well as the maximum liabilities, occurred in the years 1857, 1861, 1873, 1878, 1884, 1893, and 1896. In number and amount, 1893 was the most notable year. A financial crisis occurred in that year, as well as in 1857, 1873, and 1884. The record of 1861 is explained by the embarrassments incident to the beginning of the civil war. The other two years of maximum failures, 1878 and 1896, when considered with the years named in which crises occurred, illustrate an important principle, viz., that if the crisis is relatively the more important event, the maximum of failures occurs in that year, and is followed by a series of years in which bankruptcies are relatively small, as after 1857; while, if the depression is relatively the more important event, failures will continue large for a series of years after its beginning, and reach another very large amount in one of the severest years of the depres-

---

* Attention has already been called to the influence of railway construction in determining the degree of activity. Chapter IV, pp. 83 *et seq.*

12

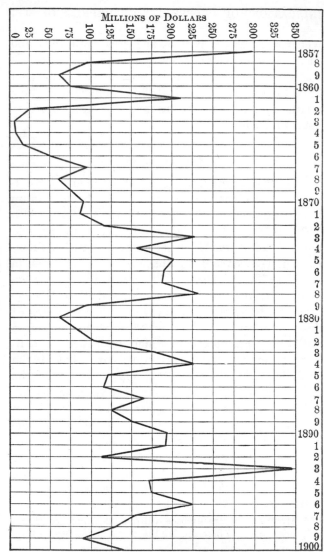

Failures in the United States.

sion, as in 1878 after 1873 and 1896 after 1893. The length of the interval between the crisis and the later maximum of failures is significant also as an indication of the continuance and severity of the depression. To illustrate, after the crisis of 1873, a maximum of liabilities was reached in 1878; after that of 1893 it was reached in the year 1896, intervals of five and three years respectively, and indicating a greater degree of severity in the earlier depression.* The diagram on the opposite page shows the volume of bankruptcies in the United States from 1857 to 1900.

SOCIAL STATISTICS

In this connection much reference has been made to social statistics, such as those of pauperism, deaths, births, and marriages.

As food supplies become more available, and communities by law, and private individuals by independent benevolence, take greater pains to provide for the unfortunate, constant changes must occur in the number of those seeking relief. There have also been frequent changes in the policy and manner of affording assistance, notably in the extent to which indoor and outdoor relief are rendered. These changes minimize the value of statistics relating to pauperism. There is an increase of deaths and a decrease of births when severe and prolonged distress exists, such as arises from war, famine, or pestilence; but otherwise the information afforded

---

* For statistics of bankruptcies or business failures, see Appendix B, p. 344, amounts as given by R. G. Dun & Co.

by these statistics is of doubtful value, as indicating prosperous or adverse conditions.   As regards marriages, the tendency towards increase or decrease in many communities is much more in accord with commercial and industrial prosperity or the opposite condition.   The value of social statistics in this connection has been the subject of much controversy.   It may be briefly stated that figures regarding pauperism, births, and deaths are reliable indications only in periods of unusual prosperity or destitution.   Statistics of marriages, particularly in countries where prudential considerations have weight, are much more valuable, but the upward and downward movement does not appear in all countries.   It is a noticeable fact that statistics of the number of marriages in Paris are much more significant of changing conditions than those for the rural portions of France.*

OTHER STATISTICS

Statistics which show an almost uninterrupted increase are those of letters and papers handled by the post-office and deposits in savings-banks.   With the increase in intelligence, improved methods of communication, and occasional reductions in the rates of postage, the number of letters sent shows an almost unbroken increase.   There is a still greater increase in the number of newspapers and periodicals handled.   The increases, however, are notably unequal in different years and reflect in a

* For statistics of marriages, see Appendix B, p. 346.

measure conditions of prosperity. Savings-bank deposits show reduction only in years of unusual distress. This fact gives much plausibility to the argument that changes in prices constitute the fundamental fact in crises and depressions. It is argued that an increase of deposits in savings-banks, which are largely supported by wage-earners, shows their condition to be as good or even better in times of depression than in flush times, when prices are high. The lower prices for some of the necessities of life, which prevail in times of depression, no doubt have an effect in maintaining the annual increase in savings-bank deposits; but it would be incorrect to assign these lower prices as the sole cause. There is a more potent reason, namely, in times of depression deposits in savings-banks are very much increased by the lodgment there of funds which in a time of more active enterprise would be invested in other ways.

All these statistics throw light upon the industrial and commercial conditions of the time to which they belong. By considering them at any time by groups, and making comparison with the years before and after, we may judge of the comparative dulness or prosperity of the period under examination. If, in addition, we are able to weigh the effect of changes in production such as those which manifest themselves in abundance or scarcity of agricultural products, also exceptional occurrences such as disturbances of a political character, our conclusions will be most nearly correct.

It is especially desirable not to rely upon one

group of statistics alone. For example, strikes or lockouts often increase the percentage of the unemployed, and thus destroy the value of statistics of employment as an indicator. But isolated occurrences, though wide-spread in their effects, can hardly change all the indications enumerated. The tables given in Appendix B include information upon the above indications. It is by no means claimed that the figures are as comprehensive as those given in works of a distinctively statistical character. It is only intended to select a few of the most striking. It is to be regretted that in many significant lines our data are so meagre; enough appears, however, to show decided tendencies, among which are the following:

1. To alternate periods of prosperity and dulness.

2. In more recent times these alternate periods are longer.

3. The upward and downward movements are more uniform and continue longer in countries of long-established industrial and commercial development, like France and England.

4. The variation between the highest and lowest point of activity is greater and the alternate upward and downward movement is more interrupted in growing countries, like the United States, where undeveloped fields are being opened. In brief, where the opportunities for enterprise and the resulting progress are greater, there the shock is more severe.

5. Before the commencement of recent de-

pressions, whether ushered in by a crisis or not, there is a large decrease in prices, a less decrease in activity, and a still less decrease in production. In fact, production often holds its own until the commencement of the depression. The lowest prices and activity, as well as diminished production, appear after the depression has begun. In former years the activity often continued until the beginning of the depression, so that the crisis seemed like a sudden breakdown in the midst of the greatest prosperity.

6. The maximum of employment somewhat precedes the date of the highest prices, and frequently precedes the maximum of production.

7. In a debtor or developing country the maximum proportion of exports to imports occurs at a considerably earlier date than the maximum of activity, and indicates that the greatest amount of business activity is contemporaneous with the maximum of consumption rather than with the maximum of production.

CHAPTER VI

INDICATIONS OF THE APPROACH OF A CRISIS OR DEPRESSION

A SUDDEN convulsion, such as a notable failure, may precipitate a crisis and cause liquidation and the slackening of enterprise. As there is no rule by which to determine when these convulsions will occur, no one can foretell the exact date of a crisis.

The convulsion is a signal for the outbreak rather than a cause. Consequences of a serious and lasting nature will not follow unless business is already upon an unstable foundation. The notable failure, or other disturbance, must concur with this instability. A crisis follows because the existing condition of affairs is clearly revealed and confidence is destroyed.

Crises occur or depressions begin without the concurrence of all the usual warnings, but there are certain indications, some of which precede at one time and some at another. These indications may be considered under three divisions:

1. Those pertaining to banks and banking, including rates of interest, the supply of money, and the condition of credit.

2. Those pertaining to foreign trade or ex-

change, including the export and import of merchandise and specie.

3. Those derived from prices and general conditions of business.

These will be considered in order.

Banks and Banking

Among the statistics pertaining to banks and banking most relied upon in this connection are those which show loans outstanding, deposits, bills or paper currency in circulation—whether issued by banks or by a government performing the functions of a bank—specie reserves and rates of interest.

Independently considered, none of these can furnish an accurate forecast of future conditions. Attention should be given to comparative figures showing the relation between two or more of these items.

Increase of Loans.—An increase in the volume of loans and discounts may be an indication of a healthy increase of business; but warning is given when there is a sudden expansion, or an expansion attended by scarcity of specie, by diminishing prices, or by sustained increase in the rate of discount.

Deposits.—An exaggerated importance has been ascribed to the indication afforded by an increase or decrease of deposits. In the usual course of events there is a slight decrease preceding a crisis, followed by a much more pronounced decrease immediately after the crisis has commenced.

Certain writers have called attention to the fact that crises have occurred without any warning in the way of a decrease in the amount of deposits, and have referred to such as exceptional.* Reference has been made to the work of M. Clément Juglar as justifying the opinion that a decrease of deposits is a forerunner of crisis. In the translation of part of his work, heretofore referred to, the translator adds in the introduction:

" The increase or diminution of deposits of course reflects a confident and successful, or a panicky and impoverishing, state of general business." †

But M. Juglar himself expressly combats this idea.

In the article on crises in M. Block's Dictionnaire Général de la Politique, after showing that on one or two occasions the minimum of deposits was not reached until after a crisis, he states:

" We insist upon these variations because some authors of considerable authority have asserted that crises were most frequently produced by a withdrawal of current accounts at the banks which caused a rapid decrease of metallic reserve. The facts prove the contrary."

In a primitive stage of banking, deposits in any country maintain a general proportion to the amount of money. Prior to a crisis metallic money

* See an article on the panic of 1893 in the Quarterly Journal of Economics, vol. viii, p. 117, by the late A. C. Stevens.

† A Brief History of Panics in the United States, translated, with an introduction, by D. W. Thom, p. 18.

diminishes, often because of foreign demands. Paper money diminishes, partly from hoarding caused by distrust and partly from increased demand within the country itself. These influences diminish the amount of money deposited with banks, and the decrease is greatest where the greatest proportion of payments is made by actual transfer of money from hand to hand. Not only is there less money in the country, but more of it is withheld from the banks in the possession of individuals. Besides, there are fluctuations in the amount so withheld which are rather seasonal than determined by the condition of business. After pay-day in large industrial communities, and when the crops are being harvested, unusual amounts are withheld from the banks.

But in the modern development of banking the actual money deposited is much less important in determining the amount of deposits, because so large a share of them represents credits obtained by loans, etc. These credits are transferred upon orders executed by depositors, and furnish a substitute for currency. In proportion as payments and settlements are made by checks, drafts, and bills of exchange, deposits maintain an increased proportion to the amount of currency in circulation. This class of deposits increases prior to a crisis rather than diminishes, because loans increase.

In the reports of the national banks, there is a striking correspondence from year to year in the volume of deposits and that of loans and discounts. Deposits show more frequent fluctuations, but rise and fall in general accord with loans and discounts. This correspondence is easily explained. Another distinction should be noted. Some deposits are the result of completed transactions, and are based upon the proceeds of sales made, amounts realized from investments, etc. Others merely represent loans or discounts, the proceeds of which are entered to the credit of the borrower. Before every crisis there is an unusual proportion of deposits which are based upon loans. If in bank statements there could be separate columns for these two kinds of deposits, the information afforded by their increase or decrease would be much more valuable.*

Paper Currency issued or in Circulation.—Undue importance has been ascribed to the statistics pertaining to this item. The importance as an indication of the amount of paper currency outstanding depends upon the system of issue. The amount naturally would afford an indication similar to that afforded by the volume of loans and discounts, because currency would be issued to keep pace with increasing demands.

There are several systems, each of which illustrates a different idea concerning the proper regulation of paper money.

First. Irredeemable paper currency, that system under which paper money is issued by a bank,

---

* The diagram giving national bank statistics in the Report of the Comptroller of the Currency for 1897, gives in a form convenient for reference and comparison the deposits, loans, etc., from 1863 to 1897. The Bank of England in time of crisis gains a large increase in deposits from banks and bankers.

or more frequently by a government, without obligation for redemption in gold, and usually endowed with legal tender quality. These issues have been in vogue in almost all countries. In this country they were tried in the period preceding the Revolution by most of the colonies, by authority of the Continental Congress in the Revolutionary War, and by the Federal Government and the Confederacy in the Civil War. They are still outstanding in Italy and some of the South American states. In all these states there may be said to be an intention to redeem in specie at some future time. The quantity increases or decreases in accordance with the exigencies of the occasion. There is, of course, a decrease when steps are taken to accomplish redemption. An increase or decrease must necessarily cause disturbance or derangement. Speculation and undue inflation will follow an increase. A lowering of prices and distress for the debtor will result from a decrease. In case of decrease, that hardship will result which must attend extrication from a serious and unnatural situation.

Second. A system based upon the so-called Currency Theory, under which paper money can be issued only against an equal amount of gold deposited (save as to a fixed amount secured by government stock or other exceptional security, as is the case with the Bank of England). The quantity increases or decreases in accordance with the supply of gold. In the time preceding a crisis the quantity outstanding will naturally diminish.

There will be a drain of gold, and as gold is the basis for the issuance of paper currency, there will be less of the latter.

Third. A system based upon the so-called Banking Theory, such as that of the Bank of France, under which there is no exact relation between the quantity of bills or currency emitted and the amount of specie on hand, but bills are payable in specie on demand. Presumably, the quantity will increase prior to a crisis to meet increased demands for loans, but this increase, as well as an increase in the amount of loans outstanding, is usually checked by raising the rate of discount. The fluctuations in recent years in the amount of bills issued by the Bank of France, as well as in the amount issued by the Bank of England under the second plan mentioned, have been so slight in comparison with earlier years, and have been influenced by such a variety of causes, as to afford little light concerning the approach of crises. But it is plain that, if under this third plan the amount of bills outstanding in excess of specie available for their redemption increases to an unusual figure, a distinctly unfavourable indication is afforded. This was the plan in vogue in the United States prior to the Civil War. Nearly all the time the proportion of specie to paper currency outstanding was very small. No feature of our banking system was more dangerous.

Fourth. A system similar to that illustrated by one form of currency in the United States, that of Government bills, or greenbacks as they are called, issued to a fixed amount and retained at that figure.* The quantity of such bills issued is invariable. The quantity in circulation, until the very eve of a crisis, will not materially change, then there will be a very perceptible decrease for obvious reasons.

It requires no reminder to recognise that, under any system, when a crisis has once commenced, or is threatened, there will be a considerable quantity of money withdrawn from circulation and hoarded. This disposition to withdraw money from circulation affords one of the strongest arguments for elasticity in the currency, and emphasizes the most serious defect in our present system.

Rates of Interest.—Wherever the law allows a rate of interest proportionate to the risk and to conditions existing at the time, it will rise preceding a crisis or panic, and often continue at a high and increasing figure for a considerable time. This happens for the same reason that the volume of loans increases in proportion to specie, namely, the existence of a strain upon credit and of a disparity between actual resources and those which the exigencies of borrowers demand. This increase in rate usually gives its warning for a considerable time. Where usury laws prevent variable rates the difficulty in obtaining loans at all will be a noticeable feature.

Relation between Specie and Loans.—The most correct indication of the approach of crises was

---

* The amount of Government notes outstanding since the Act of May 3, 1878, has been $346,681,016.

formerly afforded by the relation between available specie and the volume of loans and discounts outstanding. Of the same nature, though less conclusive, is the relation between bank reserves and loans and discounts.

A continuous decrease of specie attended by an increase in outstanding discounts is always a danger signal. The gap between the two may widen for months, and even for years, and may fluctuate from time to time, but a sudden change of large proportions, or a steady decrease of the percentage of specie is an unfailing indication of danger. The reason for this is not hard to discover. The quantity of metallic money in a country shows what part of its capital is available as money for the payment of its obligations to foreign countries, the final test of availability. For this last-named purpose, credit money cannot be used, but only money having intrinsic value—money of the Mercantile Republic, as it is called by Adam Smith.

A decrease may show merely a falling off in the resources of a country, and if met by proportionate curtailment of investments there will be no crisis. The quantity of specie may be low because of the drain to meet the expenses of war or to provide a food supply from abroad in time of scarcity. But when, in the absence of such explanation, there is a decrease of specie concurrent with an increase of discounts or loans, it is manifest that industrial and commercial ventures have not diminished in proportion to the decrease in actual resources, and that business is upon an unstable foundation. The statistics of banks in 1825, 1837, 1847, and 1857 show that in these so-called crisis years, loans and discounts reached a maximum, and that specie in banks reached a minimum; also that there was a steady progress towards such maximum and minimum for a considerable period preceding. In later years the same general tendency is apparent in crisis years, though less pronounced and with a less uniform upward and downward movement. The statistics of the Bank of England for the years mentioned afford the best illustration of the rule. They show the real nature of a crisis so strikingly that they are given at considerable length.

1. *Before and after the Crisis of December, 1825.*—The figures available for loans and discounts are the averages for quarters; those for specie reserve for specific dates: *

	Specie.	Loans and discounts.†	Percentage of specie to loans and discounts.
	(In	thousands of pounds.)	
Nov. 26, 1824..	11,448	Last quar. of 1824, 2,248	509
Feb. 26, 1825..	8,857	First " 1825, 2,466	359
May 26, " ..	6,456	Second " " 3,973	162
Aug. 26, " ..	3,683	Third " " 5,486	67
Nov. 26, " ..	3,012	Fourth " " 7,839	38
Dec. 31, " ..	1,260	(Crisis)................	16
Feb. 26, 1826..	2,309	First quar. of 1826, 9,586	24
May 26, " ..	4,383	Second " " 5,037	87
Aug. 26, " ..	6,645	Third " " 2,950	225
Nov. 26, " ..	8,998	Fourth " " 2,164	415

* See Rep. from Committee on Bank of England Charter, 1831. Apps. 6 and 88, for Bullion; App. 56, for Loans and Discounts.

† This item, styled "bills discounted" in statements, does not include public securities or long-time loans.

13

2. *Before and after the Crisis of 1837 :* *

	Specie.	Loans and discounts.	Per cent. of specie to loans and discounts.
	(In thou	sands of pounds.)	
July 2, 1833....	11,391	990	1150
July 1, 1834....	8,885	2,337	380
July 7, 1835....	6,536	3,387	192
July 5, 1836....	6,714	3,497	191
Sept. 6, "	5,161	4,527	114
Nov. 1, "	4,700	6,700	70
Dec. 6, "	3,908	9,691	40
Jan. 3, 1837....	4,221	11,398 ⎫	37
Feb. 7, "	3,831	11,425 ⎪	33
Mar. 7, "	4,118	11,217 ⎬ Crisis	36
April 4, "	4,380	11,664 ⎭	37
May 2, "	4,427	10,401	42
June 6, "	5,133	7,737	66
Sept. 5, "	6,862	4,990	137

3. *Before and after Crises of April and October, 1847 :* †

	Specie.	Loans and discounts.	Per ct. of specie to loans and discounts.
	(In thou	sands of pounds.)	
Dec. 28, 1844....	9,755	3,029	322
June 28, 1845....	10,271	4,274	240
Dec. 27, "	7,469	9,499	78
Feb. 28, 1846....	7,754	13,137	59
June 27, "	10,406	9,975	104
Oct. 10, "	8,809	6,571	134
Jan. 9, 1847....	7,471	7,490	99
Mar. 13, "	6,217	9,978	62
April 3, "	4,391	11,146 ⎫ Crisis	39
April 17, "	3,087	10,655 ⎭	28
July 17, "	4,754	9,089	52
Aug. 14, "	4,630	9,369	49
Oct. 2, "	3,852	10,399 ⎫ Crisis	37
Oct. 23, "	1,994	12,492 ⎭	15
Dec. 24, "	8,413	8,541	98
Mar. 25, 1848....	11,713	4,780	245

* Report from the Select Committee on Banks of Issue, 1840, Appendix 12.

† Report from the Select Committee on the Bank Acts, 1856–'57 (printed February 25, 1857), Appendices 12 and 13.

The amount of specie given in this and the following table is made up of the total of notes in reserve, against which specie is on deposit in the issuing department, and specie in the banking department. This change is appropriate after the Bank Act of 1844.

4. *Before and after the Crisis of 1857:*[*]

	Specie.	Loans and discounts.	Percentage of specie to loans and discounts.
	(In thousands of pounds.)		
June 28, 1856....	8,033	4,236	189
Sept. 27, "	6,019	6,520	92
Oct. 25, "	3,639	9,011	40
Dec. 27, "	6,048	6,393	94
Jan. 31, 1857....	5,441	8,263	65
April 25, "	4,241	8,500	49
June 27, "	6,710	7,985	84
Oct. 17, "	3,816	9,661	39
Oct. 31, "	2,834	11,105	25
Nov. 4, "	2,705	11,439	23
Nov. 11, "	1,462	13,233 Crisis	11
Nov. 18, "	1,552	16,003	9
Dec. 30, "	6,614	15,158	43

These tables show that in the time between the last quarter of 1824 and December, 1825, the proportion of specie to loans and discounts fell from 509 per cent to 16 per cent; between July 2, 1833, and February 7, 1837, from 1,150 per cent to 33 per cent; between December 28, 1844, and October 23, 1847, from 322 per cent to 15 per cent; between June 28, 1856, and November 18, 1857, from 189 per cent to 9 per cent.

---

[*] Continuation of the preceding Report from the Select Committee for 1856–'57, in a Return to an Order of the House of Commons, dated May 8, 1873.

These statistics show a decided change after 1825 and 1837. Beginning in 1847, fluctuations at different seasons of the year assume much greater importance, and the warning given by an unusual pressure one year before the oncoming of the crisis is plainly apparent.

In 1866, the varying proportion between specie on the one hand and loans and discounts on the other was much less noticeable than in previous years of crisis. The prominent failures at that time brought disaster without the usual warnings. Since 1866, the disturbances in the United Kingdom have lacked some of the events which in prior years immediately preceded them. While the embarrassment of great firms has aggravated the difficulty, the depressions of the last three decades have occurred in response to disturbing changes affecting the whole field of commerce and industry. Financial difficulties have been minimized. The diminished prominence of financial difficulties and of the disproportion between loans and specie is due to a multitude of causes, many of which have been potent in other countries as well. Among them are the following:

1. The growth of international financial relations, quicker communication, and the recognition of a general interest, resulting in the more ready importation of gold from abroad and in a great increase in transactions between banks and financial institutions of different countries.

2. The adoption of substitutes for money for payment of obligations and in adjusting settlements

both at home and abroad, diminishing the strain on the monetary supply, metallic or paper.

3. The great increase of bank deposits, and the dependence upon them in a larger measure for loanable funds.

4. The larger capital invested in the banking business, as shown by the growth of joint-stock banks and other financial institutions which supply demands for loans formerly made upon the Bank of England alone.

5. The establishment of the custom of increasing the rate of discount at a time when gold reserves begin to diminish.

A very important factor may be added, namely, the greater skill and prudence exercised by bankers as a result of experience.

Financiers note with extreme apprehension exports of specie. So great is this apprehension that a symptom of the disease is often mistaken for the disease itself. When there is a drain of specie, usually accompanied by an increase in loans, bank directors hastily convene and raise the rate of discount. This measure, more than any other, has tended, in more developed countries, to prevent the occurrence of severe crises in recent years, and is largely responsible for the fact that the depression feature has become relatively more prominent. The statistics of the earlier crises of 1825, 1837, 1847, and 1857 show the course of events unrestrained by the preventives which experience and prudence have suggested.

While the proportion of specie reserve was

smaller, the same general change in the proportion between specie and loans appears in the statistics of banks of the United States prior to the crises of 1837 and 1857. It is not so easy to trace the progress of the movement, because comprehensive statistics are available only by years. The following table is given by way of illustration:

Banks of the United States. Crises of 1837 and 1857 *

	Specie.	Loans and discounts.	Percentage of specie to loans.
	(In thousands	of dollars.)	
1835........	43,937	365,163	12.0
1836........	40,019	457,506	8.7
1837........	37,915	525,115	7.2
1838........	35,184	485,631	7.2
1854........	59,410	557,397	10.6
1855........	53,944	576,144	9.3
1856........	59,314	634,183	9.3
1857........	58,300	684,456	8.5
1858........	74,412	583,165	12.7

An examination of the returns of the Bank of France shows the same decrease of specie and increase of loans prior to a crisis, as in the figures given pertaining to the Bank of England; also that the conditions in the relation between specie and loans in earlier years still continue in a much greater degree in the former institution.† The

---

* See for 1835 to 1838, House Executive Document No. 111, Twenty-sixth Congress, Second Session, p. 1455; for 1854 to 1858, see House Executive Document No. 20, Thirty-eighth Congress, First Session, p. 225.

† For a collection of statistics of the Bank of France, see M. Clément Juglar's work, Crises Commerciales, tables after

Bank of France furnishes a larger share of the discounts in the country in which it is located. One reason for the continuance of the earlier conditions in the relation between discounts and specie is the greater demand for money because of the more limited use of credit and of substitutes for currency.

Relation between Available Cash and Loans and Discounts.—Similar in significance to the relation between specie and loans and discounts is that between available cash held by the banks and loans and discounts. Wherever the redemption of currency in specie is not obligatory upon banks, the proportion of available cash has much the same significance as that ascribed to the proportion of specie in the preceding paragraphs. In the United States the national banks do not redeem their bills in gold; hence, since their organization an important indication of the approach of crises is found in the decreasing proportion of available cash to loans, although the importance of this indication is diminished by the anxiety of the banks at all times to loan out their available funds and the consequent tendency to maintain only a small surplus above the required reserve. The objection may be made that both of these items—loans and discounts and available cash, as well as specie—are assets of

---

p. 399, also pp. 246, 409, 411, 415, 418, 422, 428, and 432; also, for the period from 1875 to 1885, the diagram at the end of the book. See also p. 330 of the Statistical Abstract for Foreign Countries, 1885 to 1895-'96, prepared by the British Board of Trade.

banks, and that a more correct guide could be obtained from the figures showing the relation between their assets and liabilities. But the specie, or cash, held by banking institutions, furnishes a test of resources, both of banks and their patrons, which are immediately available. Loans and discounts furnish the best indication of transactions and enterprises which rest upon credit. Safety depends upon a proper proportion between resources immediately available and those which depend upon credit. An increase in loans and discounts accompanied by a decrease in available cash is very significant.

Bank Reserves.—The proportion of bank reserves to liabilities is an important indication. These show the percentage of available assets of banks to liabilities payable on demand. Reserves relate more to the banks and show their condition, while the two former indications relate more to the situation of their customers. In time of stringency, or when the approach of a crisis is threatened, this reserve shrinks below the normal percentage. Its significance with the national banks of the United States is diminished by arbitrary regulations providing for the maintenance of a specific minimum at all times. But it is an item universally considered with a view to determining the outlook. The state of the reserve not only shows the condition of the banks, but also tends to show that of the general business community, because it indicates the extent of demands for credit both to meet payments for obligations already incurred and for prospective operations. A decreasing reserve is always watched with apprehension.*

INDICATIONS PERTAINING TO FOREIGN TRADE OR EXCHANGE, EXPORTS AND IMPORTS OF MERCHANDISE AND SPECIE

These indications may be considered under three divisions: first, relation between exports and imports of merchandise; second, relation between exports and imports of gold; third, rate of foreign exchange.

Exports and Imports of Merchandise.— As stated in the preceding chapter, a mere excess of imports is not an unfavourable indication. Its significance depends upon the situation of a country. There is a material difference in the rules applicable in a creditor country or one of matured development, as compared with debtor countries or those which are in a stage of rapid development. There are two indications which threaten a crisis. A large and long-continued excess of imports over exports in a debtor country is an indication of danger. The same is true in any country when there is a continued increase of imports beyond the

---

* Mr. R. H. Inglis-Palgrave, in his work on Bank Rate in England, France, and Germany from 1844 to 1878, has collected statistics of the reserve of the Bank of England during the years 1844 to 1878, inclusive. See his table on p. 6 and following pages, especial attention being called to columns 13, 14, 18, and 19. The tabular statement given is especially valuable, because it not only gives the amount of reserves, but also the percentages, taking 1844 as a basis. It shows the decrease of the reserve in 1847, 1855 to 1857, 1866, and 1871 to 1874.

usual proportion to exports, or a large and sudden increase in the proportion of imports. In either case there is an exhaustion of resources caused by extravagance or by the expenditure of undue amounts in providing for future development.

In considering the indications of crises afforded by a steady increase of imports out of proportion to exports, no better illustration can be found than that furnished by the foreign trade of Austria, or Austria-Hungary, prior to the crisis of May, 1873. Beginning in 1860, the exports of Austria for ten years showed a considerable excess over imports, the percentage of excess reaching its largest proportion in 1866; then a decrease in the proportion

Exports and Imports of Austria-Hungary in the Years Specified *

	Exports.	Imports.	Percentage of exports to imports.
	(Millions	of gulden.)	
1866................	329	218	150.9
1867................	407	294	138.4
1868................	429	387	110.8
1869................	438	419	104.5
1870................	395	431	91.6
1871................	467	540	86.5
1872................	388	613	63.2
1873 (Crisis in May)..	423	583	72.5
1874................	449	568	79.0
1875................	550	549	100.1
1876................	595	534	111.4

* The amount of special imports and exports, articles of domestic production or consumption, are given as affording the most accurate barometer of conditions. The figures are taken from the Statistical Abstracts for the Principal and Other Foreign Countries, compiled by the British Board of Trade.

of exports commenced. In 1870 a veritable boom began, and for the first time in many years imports exceeded exports, a condition which continued until the crash of May, 1873.

The figures on page 202, giving exports and imports, and the percentage of exports to imports, from 1866 to 1876 inclusive, before and after the crisis of May, 1873, is particularly significant in the showing made of the uniform increase in the proportion of imports until the occurrence of the crisis.

In 1874, it will be observed, the imports still exceeded exports, though by a considerably smaller percentage. In 1875 the two were very nearly equal, with exports slightly in excess. Beginning in 1876, and in every year since, with the exception of 1898, exports have exceeded imports, as was the case prior to 1870.

In the United States, for some years preceding each of the crises of 1837, 1857, and 1873, there had been a large and unusual excess of imports over exports. As already pointed out, this excess was principally due to the enormous amounts expended in construction looking to the development of the country. After 1873 the indications afforded by changes in the relation between exports and imports are not so significant as regards the approach of crises.

Prior to the depression of 1882–'84 there had been for six years, from 1876 to 1881 inclusive, a large excess of exports, averaging from 1877 to 1881 inclusive over $200,000,000 per annum. This balance, partly from deficient harvests in 1881 and partly from increase of importations, suddenly dropped to a little less than $26,000,000 in 1882,* a year in which construction was conducted on an enormous scale. In this instance we have an illustration of the indication afforded by a sudden increase in the proportion of imports. In 1883 and 1884 there was an excess of exports, but much less than in the years preceding 1882. Prior to the crisis of 1893 there was again a sudden change in the relation between exports and imports. For the period of eight years preceding, the excess of exports had been much less than in the similar period prior to 1884. For three years, to June 30, 1887, there was an excess of exports; for 1888 and 1889, of imports. For the three years ending June 30, 1892, there was an excess of exports, which was not large in 1890 and 1891, but amounted approximately to $200,000,000 in 1892. The amount paid to foreign countries during the decade prior to 1893, for interest on investments held abroad, transportation, expenses of tourists, etc., has been estimated at $200,000,000 per annum. If this amount is accepted as correct, these expenses more than equalled the computed balance of exports in every one of the twelve years after 1881, except 1892, in which exports were large, by reason of deficient harvests in Europe and abundant crops at home. In 1893 there was an excess of imports. It thus appears that the threat of a crisis is not to be found in an adverse balance of trade at any par-

---

* The fiscal years ending June 30th.

ticular time, but in a marked and unusual change, as when the proportion of exports to imports is greatly decreased in a single year, as in 1882 and 1893, or the continuance of an abnormal excess in the proportion of imports, as in the case of the three previous crises.

A second class of indications of crises is derived from more minute analysis of trade statistics.

Chief among these is an increase in the importation of articles for which there is a competing domestic supply, which in ordinary times has satisfied the demand. To illustrate, let us suppose that certain articles are manufactured in two countries under such circumstances that neither ordinarily calls upon the other for a supply. One country begins to import these articles from the other. This may indicate that the importing country is increasing more rapidly in wealth, or that the exporting country is gaining superior advantages, but presumably it shows overaction in the importing country. Less significance is attributable to increased importations of food and primary necessities, such as frequently occur in European countries, and occurred in the United States in 1837. These increased importations are traceable to natural causes. But, as stated, if there continues to be an importation of articles, the supply of which is not determined by natural causes, and for which there is competing production, it is an indication of overaction. In new and developing countries more than elsewhere prices rise in a time of active enterprise, and there is a great increase of demand for commodities from foreign countries which are usually supplied at home.

In analyzing import statistics much attention has been given to increase in the importation of luxuries. This increase may indicate danger. It is often associated with a season of extravagance in other directions. The importation of ornaments is said to have attracted the attention of the Roman Senate to such an extent that severe prohibitions were adopted. Foreign writers have frequently spoken of the great increase in the importation of articles of luxury at different times in the United States. This increase cannot, however, be accepted as unfavourable, if proportionate to increasing wealth.

Export or Import of Gold.—The export of gold does not necessarily indicate the approach of a crisis, but important deductions may be made from the statistics of its export and import.

Every country will, under normal conditions, have a certain share of the gold or primary money supply of the world. The different countries have been compared to reservoirs of water, of various sizes, connected by pipes. All the reservoirs will maintain the same level. The share of each country is determined primarily by its wealth. There is a tendency for metallic money, which is a form of wealth, to maintain in every country a fixed proportion to other forms of wealth. But the share of each is affected by the volume of its trade and other incidental circumstances, among which are established methods of transacting business, the habits of its people and, notably, its currency system.

The currency system affects the gold supply. Paper money displaces gold, and causes it to be sent elsewhere in a less or greater proportion, according as it is absolutely based upon a deposit of gold, is redeemable in gold on presentation, or is not redeemable at all.

Methods of transacting business influence the supply. Where balances are largely settled at clearing-houses, and checks are generally employed, less currency and less gold are required. In this particular the contrast between England and France is very marked. The latter country makes less use of clearing-houses and checks, and accordingly requires a larger supply of gold and silver, the latter metal being extensively used.

The habits of the people exercise an important influence. After the Franco-Prussian War it was found that the French peasant proprietors had hoarded large sums of gold. In the great emergency created, these amounts were brought out and assisted in the payment of the indemnity. Frequently, when native grandees in India die, it appears that they have been accumulating a great stock of gold, much of it in the form of ornaments, which for years has been kept out of circulation. All this hoarding tends to increase the demand on the gold which is in circulation as money. The peasant or grandee who hoards causes so much of the world's capital to be idle. The benefit accruing in time of crisis or emergency to countries in which quantities of gold are withheld from general circulation, is obtained at the cost of diminished activity and volume of business under ordinary conditions.

M. Paul Leroy-Beaulieu quotes figures to show that France, in 1885, had a circulation of metallic money amounting to 215 francs per capita; England and the United States had, respectively, 86 and 68 francs per capita.* Of course, if the quantity of coin in circulation had been based upon per capita wealth at that time, England would have shown the largest quantity per capita, France next, and the United States the least.

There is then a normal share of gold which belongs to each country. If any one has more than its share, it will export. It is easy to recognise that from a gold-producing country, such as Australia, South Africa, or Alaska, the greater part of the gold mined will be exported. Likewise, if gold is held in any country in such quantity that it can be invested elsewhere more advantageously, either in loans or in purchases, or can be sent abroad in payment of debts, it will be exported. If it is invested in loans abroad, it is an indication of surplus capital, and makes a favourable showing. If invested in purchases at low prices, it shows ability to draw upon other countries for an increasing share of objects of utility. If the purchases show that home prices are higher than foreign, and a supply of things usually obtained at home must be obtained from abroad, the export of gold is a sign of danger. Thus, an important question in determining the sig-

* Traité d'Économie Politique, vol. iv, pp. 190–191.

nificance of shipments of gold, is the nature of the purchases or investments to be made with it.

The specie exports and imports of this country have furnished distinct indications prior to each period of disturbance, but their significance cannot be understood without an examination not only of our general situation, but also of the particular situation at different times.

The General Situation. — This country, now and for the last fifty years, would naturally export gold. In the nine years from 1891 to 1899 inclusive, the total value of the gold production of the world, according to the best estimates, was $1,846,232,200.* Of this amount the United States produced $434,207,000.† Thus, its production for this period of nine years was 23.5 per cent of that of the whole world; in 1891 and 1896 it exceeded one-fourth of the whole. To this must be added a considerable quantity mined in the British possessions and counted in the statistics of gold production for those localities, but mined by citizens of the United States and brought to this country. It is needless to say that so large a per-

* See the Report of George E. Roberts, Director of the United States Mint, for 1900, p. 105, for production by years.

† Ibid., p. 104. An unofficial report of the Director estimates the production in the United States for 1900 at $79,322,-281, that of the whole world at $255,000,000 to $258,000,000. According to this estimate, in that year the United States produced more than thirty per cent of the whole. The disturbances in South Africa greatly diminished the supply. The gold product of the Transvaal in 1900 is estimated at $8,200,-000.

14

centage, amounting to nearly one-fourth of the gold mined, is more than the normal share of the United States for metallic money or other uses, and naturally we should export gold just as we do wheat or cotton.

Situation at Different Times.—The history of the movement of the precious metals in the United States, if considered with a view to indications, must include information as to the particular situation in successive periods. There may be said to have been five distinct periods:

1. *The Non-producing Era, extending from the Foundation of the Mint in 1792, to and including 1847, the Year preceding the Beginning of Gold-mining in California.*—During this period the total value of gold mined in the United States did not exceed $25,000,000; the production of silver did not exceed the comparatively insignificant sum of $400,000.* During these fifty-six years the United States was naturally an importer of the precious metals.†

Although the movement of the two metals was much affected by changes in laws pertaining to currency and banking, the general tendency was towards excess of imports. From 1825 to 1847

---

* Report of the Director of the Mint for 1900, p. 208.

† As regards the relation of gold to silver in the currency, this era was divided into two periods: the first from 1792 to 1834, in which the ratio of silver to gold in the coinage was 15 to 1, which overvalued silver, and excluded gold from general circulation; the second, after 1834, in which there was a ratio of 16 to 1, which overvalued gold, and excluded silver from general circulation.

inclusive, there was a balance of imports of gold amounting to very nearly $40,000,000, and from 1821 to 1847, a balance of imports of silver slightly in excess of that amount, making a total balance of imports of gold and silver of approximately $80,000,000.*

An apparent exception to general tendencies in crises and the time preceding them is to be noted in the year 1837 and the three years preceding. As there was a crisis in 1837, and feverish activity for some years preceding, we should expect to find an excess of exports of specie; but, on the contrary, there was an excess of imports of gold and silver in each year, amounting in the aggregate to $36,105,256 in these four years. The following causes contributed to this exceptional condition:

First. Borrowing on a large scale from Europe, which required the transfer of specie to this country. The Bank of the United States alone borrowed $20,000,000.

Second. Increased productiveness of mines, especially gold mines in Russia and silver mines in Mexico, which afforded larger supplies of gold and silver to all commercial nations.

Third. Increased purchases of our cotton and other products at increased prices until 1837.

---

* See Report of the Director of the Mint for 1900, pp. 246–247. Figures showing the movement of gold are given from 1825; those pertaining to silver from 1821. Prior to 1821 imports and exports of specie were not reported separately from merchandise. Of the balance of gold in this period, $20,000,000 were imported in 1847

Fourth. The issuance of the specie circular by President Jackson, requiring payment for public lands in specie.

Fifth. The prohibition by many of the States of the circulation of bank-notes for small sums, making necessary larger supplies of metallic money for change.

The exceptional movement of specie in 1837 and the years prior to the crisis of that year is referred to because it shows the danger of relying upon one kind of statistics, and also because it goes to confirm the statement made elsewhere that an abundance of capital or money rather than a scarcity may be a cause of crises and depressions.

2. *The Period from the Development of Gold-mining, after the Discovery of Gold in California in 1848, until the Issuance of Paper Money in 1862.*—This was a period in which gold was exported every year in large quantities, with the exception of the years ending June 30, 1849 and 1861, in which latter year were marketed the large crops of 1860. In these years, the total product of our mines was over $700,000,000. The aggregate excess of exports of gold during this period was more than $400,000,000. The surplus of the domestic product, amounting to over $300,000,000, was retained. The latter sum may be regarded as the share of the United States in the increased gold supply of the world.

3. *The Period of Exportation because of the Suspension of Specie Payments.*—This period in-

cluded fifteen years, from 1862 to the summer of 1877. During these years gold was, except for the payment of customs duties and interest upon part of the public debt, mere merchandise, and was accordingly exported in large amounts, reaching an aggregate of more than $630,000,000. The domestic production continued, but the export was practically of the whole quantity mined. Although resumption was not accomplished until January 1, 1879, this period practically came to a close in 1877, when preparation for resumption caused gold imports to begin.

4. *The Period of Eleven Years beginning July 1, 1877.*—As already stated, the preparation for resumption caused exports of gold to cease and imports to begin about June 30, 1877. This period continued until June 30, 1888, and may be considered one of normal conditions, during which there was no disturbance either from redundant or irredeemable paper money, as in the prior period, or from depreciated silver, as in the succeeding. Except in 1884 and 1886, there was an excess of imports during these years amounting to approximately $220,000,000, and the gold mined in this country was retained at home. The very large excess of importation in 1880 and 1881, amounting in the latter year to $97,466,127 (the largest balance in any year until 1898), fell off to $1,789,174 in 1882, from which there was a rise to $6,133,261 in 1883, but a balance of $18,250,640 was exported in 1884. In this sudden change in 1882 in the proportion between exports and imports of gold,

there was a significant indication of the approach of the crisis of that time.*

5. *The Period of Silver Inflation and Uncertainty as to the Standard from June 30, 1888, to and including the Fiscal Year 1896.*—Prior to 1888 for ten years, silver bullion of a value not less than $2,000,000 per month had been coined into silver dollars under the Bland Act of February, 1878; but the effect seems not to have been especially felt, largely because of the contemporaneous withdrawal of national bank-notes from circulation, in which there was a reduction of $106,000,000 between 1882 and 1888, and a consequent void in the supply of currency. About the year 1888 this increase of silver dollars resulted in a redundant currency, and the fear of a departure from a gold basis caused numerous securities to be sent to the United States for disposal, which had theretofore been held abroad. This was accompanied by serious apprehensions at home. The Act of June, 1890, providing for the purchase of 4,500,000 ounces of silver per month and the issuance of currency certificates therefor, greatly increased the volume of currency and the distrust of the permanence of the gold standard, a distrust which was promoted by popular agitation for the free coinage of silver, and was not removed by the repeal of this act in the autumn of 1893. The balance of exports of gold during this period amounted to $320,000,000. Exports were

* Fiscal years ending June 30th are referred to in this paragraph.

especially large during the year ending June 30, 1896.

In July, 1896, imports of gold again commenced, and, with some fluctuations (especially in the four months of the following year, from April 1st to August 1st), continued until the end of 1900. They were especially large in the year 1898. The large excess of imports in the last few years, however, would not have occurred without the combined influences of unequalled prosperity and a movement for the restoration of that share of gold which we had lost.

In reviewing these periods, it appears that the exportation of gold for 1851 and for succeeding years, was due to the large quantity mined in this country. Incidentally, this large production stimulated speculation, as well as legitimate enterprise, and was a factor in causing the panic of 1857.

The large exportations after June 30, 1862, were due to the abandonment of a specie basis. These exportations, which continued until June 30, 1877, were made the more necessary by the large expenses of the war, and by extravagant expenditure and the great development of the country in the years succeeding the war. The importations from June 30, 1877, filled the void created by the absence of gold from the currency. In the four years after the beginning of this period these importations were increased by unusually large exports of merchandise. The exportation of gold beginning in 1888 was due to the increase of silver money under the Bland Act, and later, by the

Act of June, 1890, both of which caused distrust regarding the monetary standard. There was a redundancy of instruments circulating as money, and consequently a tendency to send abroad that kind of money which had a better quality elsewhere, but no better quality here.

The large excess of importation in the fiscal years 1861, 1880, 1881, and 1898 may be regarded as most significant in indicating a prosperous condition. Each of these years witnessed a deficient food supply in Europe. The year 1898 also showed the effect of a greatly increasing foreign demand for goods manufactured in the United States.

Circumstances under which Excess of Exports of Gold indicates the Approach of a Crisis.—First, when gold is required for purchases from abroad which are made at high and rising prices. This indicates overaction and concurs with unusual increase in the prices of domestic supplies. Especially is this true, if in a time of rising prices gold is exported for commodities usually supplied by domestic production. Such a condition cannot long continue without a reaction and ensuing depression. The indications which are significant in connection with the imports of merchandise apply to the export of gold. On the other hand, the export of gold for purchases when prices are low is not an unfavourable condition. It indicates purchases upon advantageous terms.

Second, when the export of gold is attended by a scarcity of money and a marked increase in the rate of discount, it is a decidedly unfavourable indi-

cation. This is of the same kind with those
indications noticed in the conditions of banks. A
steady increase in the rate of discount, or a decrease
in the supply of loanable funds attended by a
marked decrease in the supply of gold, is a sure precursor of crisis. The only question is how long
this condition can continue without a crash.

Third, an unusual balance of exports of gold,
not explained by surplus production, continued for
a considerable time, or a sudden withdrawal of
large amounts, is one of the most unfavourable
indications. It is to be noted that there is an exceptional sensitiveness in financial centres on the
subject of gold exports, and sometimes an export
entirely normal is interpreted as showing instability
and destroys confidence when there is no reason for
distrust.

It should be added that, when for a succession
of years gold is withdrawn from circulation by
reason of the substitution of inconvertible paper as
money, the conditions which exist are sure to vary
from normal lines. Credit will rest upon a false
basis, and the inevitable tendency will be towards an
increase in the quantity of paper money outstanding and a dangerous expansion of credit.

In many respects the phenomena of a balance of
gold exports are similar to those arising from a
balance of merchandise imports. The two are expected to appear contemporaneously; but in essential
particulars they differ. Some differences depend
upon the question of gold production. In countries
like Australia and a portion of South Africa, where

gold-mining is a leading industry, gold exports are naturally classed with merchandise exports, and an export is a favourable indication. In non-producing countries like England and France, where the use for money is the prevailing demand, import is a favourable indication. There is another difference in a noticeable tendency towards contemporaneous decline in gold reserves in all the great financial centres. That which is lost in one country is not gained in another. This decline is explained by the withdrawal of considerable amounts to be hoarded or retained in circulation outside of banks, and to some extent by the transfer of gold to countries outside of the most advanced industrial and commercial circle. The influences which cause gold to be hoarded or retained in circulation outside of banks are not unlike those which affect the circulation of paper money. International credits or payments frequently cause an excess of imports of gold in a country to coincide with an excess of imports of merchandise. Again, a large demand for money, manifesting itself in high rates of interest, may cause gold to be retained in a country contemporaneously with an unusual balance of imports.

Rate of Exchange.—The rate of exchange with foreign nations is, in many respects, a more significant indication than the export or import of gold or of merchandise. It may be said to be freer from exceptional influences. A high or rising rate of exchange indicates an increase of indebtedness worthy of careful attention and an analysis of

causes. It is obvious that an increase in the rate
of exchange will tend to check importations and increase exports. When the rate has reached a certain point, gold will be exported to settle adverse
balances.

While, generally speaking, the export of gold is
attended by a high rate of exchange, of which it
may be said to be the consequence, at times this is
not so. The export of gold contemporaneously
with a low rate of exchange indicates the sending
away of a surplus for favourable purchases or investments abroad. Likewise, the concurrence of a low
rate of exchange with an excess of imports of merchandise indicates a credit balance, which enables
the importing country to make large purchases
from other countries.

The question of the significance of balances on
merchandise account and on shipments of gold, as
well as that of rates of exchange, is largely one of
comparative prices. If, by reason of exceptional
advantages in production, staple articles are made
or produced at a lower figure in one country than
in others, or if, by reason of depression, consumption
is diminished, so that slackened demand lowers
prices, exports will increase, and naturally there
will be imports of gold and lower rates of exchange.
This export movement will continue until home
prices rise to a point at which exportation is no
longer profitable. *

The point worthy of most careful study in these
price fluctuations is the cause of the rise or fall.
If there is a rise, does it indicate excessive activity?

Is the change from circulating to fixed capital excessive? Is the rise in the prices of imports out of proportion to the rise in the prices of those exports which are usually sent in exchange for them? Upon the analysis and correct answer to these questions, rather than upon more general indications, will depend the success of the observer in forecasting the approach of a crisis or depression.

As regards universality, or the contemporaneous appearance of indications in all commercial communities, there is a decided difference between those enumerated under this division and those afforded by banking statistics. Rates of interest, scarcity of money, and increase of loans are more nearly contemporaneous in all countries. All countries feel the effect of scarcity of money in any one. Unfavourable balances of trade do not appear in all countries at the same time, and thus they show more correctly the unequal degree of prosperity in different localities. Financial conditions respond more promptly to the changing movement of affairs than those which are commercial and industrial. At a later time, unfavourable conditions in commerce and industry manifest themselves and extend their influence everywhere.

PRICES AND GENERAL BUSINESS CONDITIONS

The condition of business is most healthy when its operations are characterized by enlightened conservatism. Steady, not sudden, increase in trade is the basis of enduring prosperity. A pronounced variation from the usual trend of events is always disturbing in its effect, even though in response to increased activity, and when it may seem to promise the best of results. The business man does not fear, but rather welcomes innovation. On the other hand, modern business finds one of its greatest dangers in innovation. It is rare that material change in production or trade can occur without bringing with it substantial loss. It is probable that these changes will not be met by such careful adjustment as the situation demands. In rapid progress in industrial and commercial affairs, or in the development of new fields of production, lies one of the most serious dangers of depression.

It is necessary to make a careful survey of conditions, not alone in one country, but in all. Every famine or other calamity which entails loss upon part must have its effect upon the whole of the great aggregate. The prevalence of an undue degree of speculation or of extravagant expansion, even in the production of staple articles, is one of the surest signs of approaching collapse.

One of the most significant indications of danger is an increase in the number of business failures, or in the aggregate of liabilities. The significance of the indications to be derived from bankruptcies depends very largely upon an analysis of the circumstances of the different cases. An increase of failures not directly traceable to unskilful or fraudulent management, or insufficient capital, furnishes reasons for caution. It indicates excessive and unwholesome competition. Before almost every crisis there is a progressive increase in the number of failures and the amount of liabilities. At such times, one leading feature is the epidemic of speculation. As speculation bears a greater or less proportion to the volume of business, the danger of crisis is greater or less; and in making investments, that enterprise is safest which avoids speculation, adheres to safe and conservative methods, and does not attempt operations without the necessary capital and the ability to maintain them. As stated by Mr. Bagehot:

" Part of every mania is caused by the impossibility to get people to confine themselves to the amount of business for which their capital is sufficient, and in which they can engage safely." *

One other tendency peculiarly noticeable in the United States is the disposition to engage in occupations for which there has been no preparation. There is a prevalent contempt for expert knowledge, largely due to the ingenuity and ready adaptability of the people for new work and the numerous instances in which men have achieved conspicuous success in ventures for which they had little or no preparation. If a general average were taken, however, it would appear that of those who have made essay in untried fields the number who have failed has been far greater than the number who have succeeded, and the failures have been more striking than the successes. In the competition which now prevails in every branch of life, it is

* Collected Works, published by the Travelers' Insurance Company, vol. iv, p. 567.

not reasonable to expect success in vocations in which there must be competition with those who have had thorough training and preparation for the work.

Though it may seem remote from this subject, it may be remarked that in the period preceding every crisis, there is a notable absence of scrutiny in the examination of the skill and trustworthiness of those to whom capital is intrusted for management. In the buoyant spirit of the time, a desire for increase of activity causes the investor to be less critical, and thus to aid in the creation of unprofitable enterprises and opportunities for fraud.

Prices of Commodities.—In the season of activity which precedes a crisis prices rise. This rise begins after the worst point in the previous depression has been reached. Attention has already been called to the fact that the rise in prices is unequal in different commodities.* Iron and steel in their various forms, as well as other commodities required for construction, and those which supply new demands of consumption, show the most striking increases. During a depression prices of these commodities fall first and most notably. The prices of other commodities do not fall so much or so early. In the preceding season of expansion they do not rise so much, and, in their rise, as well as in their fall, they show, for the most part, only a remote effect of the activity or inactivity of the time.

Lumber and coal command greatly increased

* Chapter III, pp. 52–54.

prices in the activity preceding a crisis, but the increase is by no means so large as is the case with iron and steel. It is much easier to open a new coal mine, or enlarge the output from those in existence, than to provide the plant for increased production of iron and steel. An increased supply of lumber also is more readily obtained.

In Chapter III, attention has already been called to the tendency of prices of iron and steel to reach and pass their maximum some time before the crisis occurs, though if the crisis be precipitated by an unexpected failure, the interval will be short or the high prices may continue until the very outbreak of the crisis.*

Prices of Iron and Steel in the United States: Prices Prior to and Succeeding the Crisis of 1873. —In the United States, prior to the crisis of September 18, 1873, a low price level appeared in almost all grades of iron and steel in January, 1871. This was followed by a rapid and almost unbroken rise, culminating in the months of October and November, 1872. A maximum price of rolled bar iron, $118.72 at Philadelphia, was reached in October, 1872. The price fell, with slight fluctuations, to $80.64 in September, 1873, the month of the crisis.

Standard sections of iron rails, prices quoted at the mills, fell from a maximum of $88.75 in November, 1872, to $75 in September, 1873.

Steel rails showed less decline prior to the crisis, reaching a maximum of $122.50 in March, 1873, and falling to $118 in September. Cut nails fell

---

* See Chapter III, pp. 55–56.

from $6 per keg of 100 pounds in October and
November of 1872 to $4.75 in September, 1873.
Anthracite foundry pig-iron fell from $53.87½ in
September, 1872, to $42.50 in September, 1873.*
Reasons for the slower decline in price of steel
rails, applicable also in the case of iron rails, can
be found in the smaller number of mills for their
manufacture, and the consequently increased opportunity for combination; also in the more general
custom of manufacturing in compliance with
orders. In the depression which followed the
crisis of 1873, prices of a majority of the varieties
of iron and steel fell to a minimum in the latter
part of the year 1878, though steel rails and standard sections of iron rails fell to a minimum in the
closing months of 1877. The month of November,
1878, may, however, be selected as the turning-
point. At that date, No. 1 anthracite foundry pig-
iron had fallen to $16.50 per gross ton, less than
one third the price of September, 1872.

*Prices Prior to and Succeeding the Crisis of
1884.*—In the expansion which followed 1878,
prices reached their maximum in the months of
January, February, and March, 1880, but the
highest figures were maintained only for a very
short time. Anthracite foundry pig-iron, which
had fallen to $16.50 in November, 1878, rose to
$41 in February, 1880; rolled bar iron to $85.12
in the same month; steel rails to $85; cut nails to

---

* The prices given are taken from the Statistical Abstracts
of the American Iron and Steel Association, by James M.
Swank.

15

$5.25, in the months of February and March. After the month of March, 1880, there was a sharp decline, though interrupted by numerous fluctuations. A steady decline commenced after the closing months of the year 1882, and continued until another minimum was reached in the summer of 1885. The crisis of May, 1884, occurred in the midst of this downward movement, and seems to have exerted but little influence upon the iron market. Anthracite foundry pig-iron fell to $17.75 in the months of June, July, and August of 1885, and then began to rise. Rolled bar iron fell to $40.30 in May of the same year, and then was quoted at $40.32 for the remaining months of the year. Steel rails fell to $26 in the month of April.

Prices Prior to and Succeeding the Crisis of May, 1893.—After the minimum point in 1885 there was an upward movement continuing until the earlier months of 1887, the months of February and March of that year showing maximum prices in most varieties of iron and steel; this maximum was succeeded by a fall in prices, which for most varieties reached a minimum in May and June, 1889. This minimum was followed for a short time by rising prices, which reached a maximum in January, 1890. In the two decades after the maximum prices of 1880 the trend of prices differed from that in the preceding decade. Fluctuations were much more frequent. For nearly eighteen years the general tendency was downward, though interrupted by brief revivals in prices in the years 1882, 1886, 1887, 1890, and 1895. The rise in price which occurred in 1887 and other years proved to be greater than the increased demand would sustain. The general statement may be made that during this long period from 1880 to 1897, in fact, until 1898—for there was only a slight rise in that year, and the average prices of several forms were less than in 1897—the demand did not keep pace with the increasing supply, and improvements in production were constantly exerting their influence. The increase in price in the United States in 1887 was greater than in other countries. The reasons for the difference may be found in the exceptional demands in the year 1887, in which year occurred the most extensive railway building and the greatest consumption of steel rails. There was an exceptional deficiency in the home supply. There was also a revival of general activity in this country, the effect of which was conspicuous. It should be further noted that the crisis of this decade was much less severe than that of 1873, and the downward movement succeeding it, though long continued, manifested a less decline in prices.

After the high prices of 1890 there was a fall, which continued until the month of July, 1897. This fall was more uniform than those after 1880 and 1887. It was interrupted only by a temporary revival beginning after April, 1895, and continuing until the latter part of that year.

The figures on page 228, giving representative forms of iron and steel, show the extent of the fall.

	Old iron T rails at Philadelphia.	No. 1 Anthracite foundry pig-iron at Philadelphia.	Gray forge pig-iron at Philadelphia.	Gray forge pig-iron, lake ore mixed, at Pittsburg.	Bessemer pig-iron at Pittsburg.	Steel rails at mills in Pennsylvania.	Best refined bar iron from store, Philadelphia. (Per cwt.)	Steel billets at mills at Pittsburg.
	dollars	dollars	dollars	dollars	dollars	dollars	dolls.	dollars
Dec., 1889.	27.25	19.25	17.25	18.25	23.75	35.00	2.15	.....
Jan., 1890.	27.50	19.90	17.90	18.00	23.60	35.25	2.20	.....
May, 1893.	17.50	14.85	13.00	12.25	13.51	29.00	1.75	21.69
July, 1897.	11.50	11.75	10.19	8.36	9.39	18.00	1.25	14.00

Beginning in July, 1897, prices showed an upward tendency, but increases were slight until the beginning of 1899; then there was a very rapid rise until the end of the year.

In the examination of these price movements several marked tendencies appear:

1. The interval between the date of maximum prices and the succeeding crises is longer in later years. This interval continued for a few months prior to the crises of 1825 and 1837, nearly a year prior to that of 1873, and several years prior to the crises of 1884 and 1893. This longer interval may be explained by the greater ability to carry accumulated stocks in expectation of a rise, the larger influence of speculation, and the absorption, whenever prices decline, of large quantities by the wider markets now existing.

These influences explain another tendency, viz.:

2. In later years fluctuations are more frequent. In the period after the downward price movement has commenced, the market price breaks

and then is restored again. It is evident that abundant capital for construction is waiting for investment, and, even in case of a slight decline, purchases are large and tend to bring prices to the former level.

3. Since 1873 the maximum price reached in each cycle tends to be less than that in the preceding cycle. This is due to invention, to the lower cost of manufacturing upon a large scale, and improvements in transportation. This tendency to lower prices is a part of the progress of the time and an essential feature in each depression.

4. The upward movement of prices continues for a much shorter time than the downward movement. The upward movement preceding the maximum of October and November, 1872, continued for one year and nine months. The succeeding downward movement lasted until November, 1878, or six years and one month. Then an upward movement continued until February, 1880, or one year and three months; the succeeding downward movement lasted approximately five and one-half years, to the summer of 1885, to be followed by a rising movement, interrupted in the United States in 1888 and 1889, of four and one-half years, or until January, 1890. It is to be noticed, however, that the rise in most grades of iron and steel for a year after the summer of 1885 was very slight. After January, 1890, the downward movement continued for seven and one-half years to July, 1897, when prices for a year were almost stationary, to be followed by rising prices, which continued until

the end of 1899, or less than one year and a half. The average prices by years from 1870 to 1900 are given in Appendix B, and the rise and fall of anthracite pig for the same years and of Bessemer pig from 1886 to 1900 are shown by the following diagram:

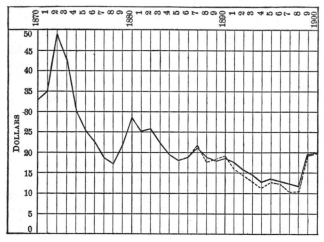

Average prices of anthracite and Bessemer pig-iron.
Solid line, anthracite.   Dotted line, Bessemer.

5. The rapid rise which precedes a maximum price rarely continues for more than a year. If we take anthracite and Bessemer pig-iron as the best standard, it will be noticed that prior to the maximum price of anthracite, September, 1872, when the price of $53.87½ was reached, prices rose from $37 in January of that year, showing a rapid rise for eight months; prior to the maximum of $41

in February, 1880, prices rose rapidly from $20.75 in August, 1879, or for six months; prior to the maximum of $19.90 in January, 1890, there was a rise from $17 in May, 1889, or for eight months; prior to the maximum of $25 for Bessemer pig-iron in December, 1899, there was a rapid rise from $11 in January of the same year, or for eleven months. In many respects the rise in 1899 was the most remarkable of all, because it had been considered by iron manufacturers in the preceding years that the equipment for production was sufficient to promptly meet any increase of demand, and yet the rapid rise in that year was unprecedented. The great increase in the price of iron and steel in that year, with the steady increase in production after 1894, proves the more general use of these products for a greater variety of purposes and over an enlarged area.

Prices of Securities; Stock Quotations.—The indications derived from the prices of securities cannot be understood without a brief review of the nature and distinctive features of this species of property.

Securities may be divided into two classes: First, those which promise a fixed return in the way of income, and of which the principal sum is payable at a definite time, such as Government, State, municipal, and railway bonds, and mortgage notes. Second, those the return or income from which depends upon the profits derived from the enterprises which they represent, such as railway and industrial stocks. The income upon these is not fixed, but is contingent upon the success of the operations in which the companies are engaged.

Two general factors primarily determine the price of securities:

1. Their income, or the return which they promise to pay.

2. Certainty of payment, or the degree of assurance of obtaining the income promised.

The prices of securities, particularly those of the second class, are affected by so great a variety of circumstances that it is exceptionally difficult to derive any general principles from the history of their rise and fall, but certain tendencies are plain.

1. Prior to an improvement in conditions they rise earlier than the majority of commodities, and prior to a crisis or depression they fall earlier. In the case of stocks the rise and fall is greater than the average rise and fall of commodities.

2. The rise in the price of speculative and non-dividend paying stocks prior to improving conditions occurs later than that of other securities. Before a depression these fall earlier and experience a greater loss in price than those which are regarded as safe investments.

3. Not only are the general changes in prices of stocks greater, but the temporary fluctuations are much greater than in the prices of commodities.

4. All stocks, or securities of the second class, are very much more influenced than other securities or commodities by speculation and by conditions peculiar to them, such as the general interest in stock quotations, their ready sale at the Stock Ex-

change, and the partiality of investors for this species of property.

As regards the first tendency. The earlier
rise of securities, prior to an improvement of conditions, is primarily due to the fact that securities are
more keenly affected by the condition of the money
market than any other species of property. After
the severest stage of a depression, money accumulates in banks and financial centres, and awaits investment. Profitable investments in industrial enterprises are scarce. There is a disposition to look to
undertakings already tried rather than to new ones.
This money, which is often redundant in quantity,
is available for the purchase of securities. In the
same connection there is another influence causing
the rise in prices to be greater than in those of commodities, as well as earlier. In time of abundant
supply of money, rates of interest go down. A
security which promises a certain return not only
feels the effect of more abundant money, but also
that of lower rates of interest. To illustrate, at a
time when the rate of interest is 6 per cent, a stock
which promises to pay that amount annually as a
dividend is naturally worth 100 per cent, but if
rates of interest fall to 4 per cent, this stock would
naturally rise to 150. Prices of commodities, for
the most part, respond only to the influence of
greater supplies of money and greater demands,
while securities are influenced not only by the
greater demand for them and the greater supply of
money, but also by changing rates of interest.
When the depression comes to an end, and quickened

activity begins, this influence of lower rates of interest is partially neutralized by increasing demands for money, but, as stocks gain the benefits of increasing prosperity, the rise in their price is usually well maintained.   In addition to other influences which promote an earlier rise or fall, there must be mentioned the more careful study and attention to the financial situation which is given by dealers in the stock-markets and in great financial centres.   They often forecast the grounds for a rise or fall in prices before the general public is awake to the situation.

Prior to a depression, the earlier fall, especially of the second class of securities, is caused by conditions opposite to those which prevail in a time of improving conditions.   At such a time money is less plentiful, rates of interest go up.   The prevalent scarcity of available funds is intensified by the withdrawal of investments in stocks for the maintenance of existing industrial or commercial enterprises. In like manner prices fall and money is withdrawn for the sake of retaining merchandise or other property held on speculation, and thus the quantity of money for investment in stocks is still further decreased.   Just as a fall in rates of interest causes a disproportionate rise in stocks, so now the higher rates of interest cause a disproportionate decline. In the examination of the prices of stocks, as of all prices, there are three periods to be considered: first, the end of the depression, when money is redundant and business is slack; second, the time of healthy activity; third, the season of excessive and unhealthy activity. All these conditions exert a peculiar influence upon the stock-market.

Second, the fall in the prices of speculative and non-dividend-paying stocks is greater. The influence of the money-market is more severely felt by these securities in the time preceding a depression. The increased demand for money to be invested in other enterprises, and the scarcity of money, which causes the fall of all securities, has especial influence upon those which do not promise an assured return. Investments in the stock-market are made from the surplus funds of the people. They are for the most part made by those who possess a considerable surplus. When this surplus diminishes, the first tendency is to dispose of property which has no reliable value or which does not promise an income. Under the influence of these factors speculative stocks are first disposed of. A time will come when speculation and manipulation are ineffectual to sustain their prices. It needs little further argument to show why stocks of this class are the last to rise. The income from all has diminished, and the element of caution dominates the investing public. Investors are slow to purchase securities of doubtful value.

Third, temporary fluctuations in the prices of stocks are greater than in those of commodities, because the prices of stocks are affected not merely by the aggregate quantity of money available for investment in the country, but also by the varying quantity available for transactions in stocks. This quantity changes not only from month to month, but from day to day. An unfavourable bank statement immediately affects the stock-market. It is also affected by the unequal payments disbursed by the National Treasury and by withdrawals from financial centres for the handling of crops. Consequently, two successive weeks, or the same week, may show great changes in the price of stocks. Of course we must recognise the very potent effect of speculation in the stock-market at all times, and it is probable that a greater portion of the money used for transactions in stocks is borrowed than is the case with any other species of business transactions.

Fourth, the price of stocks is very much influenced by conditions peculiar to themselves, most of which tend to raise the price. They are readily sold, and, by reason of the issuance of shares, they are easily divisible. These facts make it possible to realize upon the whole or a part of the investment at any time. Their prices are quoted each day in the daily papers and carefully watched. Their very fluctuations make them the favourite investment of many moneyed men. The existence of a very large element whose business is that of dealing in stocks, and whose profits are realized from commissions on transactions, or from speculation, affects their prices and causes greater fluctuations. The general effect of these extensive dealings is towards higher rather than lower prices. Other influences peculiar to stocks tend to increase fluctuations. The weekly reports as to traffic receipts and the frequent bulletins as to the condition of wheat, corn, or other commodities which form a large share of the traffic of railways have this tendency. A " corner," or any event which creates a sudden demand for money, causes the sacrifice of many stocks and depresses their price. The weakness thus created communicates itself to the whole list. A notable rise or fall in one stock has its effect upon the whole market. Prices are also influenced by other incidental factors, such as the desire of one railway corporation to obtain possession of another for the purpose of increasing its own value.

The tendency towards an earlier response to changing conditions in the price of stocks may be illustrated by numerous instances. Prior to the crises of April and October, 1847, in the United Kingdom, prices of stocks reached a maximum in July and August, 1845. In the year 1857 industry and commerce in the United States continued with their usual vigour to the very eve of the crisis in August, but the stock-market in the summer months of the preceding year gave warning of that which was to occur.* The high prices of December, 1856, were not equalled at any time during 1857, and after January, 1857, the fall was very marked. New York Central, which had been quoted at $94\frac{1}{4}$ as a maximum in December, 1856, fell to $90\frac{7}{8}$ in February, 1857, and to $84\frac{3}{8}$ in the following June; the lowest price of the year was 53

---

* In a previous chapter it has been stated that there is often an indication of a crisis one or two years before its actual occurrence, and often at the same season of the year. The crisis of 1857 occurred in the month of August. A year previous (in 1856) there was an unusual fall in the prices of stocks, and lower prices continued until near the close of the latter year.

in the month of August. To illustrate the greater fall of stocks in which there is a larger element of speculative value, New York & Erie, which was quoted at $62\frac{3}{8}$ in December, 1856, fell to $9\frac{1}{2}$ in October, 1857. Illinois Central, one of the best sustained in price of the railway stocks at that time, fell from 122 in December, 1856, to $75\frac{1}{4}$ in October, 1857. Thus it appears that the two more reliable stocks lost less than half in their price, while the more speculative fell to less than one-sixth. It has been stated that the year 1879 was one of the least prosperous in the United Kingdom. All indications point to this year as the least prosperous of that decade, yet in a majority of the leading railway stocks the price was higher in 1879 than in 1878, indicating that this species of property rises in price earlier than the average of commodities. The rise from 1878 to 1879 is particularly noticeable in the better class of railway stocks. Prior to the crisis of 1873 in the United States, of seventeen stocks, fourteen were higher in 1872 than in 1873, while three were quoted at higher prices in 1873. Eleven showed a higher price in 1871 than in 1872. The same was true in the years prior to the crisis of 1884. Of thirteen of the most prominent stocks sold on the New York Stock Exchange, two reached a maximum price in 1880, seven in 1881, and four in 1882.

Previous to the crisis of May, 1893, stocks began to fall early in 1892. Of seventeen of the most active, five reached a maximum price in January; three in February; four in March; two, Lake Shore and Michigan Central, in April. Some of those of most stable values reached a maximum later— Chicago & Northwestern, preferred, in May (while Chicago & Northwestern, common, reached its maximum in March), Chicago & Alton in July, and New York, New Haven & Hartford in January, 1893, the latter stocks illustrating the later fall of those which yield the more reliable dividends.

There are still other factors which cause alternate rise and fall in prices, which are especially effective in influencing prices on the Stock Exchange. As a general rule, fluctuations increase with the magnitude of transactions and the strength of opposing interests to be benefited by a rise or fall. Formation of a cotton or oil exchange is usually contemporaneous with larger transactions, and thereafter fluctuations assume a prominence, day by day, which formerly appeared only at much longer intervals. The tendency to fluctuation has been greatly increased by added opportunities for information, not only by the gathering of more ample statistics, but by the prompt transmission of news by telegraph and cable. Formerly, information as to a staple crop reached the localities at which it was required only at rare intervals. We may instance the cotton crop, information concerning which, in the early part of the last century, reached Lancashire only by sailing-vessels and at irregular dates. Now, day by day, the condition of the crop is telegraphed to the great centres where it is required, and considered with care. Fluctuations, because of the magnitude of transactions, are most noticeable in stock quotations. In a table in Appendix B, there is given by months the number of times in which selected stocks reached maximum and minimum prices in each year for thirty-three years.* It would be expected that the maximum prices would occur most frequently in the months when bank reserves are highest, but such is not the case. Maximum and minimum prices occur most frequently in the months of January and December, when transactions are largest; least frequently in July and August, when transactions are smallest. It thus appears that large transactions are a very strong factor in creating both maximum and minimum prices. The following statement summarizes the results derived from this table, and shows distinctly the effect of large transactions in increasing or depressing prices:

	Number of maximum prices.	Number of minimum prices.
January...............	61	89
February.............	42	25
March...............	32	35
April.................	26	37
May..................	28	25
June.................	40	26
July.................	13	27
August	14	22
September............	40	22
October..............	36	31
November............	47	36
December	66	60

* See Appendix B, pp. 338–339. In cases where the same maximum price was reached in two or more months in the same year, it is included twice or more. To illustrate: If the same maximum price was reached in the months of January and December it is counted for both months.

There is an indication of the approach of a crisis when there is a continuous and steady fall in prices in the stock-market. A less reliable indication is afforded when there are continuous fluctuations attended by a downward tendency. The former is a sure precursor of less prosperous conditions, and the only question is how long the fall will continue before a decided change occurs. Oftentimes liquidation or realization of profits may cause the sale of unusual quantities of stocks, and depress prices in the market. But this is not necessarily a sign of danger. Prices may have been quoted at a figure beyond that which conditions justify, and the fall in prices which results is merely responsive to that fact.

The first class of securities responds to changing conditions in a much less degree; violent fluctuations are absent, and the factors which determine their price have more permanent effects.

Government securities are always a favourite investment. In this country their prices are influenced by their use as the basis for the issuance of currency by the national banks and by the requirement that certain quantities shall be held by them, and by regulations which require their use as security for numerous obligations, both to the national and to the state governments. They show little fluctuation during the changing conditions of business from year to year. A slight decline can, however, be expected a considerable time before a crisis. Not only are they affected by scarcity of money, but also by the prevalent desire for larger interest on investments.

16

It may be added that after a crisis and during a depression the prices of government securities are the first to rise, and thereafter are well maintained. Minimum prices frequently do not reach as low a point as in the preceding prosperous years, and maximum prices are frequently higher than ever before.

In the case of many securities, the partiality of investors exerts a considerable influence upon the price. There is a preference for those mortgages and municipal bonds which are near to the great financial centres from which investments are made. The census returns of 1890 show that rates of interest on mortgages are higher almost in proportion to the distance from older and more settled portions of the country. The average rate of interest on real estate mortgages in force on January 1, 1890, in Massachusetts was 5.44 per cent; in New York, 5.49; in Ohio, 6.56; in Iowa, 7.63; in Kansas, 8.68; in Montana, 10.61. This partiality is closely associated with the degree of assurance of safety, but is in a measure distinct from it.

CONDITIONS IN OTHER COUNTRIES

One of the most significant indications of the approach of a crisis in one country is the existence of a crisis in another, or such disturbance there as materially diminishes its purchasing power. Even such calamities as war or deficient food supply, which confer a temporary advantage upon other countries, must produce, in the long run, perceptible effects upon the aggregate wealth, and, consequently, upon the prosperity of all.

CHAPTER VII

PREVENTIVES

PREVENTIVES may be viewed from three standpoints—namely, those of

I. Established laws; governmental control by legislation and administration.

II. The management of banks.

III. Individual action.

ESTABLISHED LAWS; GOVERNMENTAL CONTROL BY LEGISLATION AND ADMINISTRATION

In the United States substantial benefit would result from radical changes in the functions performed by the Federal Treasury—namely, by ceasing to act as a bank of issue and also as a bank of deposit.

Issuance or Maintenance of Paper Money.— That the United States Government has not heretofore ceased to issue or maintain paper money in circulation, and to perform, as it now does, the functions of a bank of issue, is explained by a reluctance to change from established methods and by the assurance of safety which belongs to notes of

the Government. A further explanation is found
in political predilections, and in a prejudice against
banks, which is prompted by a fear of their obtaining undue control over the financial affairs of the
country. It is not necessary to discuss the question
whether the issuance of the greenbacks was essential to the maintenance of the Government during
the trying period of the Civil War. The problem
with which we have to do pertains to the present.
Nearly every civilized nation has made the experiment of issuing paper money, either with the
promise of redemption in gold on presentation, or
with the promise that it shall rest on the so-called
faith of the government; but most of them have
abandoned these issues of paper currency, and substituted some other method, retaining to themselves
only the coining of metallic money.

As has already been noticed, there are crises and
panics which do not indicate unsoundness in the condition of industry or commerce. They may arise
from derangement in the circulating medium, either
from excess or from insufficient supply. Other disturbances, more serious and permanent, are industrial or commercial in their nature, but are greatly
aggravated by the same conditions which cause the
former. Crises and panics are indirectly caused by
excessive issues of currency, which stimulate overaction and afford the opportunity for waste and extravagance. They are sometimes due to deficiency
of currency, and are always rendered more serious
by its scarcity. This scarcity does not always
coincide with a deficiency of capital. Any rational

system for the issuance of paper money should provide for changing demands and changing conditions of business. It should furnish means for contraction when money is redundant, and means for reasonable expansion when money is scarce. This quality is often described by the term " elasticity of the currency." The demand for money is not a fixed and invariable one; it varies with prices, with different degrees of confidence in enterprises, with activity of business. It changes with the seasons of the year, with the harvesting and marketing of crops.

It requires little reflection to discover that Government currency cannot meet these changing requirements. Mr. Tooke points out the difference between paper money issued by banks and that issued by the Government, when he states that the banks issue currency in response to demands, and thus supply the wants of trade, while Government paper is not issued in response to calls from those engaged in trade or industry, but by reason of the necessities of the Government. The latter creates demand rather than supplies it. It is like giving to the customer the right himself to create money whenever he needs it.*

If the Government controls the issue of paper money, the amount must either be fixed and invariable, or it must vary either in pursuance of legislative authority or under the control of the executive department. If fixed and invariable in quantity, it will not properly do its work. There will be a sur-

* History of Prices, vol. iv, pp. 176–177.

feit of currency available for loans at seasons when loans are not in demand, and a corresponding scarcity on occasions when a larger supply is required. If the quantity can be changed only by legislative authority, action will be tardy, and the time for doing something will pass without provision for the situation. If left to the executive department, it is granting an undue degree of power to this branch, and is subject to abuse and to changes with different administrations, according to their different ideas of finance. Whether managed by the legislative or executive department, those in control, however able or incorruptible they may be, are not in that immediate touch with the varied business interests of the country which is essential to the most judicious action. It is clear that the system is best which works automatically as far as possible, and eliminates in the greatest degree the management of the currency from the field of political discussion.

When a government makes provision for the redemption of its paper money in specie, another objection arises in the necessity for the maintenance of a metallic reserve sufficient to meet the calls of all who present their notes. The metallic reserve is watched in all business communities with the closest attention. It is regarded as a barometer of the stability of credit and the soundness of business conditions. When the quantity of metallic money diminishes, banking institutions having the responsibility of redeeming currency in coin, take immediate steps to check the outflow by raising the rate of discount. No such method of controlling the gold supply is available to the Treasury Department of the United States. It has no control over rates of discount. Without any means of protection it must meet the demands of those who present its notes, although those who bring them may find it more to their profit to bring discredit upon the Treasury than to sustain it. It is clearly not without reason that other nations have abandoned this perilous experiment. Their ability to expand and contract the supply of money, and thus meet the exigencies of the time, their more effective regulations for control of the metallic supply, are potent reasons why, in late years, England and France have been freer from sudden crises than our own country.

Without seeking to suggest a system to take the place of the one now in use, a brief mention of two conflicting theories, advocated with a great deal of earnestness, is appropriate.

First, the " Currency Theory," to the effect that money should not be issued by banks except as against actual deposits of gold for which the paper currency is a substitute. This is the theory which prevailed in the adoption of the Act of 1844 for the government of the issues of the Bank of England.

Second, the " Banking Theory," to the effect that money may be issued in excess of gold on deposit, provided it is redeemable in gold on presentation.

It is argued on behalf of the first theory that an issue of money not based upon deposits of gold tends to stimulate gold exports, raise prices, and increase speculation. It is argued on behalf of the other theory that prices do not depend upon the quantity of paper money in circulation, provided the issues are redeemable in gold; that the quantity in circulation will be regulated by the demands of trade, and an increase will follow rather than precede rising prices and speculative demands. Both of these conflicting theories contemplate the issue of currency by banks, and it is unnecessary to say that our present system does not have the advantages of either. It does not furnish the check upon gold exports afforded by the former or the elasticity furnished by the latter.

A further objectionable feature of the maintenance by a government of a specie reserve for the redemption of paper money is the undue influence exerted under such a system upon the business of the country by changing conditions in revenue and expenditure. In the absence of such a system, a deficiency in the receipts of the government would have only limited influence upon the general course of business affairs; but if the National Treasury must maintain a gold reserve to redeem bills presented, a decrease in specie causes wide-spread demoralization. The decrease caused by an excess of expenditures is immediately felt in the decrease of the gold reserve, and thus an occurrence which should be followed only by slight effects, greatly disturbs the money-market and the general prosperity of the whole country. This dangerous feature has been in a measure removed by the enact-

ment of the so-called Financial Bill of 1900, which
provides that the gold reserve for the redemption of
notes shall constitute a separate department of the
Treasury; but the undue influence which arises from
fluctuations in the quantity of gold in the Treasury
still remains.

The advantages of the issuance of paper currency by banking institutions are not difficult to dis-
cern.   They are in immediate contact with commercial and industrial operations, and must have a
full understanding of their various needs and conditions from time to time.   In case their issues are
redundant, their reserves in gold can be utilized for
the redemption of notes, thus restricting the circulation.   In times of stringency they can increase
their issues, and thus tide over or essentially
diminish the dangers impending.*

An examination of the discussion of the Legal
Tender Act by Congress in 1862, makes it manifest
that it was the intention to issue greenbacks only as
a temporary measure.   President Lincoln, in his
Message of December 1, 1862, seems to have taken
the view that United States notes were of doubtful expediency, and to have regarded the issuance
of paper money as the proper function of banks.
He says:

" Fluctuations in the volume of currency are
always injurious, and to reduce these fluctuations
to the lowest possible point will always be a lead-

---

* This contemplates that the national banks, or other institutions issuing paper currency, will redeem their bills in gold,
a requirement essential under any well-devised system.

ing purpose in wise legislation. Convertibility— prompt and certain convertibility—into coin is generally acknowledged to be the best and surest safeguard against them; and it is extremely doubtful whether a circulation of United States notes, payable in coin, and sufficiently large for the wants of the people, can be permanently, usefully, and safely maintained.

"Is there, then, any other mode in which the necessary provisions for the public wants can be made and the great advantages of a safe and uniform currency secured?

"I know of none which promises so certain results, and is at the same time so unobjectionable, as the organization of banking associations under a general Act of Congress well guarded in its provisions. To such associations the Government might furnish circulating notes on the security of United States bonds deposited in the Treasury. These notes, prepared under the supervision of proper officers, being uniform in appearance and security and convertible always into coin, would at once protect labour against the evils of a vicious currency and facilitate commerce by cheap and safe exchanges." *

In considering the subject of necessary elasticity of the currency, the great fluctuations in deposits of money with banking institutions must be taken into account. Accepted theories as to the issuance of paper currency are largely based upon the idea that,

---

* Messages and Papers of the Presidents, vol. vi, pp. 129–130.

except as money is shipped out of the country to settle balances with other countries, a proportion of existing currency, whether gold or paper, approximately the same from month to month and year to year, finds its way to banks or other financial institutions, and is available for loans and the ordinary uses of trade.   According to this idea, the same proportion of the currency will at all times be available in the banks for purposes of lending and for other uses of currency.   This theory fails to take into account two important facts: first, the admitted fact that larger quantities of money are withheld from banks at different seasons of the same year and under frequently recurring differences in conditions, occurring when business is entirely sound; second, the existence in time of panic of a disposition to withhold money from deposit for the purpose of hoarding.   Comptroller Knox, in his Report for 1873, gives some striking figures, showing the extent of this disposition to hoard.   The total amount of outstanding national bank currency, legal tender notes, and fractional currency on October 13, 1873, was $756,315,135.   The total amount held by the Treasury and by banks on that day was $116,496,-997, leaving unaccounted for $639,818,138.   On the same day the national banks of New York city held of legal tenders only $6,517,250, as against $32,278,530 thirty-one days previous, on the 12th of September.*   It is evident that the usual theories do not take into account a fluctuation of

* Report of the Comptroller of the Currency for 1873, p. xxxi.

this nature; yet any system which does not provide for such a situation is defective. Makeshifts have been resorted to, such as the issuance of Clearing-House certificates; but these afford only partial and temporary relief, and are quite unsatisfactory. While it may be conceded that an additional amount of paper money in time of crisis cannot restore wasted resources or prevent the depression which is sure to follow, it is nevertheless true that the prompt issuance of a further supply of currency—provided always that it is a sound currency—would greatly simplify the situation, relieve embarrassed firms from failure, and prevent the demoralization which is so serious a feature in time of panic.

The effect of the workings of our currency system in promoting crises in the past has been painfully apparent. The quantity of money has been increased when the demands of trade required no increase. In times of stringency there has been a decrease, on account of the different kinds of money employed, under the working of the inexorable law, that when different kinds of money are in use, there is a tendency to send the better quality abroad or withdraw it from circulation.

Some reforms have been accomplished. Under present laws such inflation is impossible as that which occurred in the days of greenback inflation, or under the laws of 1878 and 1890 for the coinage or purchase of silver, and the quantity of money has increased with increasing wealth and adapted itself more nearly to existing needs. But with lower prices, and that suspension of new enterprises which mark a time of diminished activity, the quantity of currency might prove more than sufficient for legitimate demands, and the disturbances of the time would be aggravated by the motley nature of our money. It is certain that until our currency system is such that the quantity can be increased or diminished, in turn, in accordance with the demands of trade and industry, the threat of crises will not be removed, and the difficulty will be greater when the crisis comes. Such adjustment is impossible under the present system. The only provision for elasticity at present is in the circulation of the national banks. The recent law makes partial provision for increase in their circulation, but the equally important object, a decrease, can only be accomplished tardily; so tardily as not to respond to the demands of the time.

The Function of the Treasury as a Bank of Deposit: The Subtreasury System.—It is equally clear that the tendency to crises would be diminished by the abolition or material modification of the Subtreasury system. The reasons for the passage of a law providing for the deposit of Government funds in the Treasury or at Subtreasuries were plain enough. A complete separation of banks from the state was advocated. The Government deposits had been left with banking institutions which had failed, so that public moneys were lost; the making of prompt disbursements was rendered impossible, and the financial standing of the Government was brought into disrepute. Coupled with the organization of an independent treasury was a regulation at the time that receipts and disbursements should be made in specie.

The first law providing for a Subtreasury was passed in 1840; in the following year it was re-pealed, but it was re-enacted in substantially the same form in 1846. The unfavorable prognostications of its opponents were not fulfilled during the time of the operation of the first law, and during the early years of the operation of the second law the results foretold did not ensue. It must be borne in mind, however, that half a century ago the amounts collected as revenue were not only very much less than now, but bore a smaller proportion to the population of the country. The strongest objection to the present system is the very irregular course of the collections and disbursements of the Treasury, which produces violent fluctuations in the amount of money in circulation, greatly increasing the pressure in times of stringency, and at other times giving an unwholesome stimulus to speculation.

In some respects the effects of the Subtreasury system are similar to those which arise from the lack of proper elasticity in our currency. Each tends to prevent harmony between the supply of money and the demand for it. But they differ in this, the system of issuing paper prevents harmony, by reason of its inflexibility and utter failure to increase or decrease when desirable. The Subtreasury system brings the same result by promoting very considerable fluctuations in the quantity of the currency.

Unfortunately these fluctuations are likely to occur in directions entirely opposite to the requirements of trade. Under the Subtreasury system there is a necessity for an aggregate amount of currency much in excess of that which would otherwise be required. In the Treasury statistics of the amount of money per capita in the country, this fact is recognised by giving separate statements of that which is in the Treasury and that which is in circulation. In times of pressure, the Treasury has sought to relieve the situation by purchases of bonds or similar expedients for increasing the money in circulation. But these purchases have not resulted in that benefit which would result from loans made by banks in the ordinary course of business. The amounts paid out by the Treasury for bonds are likely to go to those who have no urgent need, and who may withhold from circulation the currency so obtained. When loaned by banks, amounts go to those who are in need, and who employ the money received for the payment of debts and for the usual transactions of trade.

Authority now exists under the law to deposit with banks money received from internal revenue taxes, but this does not extend to customs duties.

A result similar to that caused by the establishment of the Subtreasury system has been noticed in numerous States of the Union which have regulations for the annual or semi-annual collection of taxes, under which it is provided that the amounts received shall be retained in suitable vaults by the respective treasurers until disbursed for State or

municipal expenses.   Strict penalties are provided
for violations of the rule.   The result in every case
has been very marked.   At the season of the year
when taxes are collected, a large proportion of the
currency in use in the community is withdrawn
from circulation, and serious embarrassment is
caused.   In some States, laws have been passed providing for the loan or deposit of taxes collected,
reasonable interest and adequate security being required.   The objection to the adoption of this plan
by the Federal Government is based upon the
greater magnitude of the problem, but this does not
seem to be an insuperable obstacle.   Favouritism
could be prevented by competitive bidding and
safety assured by sufficient bonds and suitable penalties.   An amount could be retained in the Treasury
sufficient to meet the probable demands for a specified time and the balance divided among those who
could comply with the requirements relating to interest and security.   The deposits now made in
banks are in the direction of this plan.   Either the
Subtreasury system ought to be abolished entirely,
or some plan adopted to prevent the violent fluctuations in available money caused by a fiscal regulation which locks up, perhaps at the very time when
most needed, a large and varying share of the supply.*

The organization of a national bank to act as
the fiscal agent of the Government has been advocated as a solution of the difficulty.   But, after re-

* For figures showing the unequal amounts withheld from
circulation in the Treasury, see Appendix B, p. 344.

peated agitation, the proposition to adopt this solution may be regarded as settled adversely. It is manifest that the disposition of the people is against it.

Certainty as to Specie Payments and the Standard of Value.—There can be no more effectual preventive of crises than the establishment of our currency upon an absolutely sure basis and the maintenance of the paper money in circulation upon an equality, not merely with specie, but with that kind of specie which is accepted as the standard by the leading nations of the world. In crises a source of danger has been more prominent in this country than elsewhere—namely, the failure to redeem paper currency in specie, or the uncertainty of its redemption. An additional source of danger has at times manifested itself in a threatened change in the intrinsic value of the monetary unit. In the crises of 1814, 1818, 1837, and 1873, besides the loss of capital and the derangement of industrial conditions, there was an aggravating feature which assumed an importance almost equal to the other calamities of the time—namely, the suspension or absence of specie payments and uncertainty regarding the time of redemption. In 1893, there was the active dread of a departure from a gold to a silver standard.

Much has been written upon the evils of irredeemable paper currency. That it promotes speculation and waste, substitutes gambling and uncertainty for careful calculation and honesty, and falls most heavily on those who are least able to bear its weight, no one can deny. To eliminate from our

17

currency all uncertainty concerning what a dollar means, and what at all times it shall mean, will do much to prevent crises in the future, and will also accomplish much in mitigating their effects when we are compelled to face them.

The Avoidance of Frequent Changes and Constant Agitation in regard to our Financial and Economic Policies.—No country in the world has suffered more than ours in this particular; not only is there frequent change in vital matters of economic and fiscal policy, but there is almost constant agitation. Other nations have passed through seasons of discussion, in which great differences of opinion have developed; but none has witnessed the same frequency of changes in the adopted rules concerning tariff, revenue, and questions of currency and banking. It is fortunate that the wounds created by frequent and violent changes have caused the growth of a conservative element willing to acquiesce cordially in policies not altogether approved, provided peace is the result. It is clearly for the benefit of this, or of any country, to continue in the same general lines of economic and fiscal policy, making changes gradually and only after sufficient warning, so that industry and commerce may forecast the future with a greater degree of accuracy and engage in enterprise with more certainty, and consequently a better assurance of success.

More Comprehensive and Accurate Statistical Information.—A study of past disturbances leads to the conviction that no severe depression has occurred which was not preceded by loud warnings. These warnings ought not to pass unheeded, and in order to recognise them promptly, it is necessary that accurate statistics be furnished. Much improvement has been accomplished in the last few years, though it is to be regretted that so much of our statistical information is fragmentary or inaccurate. Official and private publications furnish much valuable information. They include voluminous figures of deposits and louns of banks, movement of specie, exports and imports, railway earnings, wholesale prices, and the condition and probable yield of crops. A vital defect in many of them is the omission to give, for purposes of comparison, similar figures for previous months and years. Another defect is the absence of uniformity in the methods and classifications employed. These comparative statistics would afford a means of determining the trend of events, and give warning when prices are unnaturally high or any branch of business is overdone. It is also noteworthy that we do not sufficiently consider statistics relating to the course of affairs in foreign countries, the influence of which upon our own condition is of the utmost importance, by reason of the enlargement of our trade and the closer international relations of modern commerce. Other statistics, which are inadequate or lacking and which would be of great value, are those pertaining to the employment of labour, capital invested in new enterprises, amounts expended in new construction, volume of production in the various kinds of manufactures, and statistics of state banks and savings institutions similar to those pertaining

to national banks. After making due allowance
for the insufficiency of statistics, it must be said
that the failure to pay sufficient attention to those
already available is equally to be regretted.

The Relation of the State to Corporations.—
The suggestions under this head apply more to
State governments than to the National Government. In no other country is there the same degree of indulgence in granting corporate rights, or
the same carelessness in supervising the transactions
of those who obtain them. The interest of the
State in keeping them within proper limits and
securing shareholders and creditors against fraud
is not sufficiently guarded. Banks have been known
to continue in business for years after their rotten-
ness would have been exposed by even a cursory
examination. This closer supervision is especially
required for quasi-public corporations. Franchises
involving the enjoyment of rights in public property have been granted without any recognition of
the probable growth of municipalities or the unusual profits which are certain to accrue to their
owners. One field for improvement is in guard-
ing the relation between corporations and their
shareholders or patrons by more careful supervision. Another is in the relation between corporations and the public. This can be secured by a
more careful safeguarding of the rights of the public. In the relation of shareholders and depositors
to corporations under present regulations, crises are
promoted by the facilities for speculation afforded
to managers and by opportunities for dishonest and

irresponsible management. The absence of publicity in the transactions of many great corporations, which control important lines of business, conceals their actual condition, and renders it impossible to obtain accurate information. This sometimes destroys confidence in meritorious enterprises; on the other hand, it may cause undue confidence in undertakings which should not be prosecuted. The great failures of corporations which destroy public confidence and precipitate crises could, many of them, be prevented by an efficient system of public supervision.

The Management of Banks

Banks and bankers have a great responsibility in shaping the course of commerce and industry. It is for them to watch the tendencies of the time with a careful eye, and restrict accommodations when enterprise reaches the danger point. For their own preservation, as well as that of the business community, it is essential that restraints be interposed to prevent a reckless spirit of speculation and extravagance. Bankers are not in the habit of hesitating to inquire about the use to which money is to be placed. It is especially important when discounts are expanding that careful inquiries should be made, and a policy of conservatism adopted.

1. *Rules as to Lending.*—Among general rules to be observed when there is danger of a crisis, none can be stated which would be more helpful than those suggested by Mr. Bagehot:

" First.   That loans should only be made at a very high rate of interest.

" This will operate as a heavy fine on unreasonable timidity, and will prevent the greatest number of applications by persons who do not require it. The rate should be raised early in the panic, so that the fine may be paid early; that no one may borrow out of idle precaution without paying well for it; that the banking reserve may be protected as far as possible."

" Secondly.   That at this rate, these advances should be made on all good banking securities, and as largely as the public ask for them.

" The reason is plain.   The object is to stay alarm, and nothing, therefore, should be done to cause alarm.   But the way to cause alarm is to refuse some one who has good security to offer." *

He also says:

" What is wanted, and what is necessary to stop a panic, is to diffuse the impression that, though money may be dear, still money is to be had." †

This, of course, involves a reform which, though slow to come, is inevitable—namely, the abolition of usury laws.   It is difficult to present any reason for the retention of these laws, which could not with equal force have been urged for those regulations of the middle ages, which were framed to determine the prices of grain or the length of shoes which the king's subjects were allowed to wear.

---

* Walter Bagehot, Lombard Street.   Edition of 1896, p. 199.
† Ibid., pp. 66–67.

2. *Effect of furnishing Capital by Discount.*— One of the most serious promotives of crises in the United States is the fact that so large a share of the capital required in manufacturing establishments and in other enterprises is furnished by discounts obtained from banks instead of by permanent capital or by long-time loans or bonds. There is certainly an incongruity, to say the least, in providing by short-time discounts for the necessary capital employed from year to year, much of which is expended in buildings or· permanent improvements. In proportion as these enterprises depend upon short-time credits rather than upon paid-up capital or permanent loans, are they in danger of failure in time of stress. Any community in which enterprises are maintained by an undue proportion of short-time credits must be in special danger of crisis; investments will be unnaturally multiplied.

3. *Reserves.*—Numerous opinions have been expressed regarding reserves and deposits. It is clear that the established policy respecting reserves is greatly promotive of crises. Under the national banking law banks in central reserve cities, three in number, must maintain a reserve of lawful money amounting to 25 per cent of their deposits. Banks in other reserve cities, twenty-eight in number, nominally maintain the same reserve, but one-half may consist of funds on deposit with the reserve agents or banks in the central reserve cities. Other banks must maintain a reserve of 15 per cent, of which they are allowed to keep three-fifths, or 9 per cent of their deposits, with banks approved by

the Comptroller of the Currency and located either in a central reserve or reserve city. A considerable share of the deposits of banks, notably in the central reserve cities, the great financial centres, is made up of this proportion of reserves deposited by the banks of outside cities. As interest is paid upon these deposits, the banks receiving them must both invest them and have the amount readily available to meet demands from the banks depositing. This necessity has caused an increased proportion of the money of banks in financial centres to be lent upon " call loans." These call loans are secured, for the most part, by divers railway, industrial, and other stocks, most of which are held not as a permanent investment by the owners, but in expectation of a rise, or in the hope of disposing of them to permanent investors. Under ordinary conditions, payment of the loans can be promptly obtained from the borrowers. But in time of pressure or crisis, it is impossible to realize upon them promptly, so that the loans secured in this manner are not readily available for the maintenance of reserves or the meeting of outside demands. At such times it has been noticed that commercial credits form a much more satisfactory resource than call loans. It is unnecessary to state that these large amounts invested in call loans greatly promote speculation. They increase the volume of transactions and give an unnatural impetus to prices. It is a question whether it would not be better for those banks which have the responsibility for the maintenance of reserves to do away entirely with interest on deposits, or at least to pay a merely nominal rate of interest. The abolition of interest on reserves deposited was recommended by a committee of the New York Clearing-House after the crisis of September, 1873. If interest is to be paid upon these reserves, lenders must be found to take them. If the demand for loans is slack, an increased effort is made to find borrowers. When this season of slack demand is followed by one of active demand, as in the changing conditions it surely will be, there will not be a sufficient supply of money. There are minimum and maximum demands for money in the same year and at short intervals. Call loans, under the present policy, cause the lending of the full supply of loanable funds at the time of the minimum demand, and leave no additional supply for a time when demands are at the maximum.

4. *Diminishing Proportion of Capital and Surplus to Loans.*—An examination of the reports of national banks shows that the proportion of capital and surplus to the aggregate of loans and discounts has been diminishing from year to year. Banks depend for their loanable funds more upon deposits

Years.	Capital and surplus, including undivided profits.	Loans and discounts.	Percentage of capital and surplus to loans and discounts.
	(In millions	of dollars.)	
1865 (October)	464	487	95.2
1870 "	563	716	78.6
1880 "	624	1041	59.9
1890 "	961	1986	48.3
1900 (September 5) . .	1,019	2687	37.9

than formerly. The figures on page 265, derived from Reports of the Comptroller of the Currency, show the increased proportion of loans and discounts.

In the meantime deposits have increased from $500,000,000 in 1865 to $2,508,000,000 in 1900.

While it would seem that greater stability and safety would exist if a larger share of the funds loaned by banks were made up of capital and surplus, this growing disproportion is an outgrowth of an inevitable tendency. Charges for exchange and collections, which formerly made up a considerable share of the income of banking institutions, are now largely done away with. This is rather an effect of increased competition than otherwise; but, whatever its origin, it requires an increase of profits in other directions. Deposits in banks have greatly increased, and it is anticipated that they will be more uniform, so that the proportion to loans will be more uniform than formerly. Thus, it is made possible to carry a larger volume of loans upon the same capital.

5. *Inspection of State Banks.*—After what has already been said about closer supervision of corporations, it is hardly necessary to add that regulations for the examination of state banks similar to those in vogue for national banks would have a salutary effect. Many disastrous failures would be prevented, and much dishonest and incompetent banking would be discovered in time to prevent calamity and the destruction of popular confidence, if all banks alike were subjected to rigid and frequent examination.

Individual Action

Among rules enjoining prudence and careful calculation, Professor Jevons states a very practical one:

" In making investments it is foolish to do just what other people are doing, because there is almost sure to be too many people doing the same thing." *

In the same connection is a rule, worthy of consideration—namely, to be careful about investing in undertakings from which an exceptional return has been realized. Profits in all enterprises tend towards equality. After making due allowance for the skill and trustworthiness required, risk incurred, and regularity of employment, investments afford approximately the same profit. If there is an exceptional return from any line of investment, it is almost certain that the business will be overdone.

Divers suggestions have been made in the treatment of this subject upon the necessity for higher standards of honesty and better education. The benefits of superior honesty and education are obvious enough, but their attainment must be worked out on lines other than economic.

Remedies

The only sure remedy is that suggested by Lord Beaconsfield—" the alchemy of patience."

The depression is a condition which must be recognised and met; any attempt to ignore it or to indulge in confidence when there is no ground for it

* Primer of Political Economy, p. 121.

will only involve further disaster.   It is like the period of convalescence from a disease.   A cure cannot be hastened except by the best of care and the intelligent co-operation of the patient.   At the same time there is every ground for confidence in ultimate recovery.   Too much confidence should not be placed in the action of government.   Just as good laws and efficient administration are rather essentials of prosperity than creative of it, so also they are more potent in preventing depressions than in remedying them.   So far as human agency is concerned, intelligent individual action must do the most.

It should not be forgotten that the most salutary direction in which preventives can be exercised is in securing the greatest possible equality of activity from year to year, and steady rather than sudden increase in the volume of trade and production.

Many propositions have been advanced for the construction of public works in time of depression. The danger in resorting to this method as a remedy is that people will fall into the fallacy of working for the sake of working, and will not appreciate the fact that work is valuable only in case it produces something of utility.   There is the further danger that, as numerous labourers are withdrawn from their usual lines of employment to engage in public work, they will, when times have improved, be unable or unwilling to return to their former employments, and thus the productive power of a country will be crippled.   It is true, however, that municipalities and states are greatly benefited by certain improvements which are of permanent value and to which capital may be appropriately applied, such as good roads, better sewers, paved streets, and similar public works.   At a time when materials are low and labour is unemployed, these improvements can profitably be made, provided they are carefully considered with a view to their permanent value, and not with the object of giving employment merely.

When prices are low, shrewd investors prosecute enterprises of large magnitude and permanent value. The city of Chicago afforded a notable instance of this a few years after the crisis of 1873.   Capitalists having confidence in the future of the city undertook the erection of buildings upon a very large scale.   Whole squares were covered with dwelling-houses and business blocks in progress of construction, and streets were made impassable by great masses of building material.   This showed an intelligent comprehension of future requirements for buildings, and the conviction that prices would not go to a lower point.

Education and experience must lead to a more intelligent direction of productive energy.   Patient, well-directed effort must meet the problems presented by changes from year to year.   It is best not to depend upon the government of any country for relief, but upon the individual action of its citizens.

There is much foundation for the saying of Jeremy Bentham:

"Industry and commerce only ask of the state that which Diogenes asked of Alexander—'Keep out of my sunshine.'"

CHAPTER VIII

A BRIEF ACCOUNT OF CRISES AND DEPRESSIONS IN THE UNITED STATES

I⊤ is not intended to give in this chapter a detailed history of crises and depressions in the United States, but only to point out some of the distinctive features of each with a view to obtaining a more thorough understanding of the general features of all.

An examination of the history of the United States prior to the beginning of the nineteenth century, and for some time thereafter, reveals no crises similar to those of later years. In the earlier days the colonies were separated from each other, each having its own commercial and industrial organization and separate political life. Their trade was with the mother country, or countries, rather than with each other. Each exhibited the features which are to be found in the early development of a new country—abundance of land, high wages for labour and high rates of interest, plentiful supplies of timber and of raw material, and varied fields for enterprise. To these may be added the energy and the progressive spirit of the people, which have never been surpassed. The benefits derived from these advantages were limited, however, by seclusion, and by political disturbances and the insecurity of life and property. That progressive and complex development, characteristic of later days, was lacking. The Federal Constitution might never have been adopted except for the realization that a great future in commercial and industrial development was in store, which could be secured only by a more perfect union. After the formation of the Federal Government many of the former conditions continued; but with the steady growth of the country, commerce increased rapidly and wealth began to accumulate.

Attention has frequently been called to the greater relative importance of crises, as compared with depressions, in the earlier years of the last century. The more uniform movement, in which stagnation gradually gives place to quickened activity, which is followed later by substantial prosperity and still later by feverish speculation and collapse, is more modern. This greater prominence of the crisis phase was even more noticeable in this country than elsewhere. Not only was this phase more prominent, but the disturbances were caused in a larger degree by unwise fiscal regulations, or by unsound banking and vicious currency. To these influences must be added the disturbing effect of frequent changes in tariffs and a lack of permanency in the laws and regulations affecting commerce and industry. Numerous experiments were made, some of which were attended by very disastrous results.

Mr. Albert.S. Bolles, in speaking of the century subsequent to the meeting of the first Continental Congress in September, 1774, says:

" The financial history of the United States during the subsequent period is thickly strewn with financial experiments amply rewarding investigation. In surveying the field, many transactions evincing sound wisdom and rare integrity will appear interwoven with other deeds, variously coloured by accident, dishonesty, or ignorance. If no other country can boast of making such progress during the first century of its existence as the United States, no other has committed so many and such serious mistakes. In the history of American finance, men have appeared on nearly every occasion comprehending the exigency, and whose advice, if followed, would have averted many a disaster. But measures springing from incapacity or dishonesty often teach lessons not less impressive than measures displaying the highest wisdom. It will not prove a profitless task, therefore, to garner some of the fruits lying within the field of inquiry, whether they were ripened under the watchful eye of Morris, Hamilton, or Gallatin, or whether they were the product of less skilful and less honest husbandmen." *

John Adams said in a letter to Thomas Jefferson, written August 25, 1787:

" All the perplexities, confusions, and distresses in America arise, not from defects in their Constitution or Confederation, not from a want of honour

* Financial History of the United States, vol. i, p. 3.

or virtue, so much as from downright ignorance of the nature of coin, credit, and circulation." *

THE CRISIS OF 1814

While earlier disturbances of serious magnitude occurred, by general consent this has been considered the first in the United States which displayed the general phenomena belonging to a crisis. It was precipitated by the capture of the city of Washington by the British on the 24th of August, 1814. The Philadelphia banks suspended specie payments August 31st; the banks of New York city, September 1st. The distress which culminated in this year has often been ascribed to the waste of resources incident to the war, but a more critical examination discloses more potent causes. They were:

1. Erroneous policies in regard to foreign trade and in providing for the expenses of the war. Foreign trade was greatly diminished, almost destroyed, by the Embargo and Non-Intercourse Acts beginning in 1808. The shipping trade of the country, which had yielded a large annual income, was brought to a standstill, and our products were deprived of their best markets. The fiscal year ending September 30, 1814, showed the smallest foreign trade in the history of our country. The total of imports was $12,819,831, and the total of exports $6,782,272, making an aggregate of $19,602,103, as against a total of over $42,000,000 in the fiscal year ending September 30, 1790, the small-

---

* John Adams's Works, vol. viii, p. 447.

18

est aggregate in any preceding year. So great a falling off in foreign trade could not be without serious results.

In meeting the expenses of the war too much reliance was placed upon the borrowing power and too little upon the taxing power. In anticipation of a conflict with Great Britain, Mr. Albert Gallatin, Secretary of the Treasury, previous to the commencement of the war, had recommended an increase of taxation. This recommendation was not heeded. The cost of maintaining the army and navy was defrayed by large Government loans, causing the sudden diversion of an unusual amount of capital from the ordinary channels of trade. When, after a policy of hesitancy and delay, duties were doubled in 1812, and internal revenue and direct taxes were imposed in 1813, it was found that the business of the country had so diminished that the collections of revenue were disappointing. There was so decided a change in the proportion between the receipts and expenditures of the Government that it could not fail to exercise a destructive effect upon business.   Prior to 1812, in every year, with the single exception of 1792, receipts had exceeded expenditures.* From a situation in which the receipts were double the expenditures, there was an abrupt change to one in which the expenditures were double the receipts.   At no time until the Civil War was there so disproportionate an excess of expenses over revenue as in the three years 1812,

---

* American Almanac, 1880, pp. 64-69. Loans are not included in receipts nor interest in expenditures.

1813, and 1814. In its effect upon the financial condition of the country this disproportion was much worse than in the Civil War, because there was less facility in obtaining loans.

2. The great increase in the number of banks, attended by an unhealthy augmentation in the quantity of circulation and in the amount of discounts.

The charter of the old United States Bank had expired in the year 1811. State banks took its place. Many of them commenced business without adequate capital, and issued currency without sufficient security.

If we look for any development in the period preceding 1814, marking, as is usually the case preceding crises, an advancing step in material progress, there is little to be found. There was some growth of manufactures. By reason of the Embargo and Non-Intercourse Acts and the war, foreign commerce, and consequently foreign supply, had been greatly curtailed. This gave a great stimulus to domestic manufactures. Their products were sold, however, under unusual conditions and at very high prices, so that the manufacturing development of this period cannot be called a normal one.

CRISIS OF 1818–'19 AND EVENTS LEADING THERETO

This crisis may be said to have commenced at the end of October, 1818. The restriction caused by the embargo and by the war was succeeded by an unnatural expansion in trade. From less than $20,000,000 of foreign commerce in the year ending September 30, 1814, the amount increased to over $152,000,000 in that ending September 30, 1815, and over $194,000,000 in that ending September 30, 1816.   In each of these three years the value of imports was about twice that of exports. It would hardly be necessary to go outside of this very unusual change to ascertain the cause of the crisis; but there were aggravating features of a very serious nature.

Paper money in 1815 in different localities and different months of the year was depreciated from 20 to 50 per cent, and, until the year 1817, increased in quantity.   This increase, however, was so palpably unsound that a radical change in policy was made and the quantity was suddenly restricted. The bank circulation, which had reached $110,000,-000 in 1815 and 1816, fell to $65,000,000 in 1819.*

The new United States Bank, which was granted a charter by the Act of April 10, 1816, and commenced operations later, at first issued a large quantity of bills, but afterward, in order to secure safety, made a vital change, and restricted its issues very rapidly.   Thus, while bank issues at first promoted speculation and a rise in prices, at a later time their restriction caused a ruinous fall in prices.   In no epoch of the century is it probable that the fall in prices of commodities and real estate was so marked as in 1818–'19.   Labour also was without employment, except at starvation wages.   Incidental to expansion of credits and speculative enter-

* Albert Bolles, Financial History of the United States, vol. ii, p. 329.

prises there had been, of course, a great increase of luxury and waste. A committee of the Senate of the State of Pennsylvania in making a report in 1819, and tracing the difficulty to the expansion of banking in 1814 and subsequent years, said:

" In consequence of this most destructive measure, the inclination of a large part of the people— created by past prosperity—to live by speculation and not by labour has greatly increased, a spirit in all respects akin to gambling prevailed, and a fictitious value was given to all kinds of property. Specie was driven from circulation as if by given consent, and all effort to restrict society to its natural conditions was treated with undisguised contempt."

These two crises supplement each other, but are strikingly in contrast. There was a brief season of great activity between them, but no real or permanent prosperity. The difference between them is sharply defined. In 1814 and prior thereto, there was an expansion of currency and a contraction of commerce and industry. In 1818 and prior thereto, there was first an expansion, then a contraction of currency, and an expansion of commerce and industry. At no time in our history were the destructive influences of radical changes in fiscal and economic policies more keenly felt than at the time of these two crises. They were contemporaneous with disturbances abroad. It would, however, be incorrect to regard them as caused or governed by movements prevailing in other commercial nations. While, no doubt, the distress was intensified by conditions in Europe, they were, nevertheless, distinctively local and dependent upon causes existing in our own country.

In 1815, with the close of the Napoleonic wars in Europe and the war with Great Britain, commenced a new commercial and industrial era, which was world-wide in its influence. The preceding quarter of a century had been marked by almost constant war, involving the larger part of Europe, and for a much longer time there had been frequent contests among the nations. The succeeding period, with slight interruptions, was one of peace. A new and greater development commenced. For a few years, both in Europe and America, there was a time of waiting, necessary for recovery from the exhaustion of war. Steady improvement may be said to date from the year 1819.

THE PERIOD FROM 1819 TO 1837

During this period there were frequent disturbances, but no crises of the same severity as those of the preceding or succeeding periods. In 1824 there was much activity in the formation of new enterprises and in the re-establishment of banks which had failed. The crisis of December, 1825, in Europe, caused a reaction and diminished demand for our products, and consequently lower prices in 1826. There was a stringency in the money-market in the autumn of the years 1828 and 1831. But these were mere temporary interruptions in an onward movement, which were not different in kind from those which occurred between the close of the war in 1865 and the crisis of September, 1873. This period, from 1819 to 1837, was the first which displayed in this country the distinctive features which preceded the crises of 1873 and 1893. It afforded an illustration of gradual growth, expansion, and collapse. The movement was particularly marked from 1831 to 1837, and most active from 1834 to 1837.

The eighteen years preceding the crisis of 1837 may be described as an era of internal improvements. The construction of numerous canals was begun. Many of them far exceeded in cost any public or private enterprise undertaken, or even projected, before this period.* Railway building was commenced in 1828. There was a constant movement to the westward resulting in the settlement of large tracts of land in Ohio and beyond, and causing a large increase in agricultural production. Other developments were the beginning of immigration of a magnitude sufficient to promote the more rapid development of the country, and the negotiation of foreign loans on a large scale. Withal, the most conspicuous feature of the period was the growth in transportation facilities. Development in transportation assumes an exceptional importance in a country having the large area and variety of re-

---

* The Erie Canal was commenced on July 4, 1817, and opened for traffic November 4, 1825. While this great public work was the most useful of all our canals, its entire cost of construction, from 1817 to 1836, amounting to $7,143,789, was but a small fraction of the total expenditure for canals in Ohio, Pennsylvania, New Jersey, Illinois, and other States.

sources, widely scattered, which belong to the United States.

The influence of foreign loans is shown by the fact that while imports of merchandise exceeded exports from 1831 to 1837, inclusive, imports of specie also, during all of this period, largely exceeded exports. In 1834 exports of coin and bullion amounted to $400,500, while imports of the same reached the total of $16,235,374.

The Crisis of 1837

Towards the close of this unequalled season of industrial and commercial growth, came the usual results, the excesses which cause waste and loss. Along with necessary railways and canals there was a multitude of enterprises in advance of the demand. There were others which were useless. Speculative operations attained a volume not known before. Numerous influences, financial and political, aggravated the difficulties. Among them was the refusal to extend the charter of the United States Bank, and its consequent withdrawal from business. This caused a radical change in the banking business of the country. The withdrawal of the public deposits and their lodgment with numerous State banks, familiarly known at the time as the " pet banks," increased opportunities for extending credit, and furnished the foundation for injudicious enterprises. The distribution of the surplus revenue among the States had the same effect. These events illustrate the danger which results whenever an unexpected or unusual amount of money is added to the circulation. Vicious banking and currency played a part almost as important as in 1814 and 1818.* The actual outbreak of the crisis may be located in the month of May, or the earlier months of 1837.

The crisis of 1837, or panic, as it is more frequently called, has been referred to as a great calamity. Doubtless it brought keen distress to many individuals and witnessed the failure of many enterprises, but the preceding period marked the commencement, under entirely new conditions, of the industrial and commercial growth of the United States. There was not only a steady increase in population and foreign trade, but domestic commerce and wealth nearly doubled in the eighteen years from 1819 to 1837. Canals costing $100,-000,000 were commenced or finished. Abundant mineral and agricultural products of the country, which had been unavailable by reason of lack of transportation facilities, were made available for distribution throughout the country and for shipment abroad. A great increase in useful articles and supplies at home coincided with the growth of wealth and an increase of demands abroad. Many of the methods of transacting business had been crude, and showed the effects of the limitations which belonged to an earlier and less progressive period; but under the stimulus of the time, these

---

* The crisis of 1837 was aggravated by the high price of wheat and other products which this country had exported in large quantities, but which at this time were imported by reason of deficient harvests.

methods were changed and a new impetus was given
to the material growth of the country. This period
witnessed the beginning of great cities like Chicago,
which before that day were not known. The great
agricultural States of the Middle West assumed that
importance which assured their future growth and
prominence as great commonwealths. It would be
expected that such rapid development would be
attended by excess and loss. That increase of en
terprise which was normal and represented increasing wealth was attended by speculation everywhere.
The transportation facilities which brought great
areas of land nearer to the seaboard and to wider
markets, led to the purchase, at speculative values,
of other lands still more remote. Instances were
not lacking in which lots in cities and farms were
quoted, and even sold, at higher prices than have
been realized for them from that day to this.
Although the calamity was sharp, nevertheless the
overaction and speculation were but incidents of our
superabundant vitality and growth, such as are sure
to attend rapid development.

The Period from 1837 to 1857

A period of depression followed the crisis of 1837.
Liquidation was necessary, and there were many
failures. The buoyancy of the time was such that
an early attempt at revival was made, but in 1839
there was again a reaction and a multitude of failures. The great inflation of the currency and the
effects of excessive enterprise were not yet remedied.

The situation was greatly aggravated by the suspension of the United States Bank and other banks. Bank failures were even more numerous than in 1837. In the summer of 1843 the end of the depression may be said to have been reached. In 1848 there was again a maximum of discounts and a great falling off in specie, but there was no crisis to be compared with those of 1837 and 1857. The crises occurring in Europe in 1847 exercised little influence here, for scanty food supplies there caused exportations to be very large. In this way any unfavourable effects were neutralized.

The war with Mexico, from 1846 to 1848, had some effect in checking enterprise and that forward movement which would lead to a crisis. Its effect upon business was certainly slight. The discoveries of gold in 1848 and 1849 afforded new resources and a new field for investment, thus tending to prevent the depression which otherwise might have occurred. The Crimean War in 1854–'55 caused increased demand and prices for American products.

The years preceding 1857 make up a period of remarkable growth and prosperity marred by intermittent checks or disturbances, most of which can be termed financial. A great deal of capital was absorbed in the completion of canals commenced or projected prior to 1837; but in the latter part of the period, activity in the construction of railways succeeded that in canals. Railway building, which in no year preceding 1849 had reached 800 miles, amounted to 3,642 miles in 1856. The increase of immigration and the growth of population proceeded in much the same ratio as prior to 1837.   Defective currency and unstable banking had a less destructive effect than in the previous period, though still very noticeable.   At all times the proportion of specie held by the banks to their loans and circulation was dangerously small, even when the most conservative management was maintained.

Crisis of 1857

Industry and commerce were much less affected in 1857 than in 1837.   The financial disturbance was comparatively more prominent, and the depression of 1857 and succeeding years was less severe and less universal in its effects than the previous one. As distinguished from other crises, the outbreak in 1857 was more sudden.   There had been fluctuations in prices, with a general downward tendency, but when the crisis came in August, 1857, it was a surprise to many of the most watchful financiers. The immediate signal for its occurrence was the failure of the Ohio Life Insurance and Trust Company on the 24th of August, 1857.

Special Features of Crises and Depressions in the United States in 1857 and Preceding Years

There were decided differences between the crises and depressions occurring in the United States in 1857 and prior thereto and those occurring contemporaneously in Europe.   Disturbances occurred more frequently. There was not the same steady upward movement in activity, followed by crises and a downward movement. It is obvious that there were vital differences in conditions. There were some reasons tending to make the distress here less severe.

First, there was a smaller quantity of capital available for investment in this country. In European countries the quantity was not only larger, but it was more mobile. In a time of rising prices and promising ventures this capital was made available to promote the upward movement. In the United States the smaller quantity of capital, showing its effect in greater rates of interest and greater increase in the rate of interest in times of expansion, tended to check extravagant enterprise, which otherwise might have reached unprecedented proportions. This limitation, as a check upon extravagant enterprise and waste of resources, was especially noticeable in the earlier part of the century. Except in times of unusual excitement only the most obvious and favourable fields were exploited.

Second, we were aided by the great growth of the country, which was stimulated by immigration and the development of great areas of territory, and aided by opportunities for profitable investment, such as those created by the discovery of gold in California. All these afforded increased demands for products, tended to prevent over-production in any line, and limited the effects of overaction.

Third, while the banks promoted crises by their instability, yet the warnings given by their frequent failures diminished confidence and the danger from too great a volume of enterprise.

THE PERIOD FROM 1857 TO 1873

Attention has already been called to the very large number of failures in the year 1857. The depression which followed the crisis reached its worst point in 1859. There would have been a more pronounced revival in that year but for deficient crops. There was a decided improvement in 1860. Exceptional conditions commenced with the war in 1861, which prevented a movement in business uniform with that abroad, and gave a distinctive character to the succeeding period. The great demands incident to the war and the general employment of labour caused by these demands and by the withdrawal of so large a body of men as soldiers prevented the possibility of depression. The issuance of paper money, which soon depreciated in value, made the payment of debts easier, and tended to prevent bankruptcies.

In 1865, with the end of the contest, there was that exhaustion which results from war. For some time the productive energy of the country was busy filling the void. In addition to these influences, it must be said that this great contest, unfortunate as it was, gave rise to a great and immediate awakening, at least in the Northern States. There was a new birth as a nation. Manufactures, fostered by the adoption of a high protective tariff, had received a great stimulus from the unusual home demand. Agricultural production was increasing rapidly. The return of much more than a million of men to productive industry seemed to cause no embarrassment. All could find employment. With slight reactions in 1867 and 1869, the onward movement continued until 1873.

CRISIS OF 1873

Just as, by a unique distinction, Sir Edward Coke's reports are styled " *The* Reports," so the crisis of 1873 may be called " *The* Crisis." All the phenomena which belong to a crisis period appear at this time more clearly than at any other. The general causes which lead to disturbances were so plain as to eliminate from attention those exceptional features which are often mistaken for the true causes. There was an enormous absorption of circulating capital in fixed capital. Railways, as well as docks, buildings, and factories, had been constructed on an unprecedented scale. All the equipment for future production was increasing at a more rapid pace than ever before. In these expenditures we have the effect of capital invested for objects not immediately remunerative. The opening up of wide areas of territory in the West for settlement by farmers, while greatly increasing agricultural production, rendered less valuable, in some cases almost useless, very large tracts near to the Atlantic seaboard. This illustrates the effect of supplanting old fields and methods by new. Railroads preceded settlement, while in previous eras they had followed it. The effect of direct waste and loss was plainly visible. Waste and extravagance, greatly stimulated by an inflated currency, were seen on every hand. A different style of living had been adopted everywhere, whether based on increased income or not. Speculation greatly increased; foreign loans were contracted extravagantly; conservatism in business calculation and economy in expenditure were disregarded. The progressive movement was greatly increased by the opening of the Suez Canal, as well as by the progress of invention and the larger scale upon which operations were conducted everywhere.

The crisis of 1873 did not come without loud warnings. In the two preceding years, at the autumn season, money was scarce and rates of interest were high. On the 2d of October, 1871, bank reserves in New York city exceeded requirements by only $3,666,943. On the 3d of October, 1872, there was a deficiency in reserves of $1,131,-436. On the 28th of February, 1873, a deficiency appeared again, and, although there was an increase of reserves in June, rates of interest were high and displayed abnormal fluctuations.

There has been much interesting conjecture whether this crisis would have occurred had not Jay Cooke & Co. failed on the 18th day of September, 1873. This conspicuous failure was a mere incident. The outbreak was the result of inevitable tendencies, and was sure to result from the combination of the extravagant and progressive movements of the time.

The depression which followed 1873 was severe and unprecedented. It continued in most branches of business until the end of 1878, and in some lines until 1879; but, as after 1837, so after 1873, the people of the United States reached a higher plane of consumption and enjoyment than ever before attained. After 1879, a scale of living which would have amounted to extravagance and waste in 1873 was possible without exhausting the resources of the country. The great investments in railways and other enterprises began to make their effect felt. While many railways were placed in the hands of receivers, they were, nevertheless, an influential factor in the growth of the succeeding period. They were in advance of the demands of the time, but not in advance of the demands of the near future. They were constructed when prices were at the highest point, and the haste for added mileage caused them to be built at a cost so great as to render a satisfactory return upon the amount invested impossible; yet, they were useful in the development of the country and in making increased production available.

THE PERIOD FROM 1879 TO 1890, INCLUDING THE CRISIS OF 1884

There were indications of revival in the year 1877; in some branches of trade the improvement was marked in 1878, nevertheless, this year showed the maximum number and amount of failures after 1873. A substantial and increasing prosperity was

19

manifest at the beginning of the year 1879. The opening up of new agricultural fields in the West and Northwest, which were well furnished with means of transportation, together with favourable years for crops, exerted a powerful influence at the close of this decade. Cotton production, which had languished during the Civil War and for ten years thereafter, showed a tardy increase, but in 1880 reached the same and even greater volume than it had shown in 1860, the maximum year of production up to that time. These large products of the farm were contemporaneous with increasing demand and, for several years, diminished supply in Europe. There was accordingly another advancing movement beginning in the year 1879, healthy at first, but excessive later.

The year 1881 was one of diminished agricultural production. The decrease was apparent in wheat, corn, and cotton alike. At the same time prices abroad were lower. There were troublous times at the beginning of 1882. Numerous failures occurred, and the volume of liabilities increased that year, and still more in 1883. In 1882 there was a crisis in France. But in the United States the impetus towards prosperity was so strong that the activity continued, but with material abatement in many lines. The year 1882 witnessed the maximum construction of railways up to that time, and the fiscal year ending June 30th, the largest immigration. Many indications of prosperity continued throughout the year 1883.

The crisis occurred in May, 1884, the date of

the failure of Grant & Ward in New York, with that of the Metropolitan National Bank and other institutions. The downward movement may be said to have reached its lowest point in 1886. After this there was a season of prosperity not marked throughout by the same rapid advance as after 1878–'79, but which continued with some variations in activity until 1890, and, with an interruption at that time, until 1893.

A distinction between the decade beginning in 1881 and the previous one is to be noted in the matter of railway construction. In the second decade, while the mileage of railway construction was greater, it was largely made up of lines constructed in competition with existing lines, as illustrated by the West Shore, which paralleled the New York Central & Hudson River from New York to Buffalo, and the New York, Chicago & St. Louis, which paralleled the Lake Shore & Michigan Southern from Buffalo to Chicago. In this decade also, the great trunk lines were absorbing branch lines and increasing their mileage, and engaged in the construction of branches and connecting lines to all important terminal points. The railway construction of this decade, though greater than that of the previous one, cannot be regarded as exerting the same influence in developing new territory, and it is doubtful whether it conferred so great a benefit upon the country as that between 1870 and 1880.

THE PERIOD FROM 1890 TO DATE, INCLUDING THE
CRISIS OF 1893

The depression in Europe commenced at the end
of the year 1890.   A survey of the situation affords
strong arguments that it was due in the United
States at the same time.   But while the onward
movement was checked, the actual crisis was postponed until 1893.   For this there were several
reasons:

First.   As in 1879 and the ensuing year, there
was again a deficiency in the food supply of Europe.   The exportation of food was particularly
noticeable in the fiscal year ending June 30, 1892.

Second.   It had become established that one
feature before and at the outbreak of a crisis in the
United States was the withdrawal of foreign loans.
This withdrawal did not make its influence felt here
until after 1890.   The inflation in the currency,
which was occasioned by the issue of silver certificates, beginning in June, 1890, for a time relieved
the money-market.   It must be understood that two
demands, of very different natures, cause a scarcity
of money; one to satisfy home requirements, the
other for remittances abroad.   A depreciated currency may satisfy the former, but not the latter
which in the long run furnishes the test of the
sufficiency of the supply.   It is not to be denied
that any artificial or unnatural increase of currency,
as in the days of greenback inflation, tends to postpone the coming of a crisis, but renders it more
severe when it comes.

In 1893 more than in any preceding crisis the situation was aggravated by the withdrawal of foreign investments. This withdrawal was greatly increased by the distrust of our currency. Foreign investors feared a change from a gold to a silver standard. The actual outbreak of the crisis was in May, 1893.

It must be noticed that this crisis was increased in severity by a change in the political control of the country. The threat of radical change in the tariff laws caused wide-spread distrust, and tended to create uncertainty and destroy confidence. This situation illustrates the fact that in causing crises one of the most dangerous factors is a radical change in fiscal or economic policy. Even a threat of such radical change is a potent influence in the same direction.

In many respects the crisis of 1893 was followed by distress more severe than that of 1873. There was a more rapid decrease of imports, particularly of articles of luxury. There was a larger number of bank failures; the decrease in deposits and the withdrawal of money from circulation was continued for a longer time. But it cannot be compared with that of 1873 in its intensity or in its continuance. In the year 1895 there was a slight revival. This, however, was dissipated in the following year, and the uncertainty and excitement of the presidential election of 1896 interposed an absolute barrier to any immediate improvement.

This presidential election again illustrates the danger which must ensue to business from radical changes of fiscal policy. No nation can pass through a year of doubt as to the standard of value such as that which existed in the presidential election of 1896 without paralyzing business and industry. The election of 1896 having been decided, there was a period of halting, after which the beginnings of a revival plainly appeared in June and July, 1897. Then began a healthy increase.

The year ending June 30, 1898, was one of trade statistics unparalleled in their favourable aspect. Exports exceeded imports by almost exactly 100 per cent; total foreign trade, barring a slight excess in 1892, was greater than ever before.

While 1870 to 1880 may be called a period of agricultural expansion, and 1880 to 1890 one of manufacturing expansion, that beginning in 1890 was characterized by an expansion of both agricultural and manufactured products. In this last decade one of the distinctive features was a change from an excess of imports to an excess of exports of

CEREAL PRODUCTION.*			MANUFACTURES.†		
Years.	Bushels per capita.	Increase per cent over quantity for preceding decade.	Years.	Capital invested. Increase per cent during decade.	Net product. Increase per cent.
1839....	36.06	.....	1850–1860...	89.38	84.11
1849....	37.40	40.93	1860–1870...	67.80	63.31
1859....	39.41	42.84	1870–1880...	64.10	40.01
1869....	35.98	11.97	1880–1890...	120.78	106.59
1879....	53.78	94.45	....	.....	.....
1889....	56.19	30.44	....	.....	.....

* Census of 1890, Statistics of Agriculture, p. 6.
† Ibid. Report on Manufacturing Industries, part i, p. 4.

manufactures. This change occurred in the fiscal year ending June 30, 1898, in which, for the first time, exports of manufactured products exceeded imports.

The figures on the opposite page, derived from the Census of 1890, illustrate the course of events up to 1890.

From these statistics it appears that in the decade from 1870 to 1880 the quantity of cereal production, as compared with the net product of manufactures, increased in the proportion of 94.45 to 40.01, or more than twice as much. On the contrary, in the decade from 1880 to 1890, the net product of manufactures, as compared with the quantity of cereal production, increased in the proportion of 106.59 to 30.44, or three and a half times as much.* There was an even greater increase in the capital invested in manufactures, which, between 1880 and 1890, increased 120.78 per cent.

It has already been stated that the year of greatest proportion of exports to imports has preceded the most notable season of prosperity. After June 30, 1898, the proportion of exports to imports declined somewhat, but an even more prosperous period followed. While prices of iron and steel showed a rise in the summer of 1897, the great increase did not begin until the year 1899.

---

* By reason of the different years selected in the Census Reports, it is impossible to make an exact comparison by years. The statistics of cereal production are taken as of 1879 and 1889, while those of manufactures are taken as of 1880 and 1890. It is assumed, however, that the comparison is substantially correct.

The years following July 1, 1897, show signs of a larger degree of prosperity and expansion, attended by more distinct indications of the assumption of a higher place in the world's trade and production than have ever appeared in any country.

There is a natural interest in conjectures upon the duration of this period.

The Present Outlook

Without attempting to forecast the probable date of the next crisis or depression, it will be interesting to give with some detail the indications which point respectively towards or away from such an event. While conditions at the time of the occurrence of each of the latest crises have materially differed from those of the preceding, differences in conditions at the beginning of the twentieth century are even greater. This renders prediction correspondingly more difficult. As a preliminary statement, it may be said that the possession of great wealth is not a reason why a crisis should not occur. On the contrary, the possession of great resources, or even of an abundance of available money, is one of the provoking causes of crises. This has been frequently pointed out in these pages.

Among indications at the present time looking to the approach of a crisis or a depression may be named the following:

1. There has never been a time in any country when that speculative movement which is aroused by a period of prosperity and shows itself in the

floating of securities at many times the actual present value of the property they represent, was so noticeable as now. We have passed the time when the stock and bonds of industrial corporations are counted by thousands or millions; a billion is not an unknown figure. In this large capitalization there is a great difference between the nominal value of stocks and bonds and the actual value of the property they represent. It is a serious question whether the earning capacity of these corporations is such as to pay a return upon the inflated prices at which their securities have been taken by the investing public. The failure of one of them might at any time cause a crisis and impose a check even upon the most advantageous enterprises.

2. While speculative enterprises and the development of untried fields do not constitute so large a part of the prevailing activity as was the case prior to 1873 and 1882–'84, new undertakings have been inaugurated upon a colossal scale. In the absorption of capital for increase of production or future profits, conditions are quite the same as have existed before every previous depression.

3. If we consider the prices of iron and steel, which have furnished the best barometer in the past, we are in the fluctuating period. Prior to each of the recent depressions, iron has passed a maximum of price and then has fallen or fluctuated for a time before the occurrence of a crisis. This fluctuating period seems to have commenced at the end of the year 1899. It commenced about one year prior to the crisis of 1873, four years prior to

the crisis of 1884, and three years prior to the crisis of 1893. It appears also that the consumption of pig-iron in the year 1900 fell off from that of 1899, though the production did not.* In the first six months of the year 1901, however, consumption exceeded production, while the latter was well maintained.

4. That absence of equilibrium between different kinds of production, which is a precursor of a depression, has manifested itself in certain branches, most notably in the manufacture of textiles, in which there has been over-production, and as a result there has been a decrease of activity and profit in them.

5. There are not lacking distinct indications of diminished activity and purchasing power in other countries with which we have extended commercial relations and upon whose prosperity our own, in great measure, depends. The crisis of 1893 in this country occurred two and one half years after diminished activity in European countries clearly indicated the beginning of depression there.

Among the indications, on the other hand, that a depression is not impending, may be named the following:

---

* See a communication from Mr. James M. Swank in The Bulletin of the American Iron and Steel Association for February 23, 1901, p. 30. He estimates the consumption for 1899 at 13,799,442; for 1900 at 13,177,281, a decrease of 602,161 tons. After accounting for the increased exports of 1900, he estimates the diminished consumption for strictly home use at 900,000 tons.

1. There is a vital distinction between industrial operations at this time and those in the periods preceding previous depressions. This distinction may be expressed in a word by saying that in previous instances the greater part of the activity was in new construction; now it is in the extension or improvement of the old. Railway building in the construction of new roads has almost reached a standstill; yet, in volume, the sales of steel rails and railway material compare favourably with those of former years of activity. Prior to 1873 and 1884 thousand of miles of railroads were building. The most of these railways were through undeveloped territory, as illustrated prior to 1873, or in competition with existing lines, as illustrated prior to 1884. Now steel rails are being substituted for iron upon existing lines, or heavier steel rails for lighter. Pressed-steel cars are taking the place of those constructed of wood; substantial embankments take the place of trestles. Upon railways, as well as upon highways, wooden bridges are giving way to those which are made of steel. Instead of construction preceding demand, demand precedes construction. New furnaces and rolling mills are not now being constructed in such numbers as on former occasions, but those in existence are being remodeled or provided with increased capacity. In mineral production, instead of investments in mines of doubtful profit or productive capacity, capital is employed in working those which have been found to yield abundant return. Much of the gold and silver mining, the profits of which formerly depended upon

many contingencies, is conducted in pursuance of careful calculation.

Before previous crises there was preparation for untried business or manufacturing, which was accompanied by elements of uncertainty and experiment. Now capital is expended for the better transaction of existing business or for improved methods in manufacturing. It promises a more assured and, in most instances, a quicker return. It is plain that the latter condition has fewer dangerous features than the former. Many of the former enterprises were in unexplored fields; a larger share of those of the present are in fields which have been exploited and found to be profitable.*

2. Our excellent financial condition. The money-market has experienced several extremely severe shocks, pronounced enough to cause a crisis in earlier years, and yet has recovered itself. In the autumn of 1899 the reserves were dangerously low in the banks of New York city, and the financial situation seemed as threatening as before the crisis of 1873. Money on call rose to an unusual figure. In the speculations of the month of May, 1901, losses in the stock-market occurred surpassing any previously chronicled. Bankruptcies have

---

* It will be noticed that the conditions referred to in this paragraph differ widely from those referred to at the beginning of the statement of unfavourable indications. The danger there referred to is the inflation in the price of *securities*, which represent capital. This paragraph refers to the smaller amount of waste and the more assured results in the use of *capital*.

occurred, and revelations of business mismanagement and dishonesty have been made, such as usually interpose a check upon enterprise, without apparently disturbing the forward movement.

Our additional command over the world's trade and our enlarged financial operations make it possible in case of stringency to obtain remittances from abroad more easily. Large balances abroad furnish a valuable reserve upon which to draw in case of danger.

The dangerous feature present in the time preceding every crisis for half a century viz., the withdrawal of foreign capital—is happily lacking, for the amount of indebtedness abroad has so greatly diminished as to be no longer a serious disturbing influence, and our reliance upon foreign capital for future development has ceased.

3. The monetary system of the country, while by no means perfect, is free both from the presence of irredeemable paper currency, such as was in circulation in 1873, and the silver inflation of 1893.

4. The very consolidation of great enterprises under the control of a more limited number of organizations makes a decrease of production easier, and helps to diminish that ruinous competition and over-production which operate in every time of crisis. However objectionable this concentration of industry may be from many standpoints, such as diminishing general opportunities for enterprise, fostering monopoly, and throwing men out of employment, it, nevertheless, has its favourable side as regards the probability of a crisis.

5. The sustained increase in railway earnings, the large profits of domestic transportation, and the unusual activity in ship-building, all seem to show an increase in production and the ready sale of products. They afford a distinctly favourable indication.

6. The indications pertaining to foreign trade are favourable; there is neither a marked decrease in the proportion of exports to imports from year to year, nor a sudden decrease, nor is there by any means a continued excess of imports over exports. It is true there is a slight decrease in some kinds of exports, but it does not compare with that which has been apparent prior to crises. The characteristic feature of the present situation is the maintenance for four years of an unprecedented proportion of exports. The following figures, with the percentages, give the relation of exports to imports, beginning in 1893: *

Years.	Exports.	Imports.	Percentage of exports to imports.
	(In millions	of dollars.)	
1893..........	847	866	97.8
1894..........	892	654	136.3
1895..........	807	731	110.3
1896..........	882	779	113.2
1897..........	1,050	764	137.4
1898..........	1,231	616	199.8
1899..........	1,227	697	176.0
1900..........	1,394	849	164.1
1901..........	1,487	822	180.9

From this table it will appear that in the two years from June 30, 1898, to June 30, 1900, the

* Statistical Abstract for 1900, p. 82, and Monthly Summary of Commerce and Finance for June, 1901.

proportion of exports to imports declined each year as compared with the previous year. In the past year this decline has been interrupted; but, in order to portray the whole situation fairly, it should be stated that a decrease in the proportion of exports of manufactures occurred, indicating that prices and consumption of this class of commodities were more sustained in this country than elsewhere. The increase in the proportion of exports in the year ending June 30, 1901, is for the most part explained by the increased export of the products of agriculture.

A favourable indication is found in the more minute examination of the articles imported, which displays a large increase in imports of raw material for manufacturing during the last two years. The total value of exports and imports has increased in every year since 1895, and in later years the gain has been unprecedented. Nevertheless, the congratulatory opinions which are naturally derived from these remarkable figures cannot be entertained without a feeling of caution. A depression might begin within the borders of a country in which there is a record of surpassing prosperity in its foreign trade, because of overaction at home. And in causing that overaction, a leading factor might be the very abundance of its wealth. To many the apprehension of a crisis is based upon an idea that so great prosperity as the present is necessarily followed by dangerous reaction, and that the time is approaching when another crash is due. In the great magnitude and variety of present operations sudden events may occur, such as extensive labour strikes, failures of crops, disastrous failures at home or abroad, which might assume such importance as to change the tide and cause diminished activity. Though an opinion cannot be expressed with certainty, it now seems probable than when a change occurs it will be more like that preceding 1884, when there was an abatement of activity not accompanied by a severe crisis. The falling off in commerce and industry will probably be gradual rather than sudden and sharp, as was the case in 1873 and 1893, and with much less abatement of activity.

Increase in the Production of Gold

In the present situation, no survey of probable conditions in the future is complete without consideration of the effect of the steadily increasing supply of gold, which began with increased production in the year 1891. An increase in gold, or the metal commonly employed as a basis for currency, has two opposite effects in reference to depressions. It hastens them by furnishing a more ample stock of money and stimulating extravagant undertakings, but it postpones them in so far as it creates greater buoyancy in business and readier ability to meet obligations.

The world's business for the first half of the last century increased with a rapidity such that additions to the metallic stock did not keep pace with it; that is, the increased demand for metallic money, occasioned by larger transactions and a wider extent of commercial operations, caused the purchasing power of metallic money to increase. A degree of hardship was thus imposed upon debtors. Beginning with the great gold discoveries in 1848 and 1849 a renewed impulse to activity was afforded. The annual production of gold, however, greatly diminished after 1872, and did not attain its former proportions until 1891. The resulting tendency to lower prices was still further aggravated by the adoption in the leading commercial countries of the single gold standard instead of the bimetallic standard, which latter came to be regarded as impracticable in any well-regulated monetary system. While this question is not free from doubt, it would seem that the greater production of gold will tend to postpone the approach of a depression and mitigate its severity when it comes. This greater production tends to increase prices and to maintain the supply of money required for enlarged commercial and industrial operations. At the same time it concurs with such rapid improvements in production and distribution that no oppressive or disturbing increase in prices is probable. In fact, cheapening processes are so strongly at work that the general trend of prices of commodities is likely to be downward rather than upward, notwithstanding the rapidly increasing stock of gold.

CHAPTER IX

SUMMARY AND CONCLUSION

In the preceding chapters, it has been pointed out that crises and periods of depression occur in countries where progressive forces are potent and there is rapid growth. Large accumulations of capital, which render increased enterprise possible, often furnish the basis for them; but their existence is incident to a spirit of enterprise and rapid growth rather than to great wealth. The important feature in their occurrence is the increasing proportion of expenditures in preparation for increased production, manifesting itself in the formation and prosecution of new enterprises and the building on a large scale of railroads, ships, and factories, and the providing of other means to meet increased demands. At times these expenditures for increased production attain an unusual proportion as compared with the ordinary expenditures for annual consumption or support. In proportion as expenditures are so applied, the probability of seasons of unequal activity and prosperity is increased. The beginning of a period in which large amounts of capital are invested in these new enterprises is marked by increased activity. Actuated by the profits which are obtained in such a period, expenditures of capital will not stop when provision for sufficient supply of present wants is made, but will continue until the demand is more than supplied. These influences must bring a time when enterprise is overdone and supply exceeds demand, certainly in numerous lines of production. When this time is reached, prices fall, enterprise slackens, and, as a result of falling prices and diminished employment, a change must occur. For a time, the length of which will be determined by the extent of the over-equipment for production and the exhaustion of resources, prices will be low and supply will exceed demand; but at the end of this period there is an adjustment under which conditions are better than before, because there will be a larger quantity of the necessities, comforts, and luxuries of life. The same results are caused by that derangement which occurs in a progressive society in consequence of the substitution of new appliances and new methods for those formerly in use. This brings ruin to many, displaces labour, and requires time for adjustment to the new situation.

By reason of the large profits realized in these seasons of exceptional activity a great deal of speculation and fraud is sure to occur, and these intensify the disturbances of the time.

These disturbances have occurred periodically. An examination of the rules which govern industrial and commercial movements will, it is thought, show that this periodicity is not an accident or coincidence, but the result of certain forces, the influences of which are easily traced. Its explanation can be found in the condition already set forth —namely, that at intervals of time *the demand for certain things exceeds the supply*. Whenever this demand for increased supplies arises, there is added to the productive energy theretofore applied to meet existing wants, that additional activity which is necessary to supply the new wants. Thus, in different periods the degree of activity is unequal. The periodicity is more apparent, if that for which the greater demand is developed, is something for the increased production of which a considerable time is necessary. A number of influences promote irregularity in the development of these demands and in the movement for supplying them, such as inventions or the discovery of new fields for development, or unusual accumulations of capital for investment. The effect of these influences is not, and cannot be, equal each year; but they attain that magnitude or impetus which leads to overaction, only at longer intervals.

It may be conceded that limitations in human judgment and misdirected energy contribute in causing alternate periods of activity and depression; but, after counting, as we must, on these limitations, it is difficult to tell what means could be devised by which they could be avoided.

The temporary shocks designated as panics or crises are more fitful, more dependent upon varying moods and different phases of human nature. They are also more easily prevented and not so inevitable a part of the changing movement of affairs. There is a distinct tendency towards a less degree of severity in them, and they arise more from defects in the industrial or commercial organization and errors of calculation, which time and experience can remove.

It would be too much to say that these periods of unequal activity are not calamities, but Nature herself yields her treasures in unequal portions from year to year, and in an industrial organization, in which human motive plays so large a part, where competition is sharp, and absolute co-operation is impossible, these recurring seasons of prosperity and depression seem inevitable. Their disturbing effect can be greatly diminished by legislative recognition of economic laws and by wise regulations as to currency; also by higher standards of education and consequently greater wisdom in the direction of individual effort.

Notwithstanding the exaggerated ideas of calamity which are expressed on the occasion of crises and depressions, there is no room for the pessimist in our modern business life. As M. Clément Juglar says:

" The regular development of the riches of nations does not take place without suffering or without resistance. During crises everything is arrested for a time; the social organization seems to be paralyzed; but it is only a passing torpor, prelude of grander destinies." *

---

* Des Crises Commerciales, title-page and p. 555, edition of 1889.

These periods have occurred and brought bankruptcy and ruin to many, have thrown multitudes out of employment, and caused the necessity for charity to aid those who are willing to work; but in every instance they have been followed by enlarged supplies of things which are useful and augmented opportunities for human enjoyment. We may be sure that such depressions as may hereafter occur will be but temporary checks in the great forward movement. Our aim should be to establish such a degree of steadiness in our business growth, and such standards of wisdom and honesty as will reduce their effects to a minimum.

APPENDIX A

A Selection of Opinions as to the Causes of Crises and Depressions *

WALTER BAGEHOT

" MUCH has been written on panics and manias, much more than with the most outstretched intellect we are able to follow or conceive; but one thing is certain, that at particular times a great many stupid people have a great deal of stupid money. Saving people have often only the faculty of saving; they accumulate ably, and contemplate their accumulations with approbation, but what to do with them they do not know.   Aristotle, who was not in trade, imagined that money is barren; and barren it is to quiet ladies, rural clergymen, and country misers.   Several economists have plans for preventing improvident speculation.   One would abolish Peel's Act and substitute one-pound notes; another would retain Peel's Act and make the calling for one-pound notes a capital crime; but our scheme is not to allow any man to have a hundred pounds who cannot prove to the satisfaction of the Lord Chancellor that he knows what to do with a hundred pounds.   The want of this easy precaution allows the accumulation of wealth in the hands of

---

* In the following opinions the exact language of the writer has not in all cases been followed.   In order to secure brevity or to omit matter not immediately pertaining to causes, some of them have been epitomized.

311

rectors, authors, grandmothers, who have no knowledge of business, and no idea except that their
money now produces nothing, and ought and must
be forced immediately to produce something. ' I
wish,' said one of this class, ' for the largest immediate income, and I am therefore naturally disposed
to purchase an *advowson*.' At intervals, from causes
which are not to the present purpose, the money
from these people—the blind capital, as we call it,
of the country—is particularly large and craving;
it seeks for some one to devour it, and there is
' plethora '; it finds some one, and there is ' speculation '; it is devoured, and there is ' panic.' " *

DAVID MACPHERSON
Distress in 1793

"Of the wealth accumulated in nine peaceful
years of successful commerce a very considerable
proportion was invested in machinery and inland
navigations, objects which, though generally very
productive in due time, require a very heavy advance of capital and depend for their productiveness entirely upon the general prosperity of the
trade of the country. At this time also the con-
cerns of both merchants and manufacturers were
much more widely extended and were much greater
than at any former period, a natural effect of increasing prosperity, and sometimes a cause of ensuing calamity." †

---

* Essay on Edward Gibbon. Collected Works, Travelers'
Insurance Company's edition, vol. ii, p. 2.

† Annals of Commerce, 1805, vol. iv, pp. 265–266.

W. Stanley Jevons

" The remote cause of these commercial tides
has not been so well ascertained.   It seems to lie in
the *varying proportion which the capital devoted to
permanent and remote investment bears to that which
is but temporarily invested soon to reproduce
itself.*" *

Horace White

" The antecedents of the crisis of 1873 were
identical with every other commercial crisis—
namely, speculation, the act of buying with a view
to selling at a higher price, and overtrading, or the
act of buying and selling too much on a given capital.   Most commonly these two elements are accompanied by two others—viz., the destruction or
loss of previously accumulated capital, and the rapid
conversion of circulating into fixed capital.   Speculation and destruction of capital usually go together
in preparing the way for a crisis." †

Bonamy Price

1. " What is it that makes a crisis?   You will
never understand unless you go to the root of that
great word capital.   The word capital consecrated
to the great fact that the workman must have tools,
living, shelter, and clothes while working.   There
is a division of labour and employments.   There
are the makers of goods and the traders who put the

---

* Investigations in Currency and Finance, pp. 27–28.
† Fortnightly Review, vol. xxv, p. 819.

goods where they are to be used. The latter includes shipping, railways, and canals. The test of capital is that it reappears in the goods made—that it is reproduced. When it is reproduced, when the industrial people have produced as much as they have destroyed, prosperity exists. We make to destroy.

"A nation grows rich by increase of capital, by applying their wealth, making machinery, and increasing the facilities for production.

"Nations grow poor by consuming more than they have made, by diminishing those things which keep alive industry and cause goods to be made.

"The reason why people do not buy from the shop-keepers things which they need or desire is not lack of money; it is the lack of some commodity which can be exchanged for money, and then used for the purchase." *

2. "What is the foundation of ill? There have not been bad harvests or innovations in legislation. The cause is simpler and deeper—overspending, overconsuming, destroying more wealth than is reproduced, and its necessary consequence, poverty; like a farmer who destroys not only his surplus produce, but his seed-corn and his supplies for the next year, even if expended upon drainage or some improvement ultimately useful. For an individual this is plain enough, but with a people the complications are so many and so great, and the simple facts are obscured by such a multitude of intricacies, that

* Lecture at Chicago, Ill., November 9, 1874, Chicago Tribune, November 10, 1874.

we do not grasp the vital facts. But a nation is only an aggregation of individuals." *

3. " A vast outlay on new enterprises, involving a large consumption of food and materials, whether in the way of pure waste or temporary unproductiveness, ought always to suggest a feeling of danger. . . . This excess occurs in seasons of prosperity." †

John B. Clark

" Before every commercial crisis there is a period during which there takes place very much production that does not cater to normal and permanent wants, and that, therefore, cannot . continue.

" Much production needs to be checked, and it is checked by the harsh operation of the crisis itself. The so-called ' boom ' has deranged business, and the ensuing depression is a time of painful readjustment and recuperation. It is a time of convalescence from the disease that is rudely described as an excess of production, and that really is an excess of some kinds of production and a deficiency of other kinds." ‡

Paul Leroy-Beaulieu

" 1. The very great specialization of production, the division of labour, . . . a division which is not alone personal but territorial."

---

* Bankers' Magazine, New York, vol. xxxii, pp. 95–96.

† North British Review, vol. liii, p. 467.

‡ Introduction to the translation of Karl Rodbertus's work on Overproduction and Crises, 1898, p. 2.

" 2. The habitual dependence of production upon consumption, which former is most frequently conducted without orders, with a view to future requirements rather than present, estimated and conjectured rather than always exactly calculated, a course which permits uncertainty in the regularity and non-interruption of the market.

" 3. The active rôle of speculation and of a credit which stretches the economic springs sometimes to the extreme, and at certain moments, in drawing from them the maximum effect, renders them more and more impressionable and fragile. Every perfect machine is more delicate than a crude machine. Every machine moving at a great pace and at the maximum of its speed runs the risk of derangement and of stopping suddenly at an obstacle which would barely slacken the course of a machine less complicated and operated with more prudence.

" 4. Fundamental variations in money, whether metallic or representative of forced circulation.

" 5. Very profound modifications and very sudden results accomplished in the principal branches of production, particularly following great technical progress effected upon one point or another. The sudden and permanent increase, and in considerable proportions, of certain categories of products, of a nature such that the habitual proportions between offer and demand are suddenly very much modified.

" Of these five causes of crises, the first four

concern particularly those which are called commercial, the fifth relates to general economic crises." *

LEONE LEVI

"If the predisposing cause of the different crises is considered, it will be seen that there has been a rash spirit of adventure created under the influence of successful operations and large accumulations of capital. The issuance of notes is usually subsequent to, and not antecedent to, the occurrence of the crisis. The main cause for the occurrence of crises is the sudden realization of an insufficiency of capital to meet present demands." †

J. E. THOROLD ROGERS

1. The cause exists in the function of exchange, in the expectation of unreasonable profits, and in incorrect calculation.‡

2. "A commercial crisis is the consequence of a miscalculation as to the power of endurance which capital possesses in waiting for and thereby controlling the market." #

ROBERT GIFFEN

1. "The explanation is the condition of prices for many years past. . . . Usually a great depression succeeds a great period of inflation. . . . A

---

* Traité d'Économie Politique, vol. iv, pp. 407–408. See, for a fuller statement of his views, Chapter IV, *supra*, pp. 124–125.

† Bankers' Magazine, London, vol. xxxviii, p. 316.

‡ Princeton Review, vol. lv, pp. 211 *et seq.* # Ibid., p. 219.

fall of prices, as already stated, is a usual feature in every depressed period, and accentuates and very largely creates the depression." *

2. " It is clearly unnecessary to assign any other cause for the gloom of the last year or two. Given a fall of prices like what is here described, arising from any external cause whatever, depression must ensue." †

3. " The question of low prices themselves, their origin and probable continuance, and the various consequences that may ensue, thus becomes in turn, in my opinion, the question of most interest arising out of the present depression." ‡

Martin Van Buren

" Our present condition is chiefly to be attributed to an overaction in all departments of business, an overaction deriving, perhaps, its first impulse from antecedent causes, but stimulated to its destructive consequences by excessive issues of bank paper and by other facilities for the acquisition and enlargement of credit." #

Prospective Review
Crisis of 1847

" Two causes: First, the failure of crops; second, a sudden and extensive withdrawal of capital from the ordinary reproductive branches of in-

---

* Contemporary Review, vol. xlvii, p. 806.

† Ibid., p. 808.   ‡ Ibid., p. 809.

Message, Special Session, September 4, 1837, Messages and Papers of the Presidents, vol. iii, p. 325.

dustry, to be embarked in undertakings immediately unproductive, although of greater or less ultimate utility. The inducement has been the expectation of extraordinary profits." *

BANKERS' MAGAZINE, London
Crisis of 1857

" First, American system of granting too long credits; second, too rapid extension of our banking system, arising out of gold discoveries in California; third, undue development of our railway system; fourth, war in Europe, diverting European capital to the Black Sea; fifth, frauds and peculations which, by shattering confidence, have precipitated the contraction of credits." †

ALBERT GALLATIN AND OTHERS, REPRESENTING BANKS OF NEW YORK CITY
Crisis of 1837 in the United States

" The immediate causes which thus compelled the banks of the city of New York to suspend specie payments on the 10th of May last are well known. The simultaneous withdrawing of the large public deposits and of excessive foreign credits, combined with the great and unexpected fall in the price of the principal article of our exports, with an import of corn and breadstuffs such as had never before occurred, and with the consequent inability of the country, particularly of the Southwestern States, to

---

* Vol. iv, p. 152.   † Vol. xv, p. 288.

make the usual and expected remittances, did at one and the same time fall principally and necessarily on the greatest commercial emporium of the Union." *

Matthew Marshall

" A more complete and philosophical solution of the problem is found, it seems to me, in the constitution of human nature itself, which bears with impatience the dulness of a monotonous level, and rapidly passes from one extreme to another. Enthusiasm and despondency are equally epidemic. When prices are rising and profits, even when only on paper, roll up rapidly, everybody is eager to buy. But when, after this eagerness has evaporated and suspicion succeeds to confidence, the current turns the other way, everybody desires to sell, prices fall, and, until the remembrance of the losses thus incurred is obliterated by time, nobody is willing to make fresh ventures." †

N. C. Frederiksen

" It is not the policy of the leading banks which provokes the crises. Issues of notes and other acts of the banks can aggravate or alleviate them. . . . They have taken place under all kinds of banking policy.

" Nor is it simply the character of the harvests. Good crops have helped to improve the times, and bad harvests have accelerated the eruptions. . . .

---

* Report of December 15, 1837. See Bankers' Magazine, New York, vol. xiv, pp. 781–782.

† Engineering Magazine, vol. v, p. 415.

" It is not worth while to dwell here upon the impossibility of general over-production. There is only a question of wrong production in certain branches. . . . It is hardly correct to say that credit is the cause, although crises could not have their present form without it. . . .

" The final cause of the movements is not even destruction and new formation of capital and credit, as Clément Juglar has it. . . .

" There cannot be any other reason for the whole phenomenon of ups and downs than the 'particularity' of the human mind, the waves in human appreciation. Men move together, and many are too apt to act together, to follow in the same waves of mood. . . . But it is not only, as specially developed by Mr. Mills, in the appreciation that gives or retrenches credit, that human mood appears so different and changing in periods. It is also in the appreciation which increases or decreases production and prices. All values are moved by demand and offer, and both depend, to a very great extent, on the human will." *

JAMES WILSON

1. " We are now more than ever convinced, both by principle and by facts, that the fluctuating character of the cost of the first and imperative necessities of life is the chief cause of the whole derangement of the monetarial and commercial interests of this great country, which have been

---

* Bankers' Magazine, London, vol. liii, pp. 195–197.

attended with so much *distress, disappointment, and ruin*." *

2. " It is not to high prices or to low prices that we attribute the evils complained of, but to a constant and incessant changeableness, to periodical fluctuations, to a series of years of great cheapness, followed by years of very high prices." †

JAMES A. LAWSON

" The cause is to be attributed to a sudden check given to an extensive and long-continued trading upon credit." ‡

BANKERS' MAGAZINE, London

" It is a question whether these periodically recurring difficulties are not the natural and inevitable results of causes which no human power of penetration can foresee and no amount of sagacity prevent. . . . In considering recent panics, we should examine whether there was not during and immediately preceding each of those years a large absorption of capital on objects either wholly unproductive, as war or famine, or not immediately productive, as railways and other kindred speculations." #

H. T. EASTON

" In times of prosperity credit is abused, and by this means the trader incurs liabilities which he is

---

* Fluctuations of Currency, Commerce, and Manufactures, 1840, Introduction, p. iv.   † Ibid., p. 17.

‡ Bankers' Magazine, London, vol. viii, p. 417.

Vol. xviii, p. 5.

unable to meet. This leads to a crisis, and then it is found that capital, not income, has been spent. Capital is sunk in all kinds of undertakings, and cannot be reproduced for many years. In the various crises some of the banks had lent money upon mills, railways, docks, mines, and machinery, instead of upon bills representing trade transactions." *

Charles A. Conant

" The salient feature of nearly every crisis has been the sinking of capital in unproductive enterprises. These enterprises have usually been in new fields, whose limitations have not been accurately measured by investors, or even by capitalists of presumed judgment and experience. The opening of such a field has been followed by a rush in that direction which has quickly exhausted all its possibilities, and resulted in overproduction and the loss of the capital invested. New discoveries and the opening of new continents have contributed greatly to these mistakes during the modern commercial age." †

Henry C. Carey

1. " The tendency towards crises is always in the direct ratio of the distance of consumers from producers." ‡

2. " We have had three periods of protection, closing in 1817, 1834, and 1847, each and all of them leaving the country in a state of the highest pros-

---

* Banks and Banking, 1896, p. 97.

† History of Modern Banks of Issue, p. 461.

‡ Financial Crises, their Causes and Effects, 1864, p. 5.

perity. . . . We have had three periods of that system which looks to the destruction of domestic commerce, and is called free trade. . . . Each and all of them having led to crises such as you have so well described—to wit, in 1822, 1842, and 1857. In each and every case they have left the country in a state of paralysis similar to that which now exists." *

3. " The necessity for the contraction of debt exists throughout the world in the ratio of the adoption of the free-trade system. The greater the necessity for the contraction of debt, the greater is the liability to the recurrence of commercial crises." †

ALEXANDER BARING, LORD ASHBURTON

" But this is in fact only the return of an exactly similar calamity which we suffered under in 1825, and from the same immediate cause—the sudden transition, then, through the mistaken operations of the bank, but now through the operations of the law, from a period of great abundance by bank accommodation to another of severe dearth and restriction." ‡

ROBERT BAXTER

" A provision should be made for such a contingency as a panic, so that, when hoarding interrupts the necessary flow of currency, a new stream

---

* Financial Crises, their Causes and Effects, 1864, p. 8.

† Ibid., p. 14.

‡ The Financial and Commercial Crises Considered, p. 7.

may, under proper safeguard, be created, and the course of business sustained." *

CHARLES COQUELIN

" It is, then, not true that the source of disorder is to be found in the multiplicity of banks. On the contrary, they act as a check to it. And, in fact, where have commercial crises always commenced? In London and in Paris, the localities of banks armed with exclusive privileges. These are their usual seats. There they incubated and thence extended their ravages far and wide." †

J. W. GILBART

" Although it be true that each monetary crisis is in large part produced by a distinct proximate cause, yet the primary cause of each and all is inordinate speculation, begotten of the lust of gold. . . . Men live as they journey at a railroad pace. . . . Covetousness, a maddening desire to bound at once, say from competence to riches, hurries the flies into the meshes cunningly woven for them, and the weak become the victims." ‡

EDWARD EVERETT
Crisis of 1857

" If I mistake not, the distress of the year 1857 was produced by an enemy more formidable than

---

hostile armies; by a pestilence more deadly than fever or plague; by a visitation more destructive than the frosts of Spring or the blights of Summer. I believe that it was caused by a mountain load of *Debt*. The whole country, individuals and communities, trading houses, corporations, towns, cities, States, were labouring under a weight of debt beneath which the ordinary business relations of the country were, at length, arrested, and the great instrument usually employed for carrying them on, *Credit*, broken down." *

ALFRED RUSSELL WALLACE

" Depression of trade may be succinctly defined as a wide-spread diminution in the demand for our chief manufactures, both at home and abroad." †

M. CLEMENT JUGLAR

" Crises are stated to be a natural reaction which is produced after efforts for increased production, still further increased when it is already pushed to excess." ‡

D. W. THOM

" Panics may be broadly stated as due to over-trade, which causes general business to need more than the available capital. This produces general lack of credit. There are, first, panics of circulation,

---

* The Mount Vernon Papers, p. 167.

† Bad Times, 1885, p. 13.

‡ Article on Crises Commerciales in Block's Dictionnaire Général de la Politique, vol. i, p. 588.

as in 1857, when the steadily increasing circulation doubled in nine years. Or the converse case, a sudden and proportionate shrinkage of circulation, which would cut down loans and discounts. Second, a panic of credit, as in 1866, rendering the business world overcautious. Third, a panic of capital, as in 1847, when capital was so locked up in internal improvements as to prove largely useless. Fourth, general tariff changes or changes in legislation.

" Good or bad condition of agriculture is a retarding or precipitating influence." *

M. MAURICE BLOCK

" The fact that we desire to bring to light, and from which we draw the principal consequences, is the rupture of the equilibrium between agriculture and industry." †

EDWIN GOADBY

" Every shifting is attended with a dislocation of labour, until a more stable condition is attained. A new invention of any magnitude, chemical or mechanical, involving a new industry, or the modification of an old one, means unsettlement." ‡

WILLIAM WATT

" The sum and substance of the depression of trade may be expressed by saying that the produc-

---

* A Brief History of Panics, pp. 2–6.

† Revue des Deux Mondes, mars–avril, 1879, p. 452.

‡ Prize Essay, 1885, p. 33.

tion of great classes of commodities has outstripped the cash demand for those commodities." *

J. B. Howe

" We may finish the summing up by adding that the principal loss, stated in the fewest possible words, consists in the blind misdirection of energy, enterprise, labour, and capital." †

---

* Prize Essay, p. 69.

† Political Economy and the Use of Money, 1878, p. 74.

APPENDIX B

STATISTICS

Employment Statistics, United Kingdom.
Percentage employed *

	1855.	1856.	1857.	1858.	1859.	1860.
Iron Founders	90.0	91.2	90.9	84.0	95.0	97.2
Amalgamated Engineers	96.5	96.8	96.3	90.2	96.6	98.5

All Trade Unions making Returns†

Year.	Percentage employed.	Year.	Percentage employed.	Per cent as given in the Statistical Abstract, Labour Department.
1860	98.39	1881	96.55	....
1861	95.72	1882	98.08	....
1862	92.19	1883	97.77	....
1863	94.26	1884	92 60	....
1864	97.44	1885	91.02	....
1865	97.99	1886	90.45	....
1866	96.90	1887	92.58	91.8
1867	92.66	1888	95.45	95.1
1868	91.49	1889	97.95	97.9
1869	92.58	1890	98.10	97.9
1870	95.68	1891	96.96	96.5
1871	98.19	1892	.....	93.7
1872	98.94	1893	.....	92.5
1873	98.74	1894	.....	93.1
1874	98.24	1895	.....	94.2
1875	97.51	1896	.....	96.6
1876	96.44	1897	.....	96.5
1877	95.56	1898	.....	97.0
1878	93.69	1899	.....	97.6
1879	87.50	1900	.....	97.1
1880	94.07			

* Statistical Tables and Report on Trade Unions, Fifth Report, for 1891, published in 1893, p. 80.

† Table III in article by George H. Wood, Journal of Royal Statistical Society for 1899, pp. 645–646; and figures as given

Statistics, United States. Percentage employed in Massachusetts*

1889.	1890.	1891.	1892.	1893.
98.56	97.70	99.09	98.35	91.49

The following employment statistics for the States of New York, Pennsylvania, Massachusetts, and Wisconsin give figures on different bases, showing increase or decrease in the number employed from year to year:

NEW YORK. 66 identical establishments. (From Report of New York State Labor Bureau.)			PENNSYLVANIA. 354 identical establishments. (From Annual Report of Secretary of Internal Affairs of Pennsylvania.)		
Year ending	Persons employed.	Percentage of increase.	Year.	Persons employed.	Percentage of increase.
May 31, 1891..	18,171	....	....	....	.....
" 31, 1892..	19,395	6.7	1892..	136,882	.....
" 31, 1893..	20,263	4.5	1893..	122,278	a 10.67
" 31, 1894..	15,112	a 25.4	1894..	109,383	a 10.55
" 31, 1895..	17,233	14.3	1895..	127,361	16.44
June 30, 1896..	18,999	10.2	1896..	118,092	a 7.28
" 30, 1897..	17,615	a 7.3	1897..	121,281	2.70
" 30, 1898..	20,797	18.1	1898..	137,985	13.69
" 30, 1899..	25,035	20.4	1899..	154,422	11.99

a Decrease.

The above figures were furnished by the Bureau of Labor, through Mr. Carroll D. Wright.

by the Statistical Abstract of the Labour Department, Seventh Annual Abstract of Labour Statistics, 1901, p. 76.

* Twenty-fourth Annual Report of Labor Statistics, for 1893, State of Massachusetts, issued March, 1894, pp. 128–129.

Years compared.	Number of identical establishments.	Increase in persons employed.		Year.	Establishments reporting.	Persons employed.
		Number	Per cent			
1888–1889..	1,364	1,771	0.89	1888..	1,135	71,218
1889–1890..	3,041	7,112	2.70	1889..	1,272	80,504
1890–1891..	3,745	4,966	1.72	1890..	1,364	80,880
1891–1892..	4,473	13,515	4.53	1891..	1,336	94,089
1892–1893..	4,397	a 13,034	a 4.26	1892..	1,331	90,936
1893–1894..	4,093	a 17,470	a 6.22	1893..	1,610	96,540
1894–1895..	3,629	22,861	9.02	1894..	1,460	83,642
1895–1896..	4,609	a 9,044	a 2.94	1895..	1,368	85,767
1896–1897..	4,695	8,324	2.72	1896..	1,499	80,051
1897–1898..	4,701	5,891	1.80	1897..	1,499	87,534
1898–1899..	4,740	22,936	10.60	1898..	1,499	96,248
				1898..	b 992	67,514
				1899..	b 992	75,859

Massachusetts. (Compiled from Annual Statistics of Manufactures of Massachusetts.) *Wisconsin.* (Compiled from Biennial Reports of the Bureau of Labor and Industrial Statistics of Wisconsin.)

a Decrease.   *b* Identical establishments.

These figures also were furnished by the Bureau of Labor, through Mr. Carroll D. Wright.

NOTE.—It will be noticed that the lack of uniformity renders comparison difficult, but several things are clearly apparent, namely, the falling off in employment in 1893 and 1894, followed by a temporary rise in 1895, which was again lost in 1896; and, most notable of all, the great increase in the number employed in the years 1898 and 1899.

Foreign Trade.—Total of exports and imports per capita for the United States, United Kingdom, France, and Belgium from 1868 to 1900 inclusive, and for the German Empire from 1880 to 1900 inclusive, is given on the following page:

Year.	United States. Year ending June 30th.	Great Britain and Ireland.			France.	Belgium.	Germany.
	dollars	£	s.	d.	francs	francs	marks
1868......	16.62	17	1	3	159	307	...
1869......	17.74	17	4	6	169	318	...
1870......	20.83	17	10	10	153	317	...
1871......	23.48	19	10	1	176	424	...
1872......	24.35	21	0	6	203	450	...
1873......	28.03	21	4	9	202	491	...
1874......	26.57	20	11	10	198	451	...
1875......	23.33	20	0	4	202	446	...
1876......	21.93	19	1	11	205	471	...
1877......	22.21	19	6	9	192	463	...
1878......	23.51	18	3	6	198	472	...
1879......	23.28	17	18	3	209	491	...
1880......	28.94	20	4	10	227	525	127
1881......	29.91	19	17	5	224	525	131
1882......	27.61	20	7	10	223	501	138
1883......	28.03	20	13	2	218	506	142
1884......	25.36	19	4	1	199	478	140
1885......	23.26	17	16	9	188	435	124
1886......	22.49	17	0	10	195	426	125
1887......	23.63	17	11	8	190	447	131
1888......	23.28	18	12	2	192	461	135
1889......	24.02	19	19	10	209	494	147
1890......	25.85	19	19	7	211	512	152
1891......	27.04	19	14	0	217	541	147
1892......	28.11	18	15	6	199	469	139
1893......	25.71	17	14	10	185	468	139
1894......	22.26	17	11	10	180	454	134
1895......	22.12	17	19	3	184	478	143
1896......	23.10	18	14	1	187	500	149
1897......	25.44	18	14	3	199	531	155
1898......	24.64	19	0	6	206	575	165
1899......	25.42	20	1	8	223	623	175
1900......	28.84	21	9	0	218	605	185

(See diagram, opposite page 145.)

NOTE.—It will be observed that of the countries for which statistics are given three reached a maximum of foreign trade in the year 1873. Prior to that year there had been a rapid increase; afterward there was a marked decline. The year 1880 showed in all a very great increase over the preceding year, and foreign trade was maintained at high figures for the four years from 1880 to 1883, inclusive. In the ensuing decline a minimum was reached in the years 1885 and 1886. In the following period the maximum was reached in Great Britain in 1889 and 1890; in Germany in 1890, in France and Belgium in 1891, and in the United States in 1892. In each of the European countries the ensuing decline reached its lowest point in 1894, after which year there was a steady increase in all of them until and including 1899, when France and Belgium reached another maximum. It is evident that the last depression in the United States, and also permanent improvement, did not begin until later than in Europe.

The figures for the United Kingdom are based upon the total of all exports and imports—general exports and imports, so called; those for the other countries upon the total of special exports and imports. By special exports are meant those of domestic production; by special imports, those retained for domestic consumption. The figures given for the first two countries are obtained from official computations; those for the last three were prepared by Mr. Gustavus A. Weber, of the Bureau of Labor at Washington. While general trade and special trade show substantially the same results, special trade is made the basis of the figures given, except those for the United Kingdom, in which the official computations used are based upon general trade. The figures for 1899 and 1900 in France and Belgium are subject to revision.

Exports and Imports of the United States to and from the United Kingdom, France, and Germany, for the Calendar Years 1896, 1897, 1898, and 1899. A Comparison of their Home and Foreign Valuations (French and German valuations for 1898 and 1899 are unofficial)

EXPORTS FROM THE UNITED STATES TO—

	The United Kingdom.	France.	Germany.
1896			
Foreign valuation..........	106,347,349£	313,747,000 fr.	528,304,000 marks
" " in dollars	516,846,116	60,553,171	125,736,352
Home valuation "	473,223,899	53,343,571	113,145,073
Excess of foreign valuation	43,622,217	7,209,600	12,591,279
" " "	9.2 %	13.5 %	11.1 %
1897			
Foreign valuation..........	113,041,627£	437,540,000 fr.	652,108,000 marks
" " in dollars	549,382,307	84,445,220	155,201,704
Home valuation "	482,695,024	73,665,199	136,277,886
Excess of foreign valuation	66,687,283	10,780,021	18,923,818
" " "	13.8 %	14.6 %	13.8 %
1898			
Foreign valuation..........	126,062,155£	623,000,000 fr.	876,100,000 marks
" " in dollars	612,662,073	120,239,000	208,511,800
Home valuation "	538,758,027	80,154,266	163,776,623
Excess of foreign valuation	73,904,046	40,084,734	44,735,177
" " "	13.7 %	49.9 %	27.3 %
1899			
Foreign valuation..........	120,081,188£	400,000,000 fr.	893,800,000 marks
" " in dollars	583,594,673	77,200,000	212,724,400
Home valuation "	509,926,635	70,107,127	161,405,852
Excess of foreign valuation	73,668,038	7,092,873	51,318,548
" " "	14.4 %	10.1 %	31.7 %
Totals for four years.			
Foreign valuation in dollars	2,262,485,169	342,437,391	702,174,256
Home valuation "	2,004,603,585	277,270,163	574,605,434
Excess of foreign valuation	257,881,584	65,167,228	127,568,822
" " "	12.8 %	23.5 %	22.2 %

IMPORTS INTO THE UNITED STATES FROM—

	The United Kingdom.	France.	Germany.
1896			
Foreign valuation..........	32,035,784£	224,715,000 fr.	383,250,000 marks
" " in dollars	155,693,910	43,369,995	91,213,500
Home valuation "	134,440,228	55,694,541	93,749,168
Excess of foreign valuation	21,253,682	....	....
" " "	15.8 %	....	....
Excess of home valuation..	....	12,324,546	2,535,668
" " " ..	....	28.4 %	2.7 %
1897			
Foreign valuation..........	37,933,017£	242,162,000 fr.	397,394,000 marks
" " in dollars	184,358,836	46,737,266	94,579,772
Home valuation "	159,002,286	66,730,631	98,062,278
Excess of foreign valuation	25,356,550	....	....
" " "	15.9 %	....	....
Excess of home valuation..	....	19,993,365	3,482.506
" " "	....	42.7 %	3.6 %
1898			
Foreign valuation..........	28,534,477£	210,000,000 fr.	322,900,000 marks
" " in dollars	138,679,558	40,503,000	76,850,200
Home valuation "	111,208,803	55,719,002	77,679,471
Excess of foreign valuation	27,470,755	....	....
" " "	24.7 %	....	....
Excess of home valuation..	....	15,216,002	829,271
" " " ..	....	37.5 %	1.0 %
1899			
Foreign valuation..........	34,975,472£	236,000,000 fr.	377,500,000 marks
" " in dollars	169,980,793	45,548,000	89,845,000
Home valuation "	142,327,207	70,404,908	89,579,339
Excess of foreign valuation	27,653,586	....	265,661
" " "	19.4 %	....	0.2 %
Excess of home valuation..	....	24,856,908	....
" " " ..	....	54.5 %	....
Totals for four years.			
Foreign valuation in dollars	648,713,097	176,158,261	352,488,472
Home valuation "	546,978,524	248,549,089	359,070,256
Excess of foreign valuation	101,734.573	....	....
" " "	13.6 %	....	....
Excess of home valuation..	....	72,390,821	6,581.784
" " " ..	....	41.0 %	1.8 %

AGGREGATES—THREE COUNTRIES FOR FOUR YEARS

	Exports.	Imports.
Foreign valuation in dollars........	3,307,096,816	1,177,359,830
Home valuation "	2,856,479,182	1,154.597,862
Excess of foreign valuation........	450,617,634	22,761,968
" " "	15.7 %	1.9 %

Statistics pertaining to Internal Revenue Taxes

Years.*	UNITED STATES.			UNITED KINGDOM.	
	Collected per capita in dollars.	Thousands of bbls. fermented liquors upon which taxes were paid.	Decreases or notable increases.	Total annual value of property and profits assessed to the income tax.	Decreases or notable increases.
1868....	5.17	6,146	....	£430,368,971	....
1869....	4.19	6,342	....	434,803,957	....
1870....	4.79	6,574	....	444,914,228	....
1871....	3.62	7,740	....	465,594,366	+20,680,138
1872....	3.22	8,659	....	482,338,317	....
1873....	2.75	9,633	....	513,807,284	+31,468,967
1874....	2.39	9,600	−33	543,025,761	+29,218,477
1875....	2.52	9,452	−148	571,056,167	+28,030,406
1876....	2.59	9,902	....	579,297,347	....
1877....	2.56	9,810	−92	570,331,389	−8,965,958
1878....	2.32	10,241	....	578,294,971	....
1879....	2.32	11,103	....	578,046,297	−248,674
1880....	2.47	13,347	+2,244	576,896,901	−1,149,396
1881....	2.64	14,311	....	585,223.890	....
1882....	2.79	16,952	+2,641	601,450.977	....
1883....	2.69	17,757	....	612,836,058	....
1884....	2.21	18,998	....	628,510,199	....
1885....	2.00	19,185	....	631,467,132	....
1886....	2.03	20,710	....	629,855.622	−1,611,510
1887....	2.02	23,121	+2,411	629,397,962	−457,660
1888....	2.07	24,680	....	636,154,693	....
1889....	2.13	25,119	....	645,158.689	....
1890....	2.28	27,561	+2,442	669,358,613	+24,199,924
1891....	2.28	30,478	+2,917	698,407,549	+29,048,936
1892....	2.36	31,817	....	710,752,684	....
1893....	2.43	34,554	+2,737	712,277,117	....
1894....	2.17	33,334	−1,220	706,130,875	−6,146,242
1895....	2.08	33,561	....	690,251,675	−15,879,200
1896....	2.09	35,826	+2,265	709,651,556	....
1897....	2.05	34,423	−1,403	700,447,064	−9,204,492
1898....	2.34	37,493	+3,070	729,328,295	+28,881,231
1899....	3.68	36,581	−912	758,571,709	+29,243,414
1900....	3.89	39,330	+2,749	788,023,603	+29,451,894

* In the United States fiscal years ending June 30th, are intended.   In the United Kingdom the assessment for the income tax is made for the year ending April 5th.

Bank Clearances

UNITED STATES. New York Clearing-House. (In millions of dollars.)			ENGLAND. London Bankers' Clearing-House. (Millions of pounds.)		Values (approx.) of shares sold on N. Y. Stock Exchange. (Millions of dollars.)	
		Decreases or notable increases.		Decreases or notable increases.		Decreases or notable increases.
1854....	5,750					
1855....	5,362	−388	......		......	......
1856....	6,906	....	......	....	......	......
1857....	8,333	....	......	....	......	......
1858....	4,756	−3,577	......	....	......	......
1859....	6,448	+1,692	......	....	......	......
1860....	7,231	....	......	....	......	......
1861....	5,915	−1,316	......	....	......	......
1862....	6,871	....	......	....	......	......
1863....	14,867	+7,996	......	....	......	......
1864....	24,097	+9,230	......	....	......	......
1865....	26,032	....	......	....	......	......
1866....	28,717	....	......	....	......	......
1867....	28,675	−42	......	....	......	......
1868....	28,484	−191	3,466	....	......	......
1869....	37,407	+8,923	3,602	....	......	......
1870....	27,804	−9,603	3,905	....	......	......
1871....	29,300	....	4,787	+882	......	......
1872....	33,844	....	5,893	+1,106	......	......
1873....	35,461	....	6,182	....	......	......
1874....	22,855	−12,606	5,916	−266	......	......
1875....	25,061	....	5,647	−269	......	......
1876....	21,597	−3,464	4,959	−688	......	......
1877....	23,289	....	5,018	....	......	......
1878....	22,508	−781	5,007	−11	......	......
1879....	25,178	....	4,959	−48	......	......
1880....	37,182	+12,004	5,718	+759	......	......
1881....	48,565	+11,383	6,357	....	8,197	....
1882....	46,552	−2,013	6,221	−136	7,689	−508
1883....	40,293	−6,259	5,929	−306	6,260	−1,429
1884....	34,092	−6,201	5,799	−130	5,939	−321
1885....	25,250	−8,842	5,511	−288	5,479	−460
1886....	33,374	+8,124	5,902	....	5,885	....
1887....	34,872	....	6,077	....	4,508	−1,377
1888....	30,863	−4,009	6,942	+865	3,539	−969
1889....	34,796	....	7,619	....	4,059	+520
1890....	37,660	....	7,801	....	3,977	−82
1891....	34,053	−3,607	6,848	−953	3,812	−165
1892....	36,279	....	6,482	−366	4,874	+1,062
1893....	34,421	−1,858	6,478	−4	4,550	−324
1894....	24,230	−10,191	6,337	−141	3,094	−1,456
1895....	28,264	....	7,593	+1,256	3,808	+714
1896....	29,350	....	7,575	−18	3,329	−479
1897....	31,337	....	7,491	−84	4,973	+1,644
1898....	39,853	+8,516	8,097	+606	8,187	+3,214
1899....	57,368	+17,515	9,150	+1,053	13,429	+5,242
1900....	51,964	−5,404	8,960	−190	9,249	−4,180

The following Tables show the Relative Number of Maximum and Minimum Prices reached by Certain Selected Stocks in Each Month for a Series of Years

Maxima.	1868	1869	1870	1871	1872	1873	1874	1875	1876	1877	1878	1879	1880	1881	1882	1883	1884	1885	1886	1887	1888	1889	1890	1891	1892	1893	1894	1895	1896	1897	1898	1899	1900	Totals.
January	1	3				2	3	3	3	3	1		1	6	3	4	3				2	2	1		5	8			1	1	1	3	1	61
February			1		2	6	5	1	4				1	2	1		6					1		1	3	3			2		2	1		42
March	1			1	2	1	2	1	2	1	1		2	1	1	1	4								3		6					2		32
April			1	3	4			2		3	1					5	1							2		1	2		1			1		26
May	1	4	1	2	1	1		1		2	1					1	1						7	1	1			2	1					28
June	2	2	5	2	1	1	1	2				1		1		3	1			7			11											40
July		1	2						1		4			1						1			1					2						13
August									1						4			1	1		1						1	1	1	1	1	1		14
September		1		3				1			1				3				1		4	6		3			2	3		10		2		40
October			1			1				5		2	1	1	1						4	1				1	2	2			1	11	2	36
November						1	1	1	1		2	8	3		1	1		9	4		1	2					1	1	6		1	2	1	47
December	2				1	1		1		2	2	2	6					2	7	1		2	1	7			1	2	2	2	9	12	1	66

	January	February	March	April	May	June	July	August	September	October	November	December
Totals.	89	25	35	37	25	26	27	22	22	31	36	60
1900	4	.	1	.	1	2	.	.	6	.	.	.
1899	7	.	2	1	.	1	.	.	.	.	.	4
1898	3	1	5	2	.	.	.	.	.	2	2	.
1897	3	2	.	7	3	.	.	.	.	.	.	.
1896	3	.	.	.	1	.	1	10	.	.	.	.
1895	2	2	5	.	.	.	.	.	.	.	.	6
1894	3	.	.	.	1	1	3	1	.	1	.	5
1893	.	.	.	.	.	.	9	3	1	.	.	1
1892	6	.	.	.	.	.	.	.	3	.	1	4
1891	.	.	2	.	.	3	4	3	.	.	1	.
1890	1	.	.	.	.	.	.	.	.	.	6	6
1889	2	.	6	1	.	.	3	.	.	.	.	3
1888	1	.	1	9	.	.	.	.	.	.	.	2
1887	1	2	.	.	.	.	.	.	.	11	.	.
1886	4	1	1	.	8	.	.	.	.	.	.	.
1885	7	.	2	.	3	2	.	.	.	.	.	.
1884	.	.	.	.	.	7	1	.	1	.	3	4
1883	2	2	.	.	.	.	.	2	.	4	.	4
1882	1	1	2	2	1	1	.	.	.	.	4	1
1881	3	5	1	.	.	.	.	.	.	.	.	4
1880	1	1	.	.	5	3	2	.	.	.	.	1
1879	7	1	2	.	.	.	.	1	.	.	2	.
1878	3	3	1	.	.	1	1	1	.	1	.	1
1877	1	.	2	6	.	2	.	.	.	.	.	.
1876	1	.	.	.	.	.	.	.	5	1	2	3
1875	3	1	.	1	1	1	.	.	1	3	.	.
1874	4	.	.	.	1	2	1	.	1	.	.	1
1873	.	.	.	.	.	.	.	.	.	2	8	1
1872	4	2	.	.	.	.	.	1	.	1	3	2
1871	4	1	1	1	.	.	.	.	.	4	1	.
1870	4	.	.	1	.	.	2	.	.	1	.	3
1869	.	.	1	3	.	.	.	.	4	.	2	2
1868	4	.	.	3	.	.	.	.	.	.	1	2

Minima.

Production and Consumption of Pig-iron
In thousands of tons.

Years.	UNITED STATES. Tons of 2240 lbs.		UNITED KINGDOM Tons of 2240 lbs.		GERMANY. Metric tons of 2204 lbs.		World's production.
	Production.	Consumption.	Production.	Consumption.	Production.	Consumption.	
1868....	1,431	1,416	4,970	4,438	1,264	1,299	10,400
1869....	1,711	1,567	5,445	4,754	1,413	1,501	11,575
1870....	1,665	1,863	5,963	5,245	1,391	1,510	11,900
1871....	1,706	1,925	6,627	5,625	1,564	1,892	12,500
1872....	2,548	2,810	6,741	5,509	1,988	2,501	13,925
1873...	2,560	2,690	6,566	5,498	2,241	2,830	14,675
1874....	2,401	2,500	5,991	5.271	1,906	2,234	13,500
1875....	2,023	2,000	6,365	5,464	2,029	2,316	13,675
1876....	1,868	1,900	6,555	5,677	1,846	2,123	13,475
1877....	2,066	2,150	6,608	5,770	1,933	2,094	13,675
1878....	2,301	2,500	6,381	5,484	2,148	2,202	14,118
1879....	2,741	3,432	5,995	4,795	2,227	2,171	13,950
1880....	3,835	3,990	7,749	6,175	2,729	2,663	17,950
1881....	4,144	4,982	8,144	6,710	2,914	2,835	19,400
1882....	4,623	4,963	8,586	6,867	3,381	3.409	20,750
1883....	4,595	4,834	8,529	7,001	3,470	3,418	21,000
1884....	4,097	4,229	7,811	6,578	3,601	3,584	19,475
1885....	4,044	4,348	7,415	6,492	3,687	3,646	19,100
1886....	5,683	6,191	7,009	6,008	3,529	3,382	20,386
1887....	6,417	6,808	7,559	6,439	4,024	3,900	22,171
1888....	6,489	6,674	7,998	6,996	4,337	4,373	23,575
1889 ...	7,603	7,755	8,322	7,200	4,525	4,674	25,345
1890....	9,202	8,943	7,904	6,818	4.658	4,897	27,157
1891....	8,279	8,366	7,406	6,626	4,641	4,711	25,718
1892....	9,157	9,303	6,709	5,994	4,937	4,966	26,474
1893....	7,124	6,982	6,976	6,168	4,986	5,032	24,813
1894....	6,657	6,694	7,427	6,655	5,380	5,350	25,600
1895....	9,446	9,628	7,703	6,925	5,464	5,434	28.871
1896....	8,623	8,275	8,659	7,705	6,373	6,507	30,500
1897....	9,652	9,381	8,796	7,749	6,881	7,202	32,937
1898....	11,773	12,005	8,609	7,723	7,313	7,436	35,655
1899....	13,620	13,779	9,421	8,208	8,143	8,571	39,410
1900....	13,789	13,177	8,959	......	8,494	.....	*40,000

* Estimate of London Economist.

The figures for production and consumption in the United States, and the world's production, except for the year 1900, are given by Mr. James M. Swank in the various publications of

Average Prices by Years of Iron and Steel in the United States

(Prices are given for gross tons unless otherwise specified.)

Years.	Anthracite pig.	Bessemer pig.	Bar iron.	Iron rails.	Steel rails.	Cut nails. Per 100 lbs.	Steel billets.
1868..	$39.25	....	$85.63	$78.87	$158.50	$5.17	.....
1869..	40.62	....	81.66	77.25	132.25	4.87	.....
1870..	33.25	....	78.96	72.25	106.75	4.40	.....
1871..	35.12	....	78.54	70.37	102.50	4.52	.....
1872..	48.87	....	97.63	85.12	112.00	5.46	.....
1873..	42.75	....	86.43	76.66	120.50	4.90	.....
1874..	30.25	....	67.95	58.75	94.25	3.99	.....
1875..	25.50	....	60.85	47.75	68.75	3.42	.....
1876..	22.25	....	52.08	41.25	59.25	2.98	.....
1877..	18.87	....	45.55	35.25	45.50	2.57	.....
1878..	17.62	....	44.24	33.75	42.25	2.31	.....
1879..	21.50	....	51.85	41.25	48.25	2.69	.....
1880..	28.50	....	60.38	49.25	67.50	3.68	.....
1881..	25.12	....	58.05	47.12	61.13	3.09	.....
1882..	25.75	....	61.41	45.50	48.50	3.47	.....
1883..	22.37	....	50.30		37.75	3.06	.....
1884..	19.87	....	44.05	Old iron	30.75	2.39	.....
1885..	18.00	....	40.32	T rails.	28.50	2.33	.....
1886..	18.75	$18.96	43.12	21.42	34.50	2.27	.....
1887..	21.00	21.37	49.37	22.97	37.08	2.30	.....
			Per 100 lbs.			Wire nails.	
1888..	18.88	17.38	2.01	22.23	29.83	2.55	$28.78
1889..	17.75	18.00	1.94	24.19	29.25	2.49	29.45
1890..	18.40	18.85	2.05	25.18	31.75	2.51	30.32
1891..	17.52	15.95	1.90	22.05	29.92	2.05	25.32
1892..	15.75	14.37	1.87	19.48	30.00	1.70	23.63
1893..	14.52	12.87	1.70	16.43	28.12	1.49	20.44
1894..	12.66	11.38	1.34	11.95	24.00	1.11	16.58
1895..	13.10	12.72	1.44	14.09	24.33	1.69	18.48
1896..	12.95	12.14	1.40	14.16	28.00	*2.50	18.83
1897..	12.10	10.13	1.31	12.49	18.75	1.45	15.08
1898..	11.66	10.33	1.28	12.39	17.62	1.45	15.31
1899..	19.36	19.03	2.07	20.36	28.12	2.57	31.12
1900..	19.98	19.49	1.96	19.51	32.29	2.76	25.06

* New classification adopted.

the American Iron and Steel Association.   The figures for the
United Kingdom and Germany, to and including 1899, are
taken from the annual issues of the Statistical Abstract for the
Principal and other Foreign Countries.

Statistics of Capital created and issued, and Nominal Share Capital of Joint-Stock Companies registered, United Kingdom

In thousands of pounds.

Year.	Capital created and issued.	Actual money calls on same.	Nominal capital of joint-stock companies registered.
1870..........	92,250	80,000	38,252
1871..........	109,732	93,993	69,528
1872..........	151,550	113,100	133,141
1873..........	154,700	101,150	152,056
1874..........	114,150	110,550	110,540
1875..........	62,650	60,850	82,447
1876..........	43,200	42,850	48,314
1877..........	51,500	38,600	66,800
1878..........	59,200	50,400	67,860
1879..........	56,470	47,460	75,568
1880..........	122,200	77,600	168,466
1881..........	189,400	115,250	210,711
1882..........	145,550	94,650	254,744
1883..........	81,150	76,900	167,680
1884..........	109,031	90,603	138,481
1885..........	77,972	77,875	119,222
1886..........	101,873	87,476	145,850
1887..........	111,209	93,668	170,172
1888..........	160,255	137,252	353,781
1889..........	207,037	167,804	241,277
1890..........	142,565	141,007	238,759
1891..........	104,595	76,044	134,261
1892..........	81,137	59,262	103,403
1893..........	49,141	41,953	96,654
1894..........	91,835	74,222	118,431
1895..........	104,690	84,500	231,368
1896..........	152,677	84,393	309,532
1897..........	157,299	81,694	291,117
1898..........	150,173	101,201	272,287
1899..........	133,160	....	245,939
1900..........	165,490	....	217,651

Railway Tonnage

	UNITED STATES.			UNITED KINGDOM.	
Years.	Freight carried. Tons.	Decreases or notable increases.	Freight carried. Tons.	Decreases or notable increases.
1871.....	....	....	169,364,698	....
1872.....	....	....	179,302,121	....
1873.....	....	....	190,953,457	+11,651,336
1874.....	....	....	188,538,852	−2,414,605
1875.....	....	....	200,060,651	+11,530,799
1876.....	....	....	205,965,064	....
1877.....	....	....	211,980,495	....
1878.....	....	....	206,735,856	−5,244,639
1879.....	....	....	212,188,155	....
1880.....	....	....	235,305,629	+23,117,474
1881.....	....	....	247,045,000	+11,739,371
1882.....	300,490,375	....	256,215,821	....
1883.....	400,453,439	+39,963,064	266,382,968	+10,167,147
1884.....	399,074,749	−1,378,690	259,327,886	−7,055,082
1885.....	437,040,099	+37,965,350	257,288,454	−2,039,432
1886.....	482,245,254	+45,205,155	254,626,643	−2,661,811
1887.....	552,074,752	+60,829,498	268,926,884	+14,300,241
1888.....	590,857,353	+38,782,601	281,748,439	+12,821,555
1889.....	619,165,630	....	297,506,497	+15,758,058
1890.....	691,344,437	+72,178,807	303,119,427	....
1891.....	704,398,609	....	310,324,607	....
1892.....	730,605,011	....	309,626,378	−698,229
1893.....	757,464,480	....	293,341,247	−16,285,131
1894.....	674,714,747	−82,749,733	324,457,633	+31,116,386
1895.....	755,799,883	+81,085,136	334,230,991	....
1896.....	773,868,716	....	356,468,009	+22,237,018
1897.....	788,385,448	....	374,389,246	+17,921,237
1898.....	912,973,853	+124,588,405	378,564,285	....
1899.....	975,789,941	+62,816,088	413,623,025	+35,058,740
1900.....	1,071,431,919	+95,641,978	424,929,513	....

Failures in the United States, 1857 to 1900, as reported by R. G. Dun & Co.

Years.	Number.	Amount.	Years.	Number.	Amount.
1857....	4,932	$291,750,000	1879....	6,658	$98,149,053
1858....	4,225	95,749,000	1880....	4,735	65,752,000
1859....	3,913	64,394,000	1881....	5,582	81,155,932
1860....	3,676	79,807,000	1882....	6,738	101,547,564
1861....	6,993	207,210,000	1883....	9,184	172,874,172
1862....	1,652	23,049,000	1884....	10,968	226,343,427
1863....	495	7,899,900	1885....	10,637	124,220,321
1864....	520	8,579,000	1886....	9,834	114,644,119
1865....	530	17,625,000	1887....	9,634	167,560,944
1866....	1,505	53,783,000	1888....	10,679	123,829,973
1867....	2,780	96,666,000	1889....	10,882	148,784,337
1868....	2,608	63,694,000	1890....	10,907	189,856,964
1869....	2,799	75,054,054	1891....	12,273	189,868,638
1870....	3,546	88,242,000	1892....	10,344	114,044,167
1871....	2,915	85,252,000	1893....	15,242	346,779,889
1872....	4,069	121,056,000	1894....	13,885	172,992,856
1873....	5,183	228,499,900	1895....	13,197	173,196,060
1874....	5,830	155,239,000	1896....	15,088	226,096,834
1875....	7,740	201,000,000	1897....	13,351	154,332,071
1876....	9,092	191,117,786	1898....	12,186	130,662,899
1877....	8,872	190,669,936	1899....	9,337	90,879,889
1878....	10,478	234,383,132	1900....	10,774	138,495,673

Changes in Amounts of Money in the Treasury and in General Circulation, illustrated by Increases and Decreases

Years.	Increase of amount in Treasury.	Decrease of amount in Treasury.	Increase in circulation.	Decrease in circulation.
Dec., 1878.	....	$19,401,915	$10,258,373	....
Feb., 1879.	$17,100,493	....	....	$7,042,052
May, 1879.	17,696,990	....	....	18,555,364
Feb., 1881.	22,458,006	....	....	18,848,901
Oct., 1882.	19,120,498	....	12,399,474	....
Feb., 1885.	27,450,616	....	....	6,375,838
Sept., 1887.	6,399,136	....	32,353,735	....
Sept., 1890.	....	32,969,841	61,887,372	....
Aug., 1893.	....	20,425,292	69,463,654	....
Oct., 1894.	....	19,630,566	17,054,440	....
Aug., 1895.	19,665,798	....	....	10,950,758
Dec., 1896.	17,353,201	....	3,778,654	....
Oct., 1897.	....	18,474,549	27,892,366	....
July, 1898.	34,980,125	....	....	34,237,405
Aug., 1899.	50,018,321	....	11,013,937	....

These figures show the influence of the Independent or Sub-treasury System.

Approximate Statement of the Wheat Crop of the World and of the United States, and the Cotton Crop of the United States, from 1885 to 1900, inclusive, as estimated by the Department of Agriculture

Years.	United States.	World.	Price, December 1st.	Annual cotton crop of the United States.*
	bushels	bushels	cents	bales
1885.....	357,112,000	2,093,859,000	77.1	5,706,165
1886.....	457,218,000	2,113,951,000	68.7	6,575,691
1887.....	456,329,000	2,266,331,000	68.1	6,505,087
1888.....	415,868,000	2,221,520,000	92.6	7,046,833
1889.....	490,560,000	2,075,027,000	69.8	6,938,290
1890.....	399,262,000	2,172,372,000	83.8	7,311,322
1891.....	611,780,000	2,432,322,000	83.9	8,652,597
1892.....	515,949,000	2,481,805,000	62.4	9,035,379
1893.....	896,131,725	2,559,174,000	53.8	6,700,365
1894.....	460,267,416	2,660,557,000	49.1	7,549,817
1895.....	467,102,947	2,593,312,000	50.9	9,901,251
1896.....	427,684,346	2,506,320,000	72.6	7,157,346
1897.....	530,149,168	2,234,461,000	80.8	8,757,964
1898.....	675,148,705	2,942,439,000	58.2	11,199,994
1899.....	547,303,846	2,768,295,000	58.4	11,274,840
1900.....	522,229,505	2,586,564,000	62.0	9,436,416

* The "annual crop" represents the commercial movement for the years ending August 31st.

Marriages per Thousand of Population

Years.	United Kingdom.	Germany.	France.
1870.............	8.05	...	6.0
1871.............	8.35	...	7.2
1872.............	8.70	10.29	9.8
1873.............	8.80	10.02	8.8
1874.............	8.50	9.53	8.3
1875.............	8.25	9.10	8.2
1876.............	8.75	8.52	7.9
1877.............	7.85	7.98	7.5
1878.............	7.60	7.71	7.5
1879.............	7.20	7.51	7.6
1880.............	7.45	7.48	7.4
1881.............	7.55	7.47	7.5
1882.............	7.75	7.68	7.4
1883.............	7.75	7.70	7.5
1884.............	7.55	7.83	7.6
1885.............	7.25	7.89	7.4
1886.............	7.10	7.9	7.4
1887.............	7.20	7.8	7.2
1888.............	7.20	7.8	7.2
1889.............	7.50	8.0	7.1
1890.............	7.75	8.0	7.3
1891.............	7.80	8.0	7.4
1892.............	7.70	7.9	7.5
1893.............	7.35	7.9	7.5
1894.............	7.55	7.9	7.5
1895.............	7.50	8.0	7.4
1896.............	7.90	8.2	7.5

BIBLIOGRAPHY *

De **alarmklok** op de beurs, of Beursspeculanten gedu-
rende een geldcrisis. Nieuwe uitg. *Amsterdam,
Brouwer, 1870. 8°.*

Allard, A. La crise agricole et manufacturière devant
la Conférence monétaire de Bruxelles. *Bruxelles, Société belge de librairie, 1893. 32 pp.
8°.*

—— La crise agricole; exposé didactique de ses
origines monétaires . . . présentée au Congrès
international d'agriculture de Buda Pesth. [*Bru
xelles, Société belge de librairie, 1896.*] *240
pp. 8°.*

—— La crise: la baisse des prix, la monnaie. 2. éd.
[*Bruxelles, Muquardt*] *1885. 208 pp. 4°.*

—— —— Prolégomènes à la 2. éd. [*Bruxelles, Muquardt*] *1885. 189–208 pp. 4°.*

---

* This list, compiled by Mr. Hugh Williams, Library of
Congress, is confined to books and articles in periodicals which
relate exclusively to the subject.   As no attempt whatever has
been made to include parts of books, such important articles as
Krisen in Conrad's *Handwörterbuch der staatswissenschaften,*
Crises in Say and Chailley's *Nouveau dictionnaire d' économie
politique,* *Crises* in Lalor's *Cyclopædia of Political Science,*
Crises in *Palgrave's Dictionary of Political Economy,* etc.,
have been omitted.   The list is based upon bibliographical aids
in the Library of Congress.

Allard, A. Discours sur la crise agricole et manufacturière, ses causes monétaires et les moyens d'y
remédier. Conférence donnée à la Société centrale d'agriculture de Belgique. *Bruxelles, Muquardt, 1886. 87 pp. 8°*.

—— —— Den nuværende crise i agerbrug og indus-
tri og midlerne til at raade bod paa samme. Et
foredrag afholdt i Société centrale d'agriculture
de Belgique. *Kjobenhavn, Hagerup, 1888. 68
pp. 8°*.

—— Etude sur la crise agricole, commerciale et ou-
vrière, causes monétaires en Angleterre. [*Bruxelles, Muquardt, 1888. 208 pp. 4°*.

—— Graphiques de la crise monétaire et de la baisse
des prix, 1850–1892. *Bruxelles, Berqueman,
1892. 8 pp., 5 tab. 4°*.

—— Die wirthschaftliche krisis. Aus dem französischen. *Berlin, Walther & Apolant, 1885. 47
pp. 8°*.

Armsden, J. Trade depression; or, The cause of
"cutting" and its remedy. *London, Reeves,
1892. 31 pp. 8°*.

Ashton, S. E. Commercial depression; its causes and
remedy. A plea for reciprocity. *London, Simpkin, 1879. 8°*.

Audiffret, L. G. d'. La crise financière de 1848. *Paris,
Amyot, 1848. 8°*.

Baden-Powell, G. Protection and bad times with special reference to the political economy of English
colonization. *London, Trübner, 1879. 376 pp.
8°*.

Baird, H. C. The crisis and the bank-credit system.
[*Philadelphia, 1890*] 13 pp. 8°*.

Bamberger, L. Die geschäftswelt angesichts der geschäftslage in Deutschland. Ein vortrag, gehalten im Kaufmännischen verein zu Mainz am 4.
märz, 1875. *Mainz, Diemer, 1875. 23 pp. 8°*.

Baring, A. (*Lord Ashburton*). The financial and

commercial crisis considered. 3d ed. *London, Murray, 1847. 40 pp. 8°.*

Baring, A. (*Lord Ashburton*). Beleuchtung der jetzigen finanziellen und kommerziellen krisis. Aus dem englischen übersetzt und mit einer einleitung und anmerkungen versehen von V. Nolte. *Stuttgart, Cotta, 1847. 83 pp. 8°.*

Baxter, R. Panic of 1866, with its lessons on the Currency act. *London, Longmans, 1866. 100 pp. 12°.*

Bennison, W. Causes of the present money crisis explained, in answer to the pamphlet of J. H. Palmer, and a remedy pointed out. 2d ed. *London, Wilson, 1837. 8°.*

Bergfalk, P. E. Bidrag till de under de sista hundradc aren inträffade handelskrisers-historia. *Upsala, Edquist, 1859. 139 pp. 8°.* [Reprinted from the Nordisk universitets-tidskrift. v. 5. Running title: Bidrag till handelskrisernas historia.]

Bergmann, E. von. Die wirtschaftskrisen. Geschichte der nationalökonomischen krisentheorien. *Stuttgart, Kohlhammer, 1895. 440 pp. 8°.*

Berliner, A. Die wirthschaftliche krisis, ihre ursachen und ihre entwickelung. *Hannover, Meyer, 1878. 96 pp. 8°.*

Blood, F. Inquiry into the causes of the depression of trade and agriculture. Correspondence between F. Blood and J. Bright. *Birmingham, Guest, 1879. 8 pp. 8°.*

Bona, G. della. Delle crisi economiche: studio. *Torino, Bocca, 1888. 85 pp. 8°.* (Biblioteca di scienze sociali, v. 5.)

Bonnet, V. Questions économiques et financières à propos des crises. *Paris, Guillaumin, 1859. 8°.* (Economistes et publicistes contemporains.)

Briaune. Des crises commerciales, de leurs causes et de leurs remèdes. *Paris, Bouchard-Huzard, 1840. 8°.*

Brief popular account of the financial panics and commercial revulsions in the United States from 1690 to 1857; with a more particular history of the two great revulsions of 1837 and 1857. By members of the New York press. *New York, Haney, 1857. 59 pp. 12°.*

Browning, R. The currency considered with a view to the effectual prevention of panics. New ed. *London, 1869. 8°.*

Busch, J. G. Geschichtliche beurtheilung der grossen handelsverwirrung im jahre 1799. Nebst anmerkungen mit besonderer bezugnahme auf die krisis von 1857 von H. S. Hertz. *Hamburg, Hoffmann & Campe, 1858. 166 pp. 12°.*

Busch, E. Ursprung und wesen der wirtschaftlichen krisis und angabe der mittel zu ihrer beseitigung. *Leipzig, Wigand, 1892. 111 pp. 8°.*

Cabezas, M. La crisis industrial-agrícola-social. *Madrid, Fe, 1898. 24 pp. 4°.*

Callender, W. R. The commercial crisis of 1857, its causes and results; being the substance of a paper read before the Manchester statistical society, with an appendix containing a list of upwards of 260 English failures in 1857–'58. *London, 1858. 44 pp. 8°.*

Carey, H. C. Financial crises, their causes and effects. *Philadelphia, Baird, 1864. 58 pp. 8°.*

Cargill, W. The commercial crisis and the Bank Charter act. *Newcastle-upon-Tyne, 1847. 23 pp. 12°.*

Cayley, E. Corn, trade, wages, and rent; or, Observations on the leading circumstances of the present financial crisis. *London, 1827. 47 pp. 8°.*

Chayter, H. Agricultural and trade depression. *London, Simpkin, 1880. 49 pp. 8°.*

Chevalier, M. Des forces alimentaires des états et des devoirs du gouvernement dans la crise actuelle. *Paris, Revue des deux mondes, 1847. 59 pp. 8°.*

Chitti, L. Des crises financières et de la réforme du système monétaire. *Bruxelles, Meline, 1839. 8°.*

Christians, W. Lohnerhöhung und spekulationsbeschränkung als mittel zur verhütung industrieller crisen. Ein beitrag zur socialen frage. *Berlin, F. Schneider, 1893. 20 pp. 8°.* [Aus: " Der Deutsche oekonomist."]

Clément, A. La crise économique et sociale en France et en Europe. *Paris, Guillaumin, 1886. 95 pp. 8°.*

Considérations sur les crises financières et sur la législation anglaise concernant les banques de circulation. *La Haye, Belinfante, 1858. 8°.*

Costa, A. F. La crisis politico-financiera de la Republica Argentina; carta politica al Presidente Roca. *Montevideo, Tribuna popular, 1885. 47 pp. 16°.*

Crocker, U. H. The cause of hard times. Rev. ed. *Boston, Little, Brown, 1896. 114 pp. 16°.*

—— Excessive saving a cause of commercial distress; being a series of assaults upon accepted principles of political economy. *Boston, Clarke, 1884. 40 pp. 8°.*

—— Over-production and commercial distress. *Boston, 1887. 37 pp. 8°.*

Dean, G. W. The true cause of every American panic, and depression of labour and business, and the remedy therefor, as given by G. W. Dean before the U. S. Congressional committee appointed to ascertain the causes of the depression of labour and business, and on the defects of the present tariff system, as given before the Tariff commissioners. *New York, Trow, 1884. 20 pp. 12°.*

Denis, H. La dépression économique et sociale et l'histoire des prix. *Bruxelles, Imprimerie générale, 1895. 412 pp. 8°. and Atlas, fol.*

Dupin, C. Crisis commerciale de 1839; examinée dans ses causes, son étendue, et les moyens d'y mettre un terme. Discours prononcé au Con-

servatoire des arts et manufactures. *Paris,*
1839. 8°.

Du Puynode, G. Les grandes crises financières de
la France. *Paris, Guillaumin, 1876. 403 pp.*
8°.

[Dutton, G.] The present crisis; or, The currency;
a tract of the times. By Bank Crash, Esq.
[Rochester, N. Y., Darrow] 1857. 25 pp. 8°.

Eadie, J. Panics in the money market and recovery
from their effect: being an inquiry into the practical working of the monetary systems of America
and Europe, past and present, and the phenomena
of speculations, revulsions, and panics. *New*
York, Amerman, 1873. 43 pp. 8°.

Ebstein, G. Etude sur la crise financière de 1882.
Situation présente du marché français, ses origines et ses conséquences, l'épargne et la speculation; mesures à adopter. *Paris, Librairie nou-*
velle, 1882. 50 pp. 8°.

Ehrenberg, R. Das zeitalter der Fugger. Geld-
kapital und creditverkehr im 16. jahrhundert.
Jena, Fischer, 1896. 2 v. 8°.

Evans, D. M. The commercial crisis 1847–'48; being
facts and figures illustrative of the events of that
important period, considered in relation to the
three epochs of the railway mania, the food and
the money panic, and the French revolution. To
which is added an appendix, containing an alpha-
betical list of the English and foreign mercantile
failures with the balance sheets and statements
of the most important houses. 2d ed. *London,*
Letts, 1848. 155, 103 pp. 8°.

—— Facts, failures, and frauds: revelations, financial, mercantile, criminal. *London, Groombridge,*
1859. 727 pp. 12°.

—— The history of the commercial crisis, 1857–58,
and the stock exchange panic of 1859. *London,*
Groombridge, 1859. 212, 247 pp. 8°.

Fowler, W. The crisis of 1866. A financial essay. *London, 1866. 8°*.

Frederiksen, N. C. Are we on the road towards a commercial crisis? [*Baltimore, 1899*] *29 pp. 8°*.

Frewen. The economic crisis. *London, K. Paul, 1888. 194 pp. 12°*.

Gassiot, J. P. Monetary panics and their remedy, with opinions of the highest authorities on the Bank Charter act. 2d ed. *London, 1867. 48 pp. 8°*.

Die **geld-** und creditkrise und die jetzige geschäftslage. Vom verfasser der schrift: " Die börse, die börsenoperationen und tauschungen. *Zürich, 1858. 8°*.

Germanicus. Der zweite Pariser krach. *Leipzig, Grunow, 1883. 75 pp. 8°*.

Geyer, P. Banken und krisen. Eine studie. *Leipzig, Weigel, 1865. 80 pp. 8°*.

Gibbons, J. S. The banks of New York, their dealers, the clearing house and the panic of 1857. *New York, Appleton, 1870. 399 pp. 8°*.

Gilbart, J. W. An inquiry into the causes of the pressure on the money market during the year 1839. *London, Longman, 1840. 8°*.

Glagau, O. Der börsen- und gründungs-schwindel in Berlin. Gesammelte und stark vermehrte artikel der " Gartenlaube " 4. aufl. *Leipzig, Frohberg, 1876. 366 pp. 12°*.

—— Der börsen- und gründungs - schwindel in Deutschland. *Leipzig, Frohberg, 1877. 582 pp. 12°*. [Zweiter theil von " Der börsen- und gründungs-schwindel in Berlin."]

Goadby, E., and Watt, W. The present depression in trade, its causes and remedies. The " Pears prize essays." . . . With an introductory paper by Leone Levi. 10th ed. *London, Chatto, 1885, 29, 99 pp. 8°*.

23

G[ottlieb], F. C. Ueber die gegenwärtige verkehrs-
stockung. Vortrag im Kaufmännischen verein
zu Leipzig am 25. nov. 1867. *Leipzig, 1867. 8°.*

Great Britain. *Parliament.* Depression of trade and
industry. Report of the Royal commission appointed to inquire into the depression of trade
and industry. *London, Eyre & Spottiswoode,
1886. 3 vol. fol.* (Reports from commissioners,
inspectors, and others, 9–11.) [Final report
(minutes of evidence), and Depression of trade
in France appended to 3d report.]

Gross, M. Die amerikanische krisis. Vorträge zum
verständniss der nationalen lage, gehalten im
febr. und märz 1874. *New York, Steiger, 1874.
142 pp. 8°.*

Guthrie, G. Bank monopoly, the cause of commercial
crises. *Edinburgh, Blackwood, 1864. 86 pp. 8°.*
—— Analysis of money and banking, correspondence
with Mr. Gladstone and other tracts. 2d ed.
Edinburgh, Blackwood, 1866. 8°.

Hyndman, H. M. Commercial crises of the nineteenth
century. *London, Sonnenschein, 1892. 174 pp.
12°.* (Social science series.)

Ichenhaeuser, J. Eine börsenkrisis. Ein beitrag zur
geschichte der krisen. *Zittau, P.hl, 1893. 20
pp. 8°.*

Jamieson, G. A. The present agricultural and financial depression; some of its causes, influences,
and effects. *Edinburgh, Blackwood, 1885. 69
pp. 8°.*

Jaques, H. Eine studie über handelskrisen, bank-
krisen und discont. *Wien, 1866. 8°.*

Jones, E. D. Economic crises. *New York, Macmillan,
1900. 251 pp. 12°.* (Citizen's library.) [Se-
lect classified bibliography, pp. 225–45.]

Jones, F. W. Where are we? or, The remedy for depressed trade. *London, Griffith, 1886. 64 pp. 8°.*

Joplin, T. An examination of the report of the Joint

bank stock committee, etc., etc. 3d ed. To which is added an account of the late pressure in the money market, and embarrassment of the Northern and Central Bank of England. *London, Ridgway, 1837. 122 pp. 8°.*

Juglar, C. Les banques de France et d'Angleterre aux époques de prospérité et de crise. *Strasbourg, Berger-Levrault, 1862. 8 pp. 8°.* [Reprinted from the " Bulletin d'histoire et d'archéologie de la province ecclésiastique d'Auch."]

—— Des crises commerciales et monétaires de 1800 à 1857. *Paris, Guillaumin, 1857. 28 pp. 8°.* [Reprinted from the " Journal des économistes."]

—— Des crises commerciales et de leur retour périodique en France, en Angleterre et aux Etats Unis. . . . 2. éd. Mémoire couronné par l'Institut. *Paris, Guillaumin, 1889. 560 pp. 8°.*

—— —— A brief history of panics and their periodical occurrence in the United States. Englished and edited with an introductory essay setting forth the indications of approaching panic by De Courcy W. Thom. *New York, Putnam, 1893. 150 pp. 12°.* (Questions of the day. No. 75.)

—— La liquidation de la crise et la reprise des affaires. *Paris, Chaix, 1886. 20 pp. 8°.*

[Ketchum, H. E.] The coming financial crisis and its causes. [*n. p., 1889*] *16 pp. 8°.*

Kinnear, J. G. The crisis and the currency, with a comparison between the English and Scotch systems of banking. *London, Murray, 1847. 69 pp. 8°.*

Knowles, F. C. " The monetary crisis considered "; defence of the joint-stock banks. *London, 1837. 8°.*

L., R. Etwas über die gegenwärtige geschäftsstille und die mittel zu deren beseitigung. Zeitgemässe betrachtungen von R. L. *Berlin, Puttkammer, 1876. 90 pp. 8°.*

De **laatste** geldkrisissen in de Vereenigde Staten van Noord-Amerika en de Amerikaanschen waarden. *'s Hage, Couvée, 1871. 8°.*

Lacerda, J. F. de. La crise économique due aux affaires à terme. Moyens pratiques pour résoudre cette grave question. *Havre, 1866. 8°.*

[**Laing-Meason, M. R.**] The profits of panics; showing how financial storms arise, who make money by them, who are the losers, and other revelations of a city man. By the author of "The bubbles of finance." *London, Low, 1886. 108 pp. 16°.*

The **late** commercial crisis: being a retrospect of the years 1836–8, with a plan for the abolition of the Corn laws. By a Glasgow manufacturer. *Glasgow, 1839. 113 pp. 8°.*

Laveleye, E. de. La crise économique et les chemins de fer vicinaux. *Bruxelles, Muquardt, 1879. 8°.*

—— La crise et la contraction monétaire. *Paris, Guillaumin, 1885. 8°.* [Reprinted from the "Journal des économistes."]

—— La crise et ses remèdes. *Verviers, Gilon, 1886. 94 pp. 12°.*

—— Die geld- und handelskrisen. Aus dem französischen. *Kassel, Freyschmidt, 1865. 81 pp. 8°.*

—— Le marché monétaire et ses crises depuis cinquante ans. *Paris, Guillaumin, 1865. 314 pp. 8°.*

—— Der wahre grund der seit 1873 bis jetzt anhaltenden wirthschaftlichen krisis und das einzige mittel zu ihrer heilung. Uebersetzt durch O. von Bar. *Berlin, Puttkammer, 1881. 91 pp. 8°.*

Leroy-Beaulieu, P. Das sinken der preise und die welthandelskrisen. Angebliche ursachen und vorgeschlagene heilmittel. Uebersetzt durch C. von Kalckstein. *Berlin, Simion, 1886. 48 pp. 8°.*

Lindner, M. Die asche der millionen. Vor, während und nach der krise vom jahre 1873. *Wien, Frick, 1883. 112 pp. 8°.*

Lloyd, W. W. Panics and their panaceas. The theory of money, metallic or paper, in relation to healthy and disturbed interchange. *London, Harrison, 1869. 57 pp. 8°*.

Loehnis, H. Der marasmus in handel und industrie 1877. *Strassburg, Trübner, 1878. 240, 56 pp. 8°*.

Lutwyche, A. An inquiry into the causes of commercial panics and bad trade, and a consideration of some proposed remedies. *Birmingham [1861?] 44 pp. 8°*.

M., W. The crisis; being a letter to J. W. Denison on the present calamitous situation of the country. *London, Dove, 1822. 18 pp. 8°*.

Man, E. G. The present trade crisis critically examined. *London, Wilson, 1885. 47 pp. 8°*.

Massey, B. Money crisis, its causes, consequences, and remedy, in a letter to Sir R. Peel. *London, 1847. 8°*.

Medley, G. W. The trade depression; its causes and remedies. *London, Cassell, 1885. 8°*. (Cobden club tract.)

Meyer, R. La crise internationale de l'industrie et de l'agriculture. *Berlin, Bahr, 1885. 128 pp. 8°*.
—— Politische gründer und die corruption in Deutschland. *Leipzig, Bidder, 1877. 204 pp. 8°*.

Mongredien, A. Trade depression, recent and present. *London, Cassell, [1885]. 24 pp. 8°*. (Cobden Club tract.)

Morisseaux, C. La crise économique. *Bruxelles, Muquardt, 1884. 43 pp. 8°*.

Mounder, F. The causes and cure of monetary panics. *London, 1867. 8°*.

Muret de Bort, L. Crise monétaire. De la situation respective des grands états commerçants, de la crise et de ses causes, du rôle important de la monnaie, de la bourse et du Crédit mobilier, de la Banque de France, de la production et du movement des métaux précieux, de la lèpre du lucre. *Paris, 1856. 8°.*

Neurath, W. Die wirthschaftskrisen und das cartell-wesen. (Nach dem im " Vereine reisender kauf-leute " in Wien am 14. mai, 1897 gehalten vor-trage.) *Leipzig, Klinkhardt, 1897. 37 pp. ·8°.*

Neuwirth, J. Bank und valuta in Oesterreich-Ungarn 1862–1873. *Leipzig, Duncker, 1873–74. 2 v. 8° .*

Norton, E. National finance and currency. The bank acts of 1797, 1819, and 1844, with the opera-tion of gain or loss of gold, and panics in peace or war. 3d ed. *London, Longmans, 1873. 101 pp. 12°.*

O., A. J. The cause of a crisis. *Hobart, 1894. 19 pp. 8°.*

Oechelhauser, W. Die wirthschaftliche krisis. *Berlin, Springer, 1876. 157 pp. 8°.*

On the causes and consequences of the present mone-tary crisis; or, The first principles of political economy applied to the gold supplies. *London, Groombridge, 1857. 62 pp. 16°.*

Poinsard, L. La question monétaire considérée dans ses rapports avec la condition sociale des divers pays et avec les crises économiques. *Paris, Giard, 1895. 293 pp. 18°.* (Petite encyclopédie sociale, économique et financière, 14.)

Palmer, J. H. Causes and consequences of the pres-sure upon the money market, with a statement of the action of the Bank of England from Oct. 1, 1833, to Dec. 27, 1836. *London, Richardson, 1837. 65 pp. 8°.*

—— Reply to the reflections of S. J. Lloyd on the pamphlet entitled : " Causes and consequences of the pressure upon the money market." *London, 1837. 8°.*

Perrot, F. Der fall Bontoux und der jüngste inter-nationale börsenkrach. *Heidelberg, Winter, 1882.*

48 pp. 8°. (Sammlung von vorträgen. Hrsg. von W. Frommel und F. Pfaff. 7. bd., 9. hft.)

Pike, J. S. The financial crisis, its evils and their remedy. Republished from the New York Tribune. *New York, 1867. 38 pp. 8°.*

Pommer, C. Unsere heutige wirthschaftliche lage. Neue gesichtspunkte zu einer richtigen beurtheilung derselben. *Berlin, Springer, 1877. 69 pp. 8°.*

The **prevention** of panics; or, Suggestions for an economical system of national finance in connection with the construction of public works. By a civil engineer. *London, Bailey, 1866. 58 pp. 8°.*

Putz, C. Ursachen und tragweite der krise in der kohlen- und roheisen-industrie Deutschlands. *Giessen, Roth, 1877. 54 pp. 8°.*

Raffalovich, A. La crise de Londres en novembre 1890. *Paris, 1890. 8°.*

—— Les crises commerciales et financières depuis 1889. *Paris, Guillaumin, 1900. 51 pp. 8°.* (Congrès international des valeurs mobilières.)

Rey, J. A. Les crises et le crédit. Division du travail. Banque d'escompte et banque de dépôt. *Paris, Guillaumin, 1862. 163 pp. 8°.*

Rodbertus, J. K. Die handelskrisen und die hypothekennoth der grundbesitzer. *Berlin, F. Schneider, 1858. 59 pp. 8°.*

Rodrigues de Freitas, J. J. Crise monetaria e politica de 1876. Causas e remedios. *Porto, Moré, 1876. 119 pp. 12°.*

Ross, O. C. D. Depression in trade. *London, 1885. 16 pp. 8°.*

Ruhkopf, K. Rodbertus' theorie von den handelskrisen. Darstellung und kritik. Eine studie. *Leipzig, Gräfe, 1892. 88 pp. 8°.*

S., J. Einfluss der krisen und der steigerung der lebensmittelpreise auf das geschäftsleben. Eine statistische studie. 3. aufl. *München, Ernst, 1894. 24 pp. 8°.* (Sammlung gesellschafts-wissenschaftlicher aufsätze. Hrsg. von E. Fuchs. 7. hft.)

Salomons, D. A defence of the Joint-stock banks; an examination of the causes of the present monetary difficulties, and hints for the future management of the circulation. *London, Richardson, 1837. 46 pp. 8°.*

—— The monetary difficulties of America, and their probable effects on British commerce considered. *London, Richardson, 1837. 45 pp. 8°.*

[Schuckers, J. W.] The finances; panics and specie payments. *Philadelphia, Campbell, 1874. 90 pp. 8°.*

—— The New York national bank presidents' conspiracy against industry and prosperity. A history of the panic of 1893; its organization and methods. In a series of letters to H. C. Baird. *Newark, N. J., The author, 1894. 65 pp. 8°.*

Schwarz, J. L. Die 1857er krisis. Verzeichniss sämmtlicher während der 1857er krisis auf allen plätzen der erde stattgehabten, . . . kaufmännischen zahlungseinstellungen, nebst einem wörtlichen abdruck aller in bezug auf die Hamburger krisis erlassenen verordnungen. Nach officiellen quellen bearbeitet und zusammengestellt. 1. thl. *Hamburg, Nolte, 1858. 44 pp. 8°.*

Scudder, M. L. Congested prices. *Chicago, Jansen, McClurg, 1883. 52 pp. 12°.*

Simmel, E. Die liquidirenden aktien-gesellschaften. Ein beitrag zur geschichte der handelskrisis. *Berlin, Weidmann, 1876. 51 pp. 8°.*

Sinclair, J. On the approaching crisis; or, On the impracticability of resuming cash payments at the Bank, in July, 1818. *London, 1818. 8°.*

Smith, C. M. Trade depression and wasted resources. *Sydney, N. S. W., 1887. 41 pp. 8°.*

Smith, C. W. Commercial gambling: the principal causes of depression in agriculture and trade. *London, Low, 1893. 170 pp. 8°.*

—— Original theories upon and remedies for depression in trade, land, agriculture, and silver. *London, Low, 1893. 74 pp. 8°.*

Smith, J. A. Elements of prosperity causing depression of trade. *London, 1886. 12 pp. 8°.*

Smith, W. E. The recent depression of trade; its nature, its causes, and the remedies which have been suggested for it. Being the Oxford Cobden club prize essay for 1879. *London, Trübner, 1880. 107 pp. 12°.*

Stansfeld, H. A remedy for monetary panics and free trade in currency, suggested in a brief review of the currency question. *Bonn, 1849. 8°.*

Steinberg, J. Industrie und ueberspekulation. *Bonn, Cohen, 1899. 33 pp. 8°.*

Sternberg, M. The crisis of 1876; an epitome of its causes and effects, together with suggestions as to various remedies. *London, Wilson, 1876. 102 pp. 8°.*

Stitt, J. The nature and causes of commercial crises and panics, as influenced by our monetary laws, briefly considered. *Liverpool, 1864. 29 pp. 8°.*

Stopel, F. Die handelskrisis in Deutschland. *Frankfurt a. M., Expedition des " Merkur," 1875. 61 pp. 8°.* (*His* Volkswirthschaftliche zeitfragen. hft. 1.)

Taunton, E. A remedy for panics. *Birmingham, 1846. 30 pp. 12°.*

Testelin, E. A. Economie politique; étude sur les causes et les conséquences de la crise industrielle, commerciale et agricole. *Bruxelles, Decq, 1885. 30 pp. 8°.*

Toegel, T. Die gegenwärtige geldkrise. Ein vortrag. *Mülheim a. R., 1857. 8°.*

Tugan-Baranowsky, M. von. Studien zur theorie und geschichte der handelskrisen in England. *Jena, Fischer, 1901. 425 pp. 8°.* [Translated from the Russian.]

Tutau, J. Las crisis monetarias, bursátiles, mercantiles é industriales. Conferencias dadas en el Ateneo barcelonés. *Barcelona, 1886. 151 pp. 8°.*

United States. Department of Labor. Industrial depressions. *Washington, Govt. print. off., 1886. 496 pp. 8°.* [First annual report of the Commissioner of labor.]

Vachon, M. Crise industrielle et artistique en France et en Europe. *Paris, Librairie illustrée, 1886. 320 pp. 12°.*

Wallace, A. R. Bad times. *London, Macmillan, 1885. 118 pp. 12°.*

Wasserrab, K. Preise und krisen; volkswirtschaftliches aus unseren tagen. Eine von der Staatswirtschaftlichen fakultät der Universität München gekrönte preisschrift " Ueber die veränderungen der preise auf dem allgemeinen markt seit 1875 und deren ursachen." Zugleich eine einführung in nationalökonomische studien für beamte und kaufleute. *Stuttgart, Cotta, 1889. 211 pp. 8°.*

Weber, Benno, *pseud. of G. von Pacher.* Einige ursachen der Wiener krisis vom jahre 1873. *Leipzig, Veit, 1874. 131 pp. 8°.*

Weigert, M. Die krisis des zwischenhandels. Vortrag von M. Weigert. *Berlin, Simion, 1885. 26 pp. 8°.* (Volkswirthschaftliche zeitfragen. Vorträge und abhandlungen hrsg. von der Volkswirthschaftlichen gesellschaft in Berlin und der Ständ. deputation des Congresses deutscher volkswirthe. 53. hft.)

Wells, D. A. Breakers ahead; cause of the present crisis; falling prices and business stagnation accounted for; no connection whatever between the disease and the remedy which the silver quacks prescribe. An analysis of the situation. Circulated by the Democratic honest money league of America. *Jersey City, 1896. 15 pp. 8°.*

Westrouen van Meeteren, F. W. Handels-musea en de industriëele en handelscrisis. *Amsterdam, Brinkman, 1886. 8°.*

What are the causes of the prolonged depression in trade? *Edinburgh, 1879. 22 pp. 8°.*

Williams, H. Depression of trade. *London, 1885. 52 pp. 8°.*

Williams, S. D. Trade depression and the appreciation of gold. *Birmingham, Cornish, [1886] 29 pp. 8°.*

Williams, T. H. Observations on money, credit, and panics, to which are added strictures on Manchester credits. *Manchester, 1858. 43 pp. 8°.*

Willoughby, F. S. Depression in trade. *Manchester, 1885. 15 pp. 8°.*

Willson, H. B. Industrial crises, their causes and remedies. *Washington, 1879. 8°.*

Wilson, J. The cause of the present commercial distress and its bearings on the interests of ship-owners. *Liverpool, 1843. 11 pp. 8°.*

Wirth, M. Geschichte der handelskrisen. 4. aufl. *Frankfurt a. M., Sauerländer, 1890. 706 pp. 8°.* [1st ed., 1858; 2d ed., 1874; 3d ed., 1883.]

—— Geschichte der handelskrisis im jahre 1873. *Frankfurt a. M., Sauerländer, 1874. 270 pp. 8°.*

—— Die krisis in der landwirthschaft und mittel zur abhülfe. *Berlin, Herbig, 1881. 352 pp. 8°.*

—— Die münzkrisis und die noten-bank-reform im Deutschen reiche. *Köln, Du Mont-Schauberg, 1874. 118 pp. 8°.*

—— Oesterreichs wiedergeburt aus den nachwehen der krisis. *Wien, Manz, 1876. 552 pp. 8°.*

Wirth, M. Die quellen des reichtums mit rücksicht auf geschäftsstockungen und krisen im internationalen geld-, kapital- und warenmarkt, sowie auf die agrar-, kolonial- und arbeiterfrage. *Köln, Du Mont-Schauberg, 1883. 294 pp. 8°.*

—— Die reform der umlaufsmittel im Deutschen reiche. Ein nachtrag zur "Geschichte der handelskrisen." *Frankfurt a. M., Sauerländer, 1875. 70 pp. 8°.*

Wolf, J. Die gegenwärtige wirtschaftskrisis. Antrittsrede gehalten an der Universität Zürich im sommersemester 1888. *Tübingen, Laupp, 1888. 32 pp. 8°.*

Wolowski, L. La crise financière de l'Angleterre. *Paris, Claye, 1866. 39 pp. 8°.* [Extrait de la Revue des deux mondes, livraison du 1. sept. 1866.]

Wooley, C. Phases of panics; a brief historical review. Read at the London institution on April 10, 1896. *London, Good, 1897. 78 pp. 8°.*

Yaple, A. The money crisis: its causes and remedy. *Cincinnati, Clarke, 1873. 22 pp. 8°.*

ARTICLES IN PERIODICALS

1837. The late commercial crisis. *Blackwood's magazine, 42: 210–25.*

American commercial crises. *British and foreign review, 5: 537–80.*

The moral of the crisis. *Democratic review, 1: 108–23.*

Causes and consequences of the crisis in the American trade. J. C. MacCulloch. *Edinburgh review, 65: 221–38.*

1847. The financial crisis in Great Britain. A. Baring (*Lord Ashburton*). *Bankers' magazine (N. Y.), 2: 13–16.*

1847. La crise financière et la Banque de France. H. Say. *Journal des économistes, 16: 193–207.*

La crise financière et commerciale en Angleterre. C. de Molinari. *Journal des économistes, 17: 274–84.*

De la crise financière dans la Grande-Bretagne. L. Faucher. *Journal des économistes, 18: 313–28.*

The financial pressure. *Quarterly review, 81: 230–73.*

La crise commerciale et la Banque d'Angleterre. A. Audiganne. *Revue des deux mondes, 20: 153–74.*

1848. The commercial history of the past year. *Bankers' magazine (L.), 8: 73–79.*

A chronological history of the English panic. List of the firms which have suspended payment. *Bankers' magazine (L.), 8: 81–104.*

Inquiry into the causes of the panic. " Omicron." *Bankers' magazine (L.), 8: 147–52.*

The panic on the continent. *Bankers' magazine (L.), 8: 217–24.*

The cause of commercial panics. J. A. Lawson. *Bankers' magazine (L.), 8: 415–20.*

Evidence as to causes of panic of 1847. *Bankers' magazine (L.), 8 : LVII–CXX, CXXI–CLXXXIV.*

Review of the recent parliamentary inquiry on the commercial distress of 1847. *Bankers' magazine (L.), 8: 625–33, 681–89.*

The financial pressure. *Bankers' magazine (N. Y.), 3: 225–60.*

The present commercial crisis. D. M. Balfour, *Hunt's Merchants' magazine, 18: 477–88.*

The cause of commercial panics. J. A. Lawson, *Hunt's Merchants' magazine, 19: 282–87.*

1848. La crise commerciale. H. Say. *Journal des économistes, 19: 338–43.*

La crise financière et commerciale. J. E. Horn. *Journal des économistes, 20: 15–24.*

Quelques mots sur la crise actuelle. A. Fonteyraud. *Journal des économistes, 20: 154–60.*

The financial crisis of Great Britain. T. Dwight. *New Englander, 6: 147–51.*

The crisis of 1847 and its causes. *Prospective review, 4: 152–68.*

Les crises commerciales et la liberté des banques. C. Coquelin. *Revue des deux mondes, 76: 445–70.*

1850. Restrictions on banking, the cause of commercial crises. C. Coquelin. *Bankers' magazine (L.), 10: 219–27, 308–13.*

The causes of commercial crises. By a Boston cashier. *Bankers' magazine (N. Y.), 5: 1–4.*

1851. Financial crises and the monetary system. Criticism on M. L. Chitti's Financial crises and reforms of the monetary system in Revue britannique, 1839. *Hunt's Merchants' magazine, 25: 677–90.*

1853. Commercial excitements and crises. (From Hogg's Instructor.) *Eclectic magazine, 28: 471–77.*

1854. Influence des banques sur l'entrainement des capitaux et sur les crises, discussion à la Société d'économie politique. *Journal des économistes, 2. sér. 2: 429–32.*

1855. The American crisis of 1854. *Bankers' magazine (L.), 15: 287–95.*

Crise commerciale aux Etats-Unis. J. G. Courcelle-Seneuil. *Journal des économistes, 2. sér. 5: 112–15.*

Des crises monétaires et de la question de l'or. H. Baudrillart. *Journal des économistes, 2. sér. 7: 360–89.*

1855. La crise fianancière. H. Say. *Journal des économistes, 2. sér. 8: 215–22.*

1857. The financial flurry. P. Godwin. *Atlantic monthly, 1: 112–20.*

The American panic. *Bankers' magazine (L.), 17: 785–88, 904–14.*

The financial revulsions of 1837 and 1857 [in the U. S.]. *Bankers' magazine (N. Y.), 12: 390–400.*

The panic and financial crisis of 1857. E. C. Seaman. *Hunt's Merchants' magazine, 37: 659–68.*

Des crises commerciales et monétaires de 1800 à 1857. C. Juglar. *Journal des économistes, 2. sér. 14: 35–60, 255–67.*

The financial crisis. J. S. Ropes. *New Englander, 15: 701–15.*

1858. The great failure. *Atlantic monthly, 1: 385–94.*

The commercial crisis. *Bankers' magazine (L.), 18: 1–5.*

The progress of 1857. *Bankers' magazine (L.), 18: 94–102.*

The crisis of 1857 and its causes. *Bankers' magazine (N. Y.), 12: 865–78.*

Retrospective views of the year [1857]. *Bankers' magazine (N. Y.), 12: 593–604.*

The bank acts and the credit crisis of 1857. *British quarterly review, 27: 172–96.*

Causes of the recent commercial distress. *Hunt's Merchants' magazine, 39: 553–62.*

An exposition of the crisis of 1857. *Hunt's Merchant's magazine, 38: 19–35.*

Des crises commerciales. A. Clément. *Journal des économistes, 2. sér. 17: 161–91.*

Le commerce extérieur et la crise á Hambourg. J. E. Horn. *Journal des économistes, 2. sér. 17: 245–53.*

1858. Crise économique au Chili. J. G. Courcelle-Seneuil. *Journal des économistes, 2. sér. 18: 55–70.*

The financial crisis and its cause. *Westminster review, 69: 154–79.*

1859. The commercial crisis of 1857 and the currency. *Bentley's Quarterly review, 1: 106–42.*

Causes that produced the crisis of 1857 considered. *Hunt's Merchants' magazine, 40: 19–37.*

1860. Monetary panics [correspondence]. A. Walker and H. Stansfield. *Bankers' magazine (N. Y.), 14: 497–509.*

The financial crisis of 1837. *Bankers' magazine (N. Y.), 14: 781–88.*

1861. Panics, their causes and means of prevention [seven letters]. "Lancastria." *Bankers' magazine (L.), 21: 73–76, 148–50, 222–25, 342–45, 406–10, 473–76, 543–46.*

Les crises financières et l'organization du credit en France. G. Poujard'hieu. *Revue des deux mondes, 2. pér. 33: 686–708.*

1864. La spéculation et la taux de l'escompte; aspect général de la dernière crise. P. Coq. *Journal des économistes, 2. sér. 44: 394–401.*

1865. Les crises commerciales et monétaires. E. de Laveleye. *Revue des deux mondes, 2. pér. 55: 207–33, 432–60.*

L'enquête sur le crédit; I: La crise monétaire de 1863–64 et ses origines. V. Bonnet. *Revue des deux mondes, 2. pér. 60: 391–418.*

1866. Panic of 1866. *Bankers' magazine (L.), 26: 637–41.*

Recent financial panic. *British quarterly review, 44: 125–40.*

1866. English panics of the present century. *Hunt's Merchants' magazine, 55: 65–66.*

Comptes rendus comparés de la Banque de France après les crises de 1839, 1847, 1857, et 1864. C. Juglar. *Journal des économistes, 3. sér. 2: 60–72.*

La crise financière de l'Angleterre. L. Wolowski. *Revue des deux mondes, 2. pér. 64: 927–56; 65: 176–211.*

1867. Des crises actuelles de l'industrie. L. Reybaud. *Journal des économistes, 3. sér. 8: 321–33.*

Comptes rendus comparés de la Banque de France après les crises de 1847, 1857, et 1864, année 1866. C. Juglar. *Journal des économistes, 3. sér. 6: 252–68.*

1868. On credit cycles and the origin of commercial panics. J. Mills. *Manchester statistical society. Transactions . . . session 1867–68.* pp. 5–40.

1870. Les dernières crises financières aux Etats-Unis, et les valeurs américaines. T. Balch. *Journal des économistes, 3. sér. 18: 419–29.*

1871. The causes of commercial crises and their remedies. The causes of financial panics and their remedies. *Bankers' magazine (N.Y.), 26: 357–70.*

Commercial crises. B. Price. *North British review, 53: 450–78.*

La Banque de France et la crise monétaire. V. Bonnet. *Revue des deux mondes, 2. pér. 96: 682–98.*

1872. The bank charter act and the crisis of 1866. H. Chubb. *Royal statistical society. Journal. 35: 171–95.*

1873. The panic in the U. S. *Bankers' magazine (L.), 33: 917–19.*

The American crises. *Bankers' magazine (L.), 33: 993–96.*

24

1873. Panic in Wall Street. *Harper's magazine,*
       48: 126–34.

    History of the crisis [1873]. K. Cornwallis.
       Lippincott's magazine, 12: 681–90.

    The moral side of panics. E. L. Godkin.
       Nation, 17: 238–39.

    Panics. E. L. Godkin. *Nation, 17: 206–7.*

    The financial crisis. *Penn monthly, 4: 801–3.*

1874. Bonamy Price on the causation of panics.
       Bankers' magazine (N. Y.), 29: 361–68.

    Our late panic. *International review, 1: 1–16.*

    Wall Street and the crisis. *Old and new,*
       9: 41–55.

    Commercial panics. J. C. Welden. *Overland*
       monthly, 12: 147–56.

1875. Panics and cliques. *Bankers' magazine (N.Y.),*
       29: 689–95.

    Monetary panics and the Board of trade.
       Bankers' magazine (N. Y.), 30: 1–3.

    What is the matter? Is anything the matter?
       B. B. Kimball. *Galaxy, 19: 105–10.*

    La crise financière en Hongrie. J. E. Horn.
       Journal des économistes, 3. sér. 37: 286–97.

    La crise financière de 1814 et de 1815. G.
       Du Puynode. *Journal des économistes, 3.*
       sér. 40: 173–96, 364–83.

1876. The financial crisis in America. H. White.
       Fortnightly review, 25: 810–29.

    Crise commerciale et monétaire au Chili. J. G.
       Courcelle-Seneuil. *Journal des écono-*
       mistes, 3. sér. 44: 293–95.

    The financial situation in England. E. L. God-
       kin. *Nation, 22: 344–45.*

1877. Financial panics, their causes and results.
       Abridged from the Contemporary review.
       Bankers' magazine (N. Y.), 32: 91–100.

    The cause of business depression as presented
       in the forthcoming report of the United

States silver commission. *Bankers' magazine* (N. Y.), *32 : 287–97.*

1877. One per cent. B. Price. *Contemporary review,* *29 : 778–99.*

La liquidation de la crise de 1873 et la reprise des affaires. C. Juglar. *Journal des économistes, 3. sér. 47 : 372–82.*

The responsibility of panics. E. L. Godkin. *Nation, 25 : 223–24.*

The law of panics. E. L. Godkin. *Nation, 25 : 251–52.*

Panics and sun spots. W. S. Jevons. *Nature, 19 : 33–37, 588–90.*

1878. Our commercial crises. The Gilbart lecture on banking. L. Levi. *Bankers' magazine (L.), 38 : 304–18. Bankers' magazine (N. Y.), 33 : 40–45, 118–26.*

The panics and our recuperative prospects. *Bankers' magazine* (N. Y.), *32 : 502–5.*

De crisis van 1873. N. G. Pierson. *De economist, pp. 837–63.*

Die arbeiter und die produktionskrisen. L. Brentano. *Jahrbuch für gesetzgebung, verwaltung und volkswirthschaft, 2 : 565–632.*

1879. La legge di periodicità delle crisi. Perturbazioni economiche e macchie solari. G. Boccardo. *Archivio di statistica, Roma, 3 : 385–412.*

Commercial depression and reciprocity. B. Price. *Contemporary review, 35 : 269–88.*

Ueber die verhütung der produktionskrisen durch staatl. fürsorge. E. Nasse. *Jahrbuch für gesetzgebung, verwaltung und volkswirthschaft, 3 : 145–89.*

On some effects of a crisis on the banking interest. J. B. Martin. *Journal of the Statistical society, 42 : 663–708.*

1879. Rationale of panics. F. B. Hawley. *National quarterly review, 39: 277–92.*
Depression of trade. T. Brassey. *Nineteenth century, 5: 788–811.*
Causes of commercial depression. J. E. T. Rogers. *Princeton review, 55: 211–38.*
La crise économique. M. Block. *Revue des deux mondes, 3. pér. 32: 433–59.*
1881. Unless trouble comes. J. S. Bean. *Bankers' magazine (N. Y.), 36: 270–78.*
1882. Financial crises in France. *Bankers' magazine (L.), 42: 157–65.*
1883. The panic. *Saturday review, 57: 645.*
1884. The prevention of panics. D. Wilder. *Bankers' magazine (N. Y.), 39: 425–29.*
La crise de la spéculation à New York. Les causes de la crise. *Journal des économistes, 4. sér. 26: 433–45.*
Panics and politics. H. White. *Nation, 39: 324–25.*
La circulation fiduciaire et la crise actuelle. V. Bonnet. *Revue des deux mondes, 3. pér. 62: 668–92.*
Banks and panics. *Saturday review, 58: 84–85.*
1885. Depression of trade and low prices. R. Giffen. *Contemporary review, 47: 800–22.*
La crise et la contraction monétaire. E. de Laveleye. *Journal des économistes, 4. sér. 29: 411–22.*
La crise financière de 1830. G. Du Puynode. *Journal des économistes, 4. sér. 32: 161–82.*
L'enquête anglaise sur la crise commerciale et industrielle. A. Raffalovich. *Journal des économistes, 4. sér. 32: 340–43.*
1886. Panic of 1825 and £1 note. *Bankers' magazine (L.), 46: 471–76.*
Panic of 1866. *Bankers' magazine (L.), 46: 1013–17.*

1886. Des fêtes comme remède à la crise commerciale. H. de Beaumont. *Journal des économistes, 4. sér. 33: 251–60.*

La crise économique; étude des causes et des remèdes. J. G. Courcelle-Seneuil. *Journal des économistes, 4. sér. 35: 161–72.*

La baisse des prix et la crise commerciale dans le monde; causes alléguées, remèdes proposés. P. Leroy-Beaulieu. *Revue des deux mondes, 3. pér. 75: 383–418.*

The depression of trade abroad. *Spectator, 59: 841–42.*

Causes of the depression of trade. *Spectator, 59: 1139–40.*

1887. Royal commission on the depression of trade. *Bankers' magazine (L.), 47: 106–8.*

The great depression of trade; a study of economic causes. D. A. Wells. *Contemporary review, 52: 275–93, 381–400.*

Economic disturbances since 1873. D. A. Wells. *Popular science monthly, 31: 289–304, 433–51, 577–96.*

1888. The progress of applied science and its effect upon trade. L. Playfair. *Contemporary review, 53: 358–71.*

The dislocation of industry. W. Smart. *Contemporary review, 53: 686–702.*

Panics. *Spectator, 61: 1186.*

1889. La crise économique en Italie. V. Pareto. *Journal des économistes, 4. sér. 46: 161–80.*

1890. Financial crises of the century. *Bankers' magazine (L.), 50: 201–7, 921–26, 1786–93.*

The South American financial crisis. *Bankers' magazine (L.), 50: 1253–62.*

The Baring crisis. *Bankers' magazine (L.), 50: 1933–38.*

1890. The crisis on the stock exchange: its causes and effects. G. B. Baker. *Contemporary review, 58: 680–92.*

1891. The Bank act and the recent crisis. *Bankers' magazine (L.), 51: 419–27.*

The panic of 1873. *Bankers' magazine (N. Y.), 46: 392–98.*

The crisis of 1890. *Economic journal, 1: 192–96.*

The Baring financial crisis. A. Crump. *Economic journal, 1: 388–94.*

De November-crisis. G. M. Boissevain. *De economist, pp. 63–89.*

The sources of commercial panic. B. D. Mackenzie. *Gentleman's magazine, new ser., 46: 154–75.*

The late financial crisis. H. Clewes. *North American review, 152: 103–13.*

1892. The financial outlook in 1892. W. R. Lawson. *Bankers' magazine (L.), 53: 44–57.*

Runs on banks, 1866 and 1892. *Bankers' magazine (L.), 54: 633–39.*

The depression of 1892. *Bankers' magazine (L.), 54: 779–88.*

1893. Industrial depressions: their cause and cure. F. H. Cooke. *American journal of politics, 3: 597–604.*

The financial problem and business situation discussed from a practical standpoint. G. C. Kelley. *Arena, 9: 118–29.*

A whirlwind of disaster; its lessons. E. Wiman. *Canadian magazine, 1: 517–22.*

What causes depression of trade? L. Irwell. *Chautauquan, 18: 307–13.*

The crisis in the United States and the repeal of silver purchase. F. W. Taussig. *Economic journal, 3: 733–45.*

1893. The financial situation. M. Marshall. *Engineering magazine, 5 : 411–18.*

The present depression of trade ; opinions of men of business. *Fortnightly review, new ser., 53 : 297–315.*

The financial excitements and its causes. G. R. Gibson. *Forum, 15 : 483–93.*

Phenomenal aspects of the financial situation. A. C. Stevens. *Forum, 16 : 22–32.*

La crise et le protectionnisme en Australie. A. Raffalovich. *Journal des économistes, 5. sér. 15 : 87–91.*

The crisis of 1890. M. Wirth. *Journal of political economy, 1 : 214–35.*

Panic of 1873. H. White. *Nation, 57 : 76–77.*

The genesis of a financial panic. J. T. D. *Nation, 57 : 192.*

The present crisis. J. H. Eckels and S. Pennoyer. *North American review, 157 : 129–44.*

Political causes of the business depression. W. E. Russell. *North American review, 157 : 641–52.*

The lesson of our financial crisis. H. Lieb. *Open court, 7 : 3767–68.*

Les principales causes des crises économiques. A. A. Issaïev. *Revue d'économie politique, 7 : 654–92, 985–1011.*

1894. Causes of the present business depression. H. C. Ager. *American journal of politics, 4 : 233–49.*

The artificial panic in retrospect. W. Knapp. *American journal of politics, 4 : 656–66.*

The panic and the silver movement. A. B. and H. Farquhar. *American journal of politics, 5 : 84–89.*

Commercial depression and business crises. *American journal of politics, 5 : 449–60.*

1894. The cause of financial panics.   J. W. Bennet. *Arena, 9: 493–521.*

The panic of 1893 in the United States and its connection with the credit system in Europe.   D. M. Frederiksen. *Bankers' magazine (L.), 57: 49–60.*

Depression in 1847 and 1894 compared. *Bankers' magazine (L.), 58: 613–20.*

The banks and the panic of 1893 [review of A. D. Noyes' article in the Political science quarterly].   *Bankers' magazine (N. Y.), 48: 721–26.*

De geldmarkt in 1893.   G. M. Boissevain. *De economist, pp. 106–26.*

Wage-earner's loss during the depression. S. W. Dike. *Forum, 18: 369–78.*

Facts touching a revival of business. *Forum, 18: 379–84.*

Panics and hard times. F. S. Hayden. *Homiletic review, 28: 279–86.*

Die wirthschaftliche krisis des jahres 1893 in den Vereinigten Staaten von Nordamerika. E. von Halle. *Jahrbuch für gesetzgebung, verwaltung und volkswirthschaft, 18: 1181–1249.*

The banks and the panic of 1893.   A. D. Noyes. *Political science quarterly, 9: 12–30.*

Analysis of the phenomena of the panic in the United States in 1893.   A. C. Stevens. *Quarterly journal of economics, 8: 117–48.*

Der "grosse börsenkrach" des jahres 1873. A. Schäffle. *Zeitschrift für die gesammte staatswissenschaft, 50: 1–94.*

1895. The financial situation (economically considered). *Bankers' magazine (L.), 60: 22–30.*

Depression corrected. *Edinburgh review, 182: 1–26.*

Two per cent. *Chambers's journal, 12: 321–24.*

1895. The present depression: its causes, consequences and continuation. R. H. I. Palgrave. *National review, 25: 105–18.*

Trade and industry. (The currency question —for laymen. II.) W. H. Houldsworth. *National review, 25: 213–19.*

1896. The periodicity of commercial crises as exemplified in the United States. E. V. Grabil. *American magazine of civics, 8: 366–75.*

English financial panics, their causes and treatment. *Bankers' magazine (L.), 62: 172–87.*

1897. Ueber das wesen der krisen in der volkswirthschaft. G. Cohn. *Nachrichten von der Königl. gesellschaft der wissenschaften zu Göttingen. Philologisch - historische klasse, pp. 283–305.*

1898. Panics and prices. G. Yard. *Cornhill magazine, 77: 757–68.*

1899. Les banques allemandes en cas de crise ou de guerre. A. E. Sayous. *Revue d'économie politique, 13: 142–65.*

INDEX

THE END